Modern China and International Economic Law

This book series offers an essential forum for Chinese economic law scholars, as well as international scholars interested in China's practice in the context of international economic law. It is thus the aim of this book series to publish essential monographs/ compilations in the field of international economic law that focus on China, or on uniquely Chinese characteristics. This book series above all focuses on research that closely relates current practices with past history, and future policies with current circumstances, pursuing a philosophy of understanding legal practices by combining the past and present. Accordingly, top scholars in China and beyond its borders will be invited to contribute to this project from their respective areas of focus, which can cover broad topics related to international law in the current context of China's peaceful rise, such as China's economic policy with various countries, its participation in the WTO legal system and bilateral investment treaty practices, etc.; as well as more specific topics such as China's domestic legislation regarding foreign business, its unique "one country, two systems" policy and its implications on external economic interactions between different "systems" within China.

Deming Zhao

Contemporary Export Control Law of China

中国国际经济法学会
Chinese Society of International Economic Law, CSIEL

Springer

Deming Zhao
Global Law Office
Shanghai, China

ISSN 2364-8317 ISSN 2364-8325 (electronic)
Modern China and International Economic Law
ISBN 978-981-99-9824-1 ISBN 978-981-99-9825-8 (eBook)
https://doi.org/10.1007/978-981-99-9825-8

This Springer imprint is published by the registered company Springer Nature Singapore Pte Ltd.
The registered company address is: 152 Beach Road, #21-01/04 Gateway East, Singapore 189721, Singapore

Foreword

Export Control Law is a new piece of legislation implemented in China, which has been born with the notion of protection of national security and interest as well as non-proliferation of weapons of mass destruction and their carrying vehicles, along with the process of China's confronting the abuses against China of export controls and economic sanctions by relevant countries, the United States of America in particular. Understandably ECL has a defensive or countering posture. At the same time, ECL reflects the persistent position of China to maintain the multilateral non-proliferation mechanism and exhibits the basic attitude of China as a responsible big nuclear State committed to international obligations.

Apart from vigorous discharge of the international non-proliferation obligations, ECL is a bit similar to the US export control regime in terms of some controlled activities based on national security considerations. However, there is a sharp difference in the national security notion as between China and the United States. China abides by the relative notion of national security which cares the security of other nations as well, while the United States seeks the absolute self-security so that as a hegemonic practice it does not save any effort to suppress its competitors, if any. The case in which Huawei was so suppressed has been a vivid illustration of such barbarous hegemonic addiction.

Nevertheless, China has shown self-restraint to a certain extent in tackling and countering the hegemonic practices of the United States, with a focus on reasonableness, beneficence, and moderation. China uses its tools in its toolkit of countermeasures not to the full extent and in a manner consistent with international law. Such countermeasures with moderation reflect the strategic resolve of openness to the outside world as well as the self-confidence in the prospect of development of China. "*Peace leads to mutual benefits while strife afflicts mutual damage* 和则两利, 斗则两伤". This is the intelligence crystalized from Chinese old history with a culture cherishing harmony among different people 和而不同. It remains to be seen when or whether the United States may realize such a historical and realistic rule of intellect.

With his forward-looking projection, Professor and Dr. Deming Zhao has probed and practiced export control laws and regulations for many years, though export control law is still a new area of law in China. He has already some articles published in this field. This book, *Contemporary Export Control Law of China* as he authors, has been prepared with the perspectives both strategic from the above and articulative horizontally regarding a wide range of controlled items, and with legislative commentaries on the countermeasures and insights on trade compliance practice for the business community. This book is obviously a valuable one seldom seen in the field of China export controls and economic sanctions. As his academic supervisor when he was a post-graduate student, I am very pleased to see his achievements in his practice of law as well as his theoretical works, though I earnestly expect that he continues to unleash his talent in the academic field.

Finally, I feel obliged to relate that Prof. Deming Zhao has been generous as to make financial aids to the academic activities of his Alma Mater. It is a deed of virtue highly praised in the Chinese culture as "*gratifying benefaction in return* 知恩图报" and "*not forgetting the source of one's drinking water* 饮水思源".

December 2023

An Chen
Professor of Law
Xiamen University Law School
Xiamen, China

Preface

It can be dated back to 1986 when I first encountered U.S. export control law as an undergraduate student in the International Economic Law Program at Xiamen University. A JD graduate from the U.S., after finishing his bar examination, sought to have some fresh air to teach US law in Xiamen, a beautiful coastal city in China, together with his newly wedded wife. Understandably he was very enthusiastic. Whenever he showed up in the big classroom, presenting the Export Administration Act, he occasionally unleashed some admiring words on his wife, no matter whether she was then in the classroom or visible through the window. Apart from this episode, I could barely remember his proposition that the U.S. export controls were "stupid" against China as against the Soviet Union, which would enable China to be strong by itself in the long run, while the U.S. companies afflict a loss of the market in China, and the competitors of U.S. manufacturers would make supplies to China at the same time. At that time, I was not aware that China and the U.S. were collaborating quite closely in the military arena, as against the Soviet Union then.

Thirty-one years later, upon invitation by Prof. Michael Wolffgang of Munster University, Germany, I started in 2017 to lecture in Germany on China export control regulations and Customs Law to the business community there. Lectures were later switched to online during the COVID-19 pandemic years. The lectures have left me with many "students" in Germany who were concerned about the potential extraterritorial jurisdiction of export controls of China over foreign companies.

With perhaps a sense of export control engraved in a past young mind and facing the needy lecture tasks posed to the current senior brain, I had closely followed the process of enactment of the Export Control Law of China and exhibited myself an air of vigor in commenting on versions of this piece of legislation right from the emergence of the draft in 2017 through the different legislative stages. It was comforting to note that many of my comments proved to be consistent with the subsequently amended versions or the final version of the Export Control Law of China, and I reasonably assumed that the drafters and legislators somehow shared a similar mind with me to a comfortable degree.

Though COVID-19 presented hardship to human life, it did offer some easiness for solitary reading. During the pandemic, I was a bit amused to find a somewhat origin of the dual-use item control back in 642 BC in ancient China. According to *Zuo's Biography of the Spring and Autumn Annals*, as between ZHENG and CHU, two of the States under the Dynasty ZHOU, Count ZHENG in that year took the initiative to pay a visit to the State of CHU. The Sovereign of CHU was so pleased as to promise a large amount of copper to ZHENG in return for this visit, which episode may help you to have a flavor of Chinese friendliness, but the Sovereign CHU repented his idea later. As a compromise, he sought a pledge from Count ZHENG "never to use the copper to make weapons". Count ZHENG kept his promise and made three big bells out of the copper in his State, which was of course quite sounding. This was an instance of dual-use export and end-use control based on an insecure psychology, which was equivalent somehow to the national security uneasiness in modern times.

Over many years of customs and trade compliance study and practice, I still find the export control issues far from boring. My advice has covered issues of dual-use nuclear, missiles, chemicals, and occasionally military items. In 2013, we succeeded in convincing the export control authority that a given exported material was not capable of missile usage, nor falling within catch-all controls, so that the export items seized by the customs were not subject to export control, and thus, the export business of the client stood clear of a collapse.

Probably due to all the foregoing flashes, when Prof. An Chen encouraged me to write something several years ago, the idea of *Contemporary Export Control Law of China* prompted itself in my mind.

Export Control Law of China is obviously an important topic to the business community. I hope that the readers of this book can sense the underlying psychology of the same law at least from the following perspectives: (a) it was enacted largely as countermeasures against the foreign abusive practice of export controls, a defensive rather offensive posture; (b) it reflects a certain extent the Chinese modernity with an element of self-restraint in its extraterritorial reach; and (c) it has a consideration for the business community as it unilaterally controls much fewer items than the export controls in the U.S., EU, or UK, and it normally and tolerantly does not control items only because that a foreign country controls the same against exports to China, such as the duel use items controlled under Wassenaar Arrangement, most of which items are not controlled by China.

I must hereby express my gratitude to Prof. An Chen for his constant pressing encouragement, to Prof. Michael Wolffgang of Munster University and Prof. Wei Xiao of Xiamen University for their recommendations, and to Mr. Tingfeng Jin, Ms. Wentong Zhou, and Ms. Chi Zhang for their assistance in preparing this book. Finally, my thanks to the Springer editing team for their generous patience and an air of calmness each time I made an apology for delays in preparing this book.

November 2023

Deming Zhao
Chair Professor of An Chen International Law
Partner, Global Law Office
Shanghai, China

Contents

About the Author

Dr. Deming Zhao LL.B., LL.M. and Ph.D. in Law (Xiamen University); LL.M. (UCL, London); Visiting Professor, Shanghai Foreign Economic and Trade University; Chair Professor, An Chen International Law.

Dr. Zhao is currently a partner of Global Law Office, one of the leading Chinese law firms in China. Apart from his corporate, shipping, and dispute resolution practices, Dr. Zhao was one of the pioneers who developed the legal practice of customs and trade compliance in China, which is inclusive of export controls and economic sanctions. Dr. Zhao was also named as one of the *Top 20 Lawyers of Client Choice in China*, in the first survey of this nature by ALB in 2012, for "his practical experience in very specialized areas" and "his consummate professional skills". He has also been recommended by Chambers as *the top-ranked lawyer in the practice of Customs, Export Controls and Economic Sanctions* in 2021, 2022 and 2023. Dr. Zhao occasionally writes traditional Chinese poems in his spare time and is close to completing the translation from English into Chinese *Stray Birds* by Rabindranath Tagore and started to translate some poems by William Butler Yeats, with the only aim of revealing some of their poetic beauty in Chinese language. e-mail: zhaodeming@glo.com.cn; dmzhao@vip.sina.com

Abbreviations

AFSL	Anti-Foreign Sanctions Law of China
ASB	Anti-Smuggling Bureau
ATT	Arms Trade Treaty
BTWC	Biological and Toxin Weapons Convention
CMC	Central Military Commission
COCOM	Coordinating Committee for Multilateral Export Controls
CWC	Convention on the Prohibition of the Development, Production, Stockpiling and Use of Chemical Weapons and on their Destruction
EAR	Export Administration Regulations
ECCN	Export Control Classification Number
ECL	Export Control Law
ECRA	Export Control Reform Act
GAC	General Administration of Customs
GATT	General Agreement on Tariffs and Trade
IAEA	International Atomic Energy Agency
ICP	Internal Compliance Program
ISO	International Organization for Standardization
MOFCOM	Ministry of Commerce
MTCR	Missile Technology Control Regime
NPT	Non-Proliferation of Nuclear Weapons
NSG	Nuclear Suppliers Group
OPCW	Organization for the Prohibition of Chemical Weapons
PUEL	Provisions on the Unreliable Entities List
SASTIND	State Administration of Science, Technology and Industry for National Defense
UN	United Nations
WMD	Weapons of Mass Destruction
WTO	World Trade Organization

Chapter 1
Introduction

This chapter serves as an introduction to the export control rules of the People's Republic of China ("PRC" or "China", for the purpose of this book only, not including the Hong Kong Special Administrative Region, the Macau Special Administrative Region, and the Taiwan Region which are deemed for the import and export purposes as the special customs territory outside the customs territory of China). The term "export control" used in this book can be defined as a licensing and other restrictive or prohibitive control framework designed to regulate the outbound flow of goods, technologies (including software), services as well as their data (collectively as "items") for the purpose of non-proliferation control of weapons of mass destruction ("WMD") or national security or interest considerations.[1] Such items normally include but not limited to nuclear items, military items and "dual-use" items.

Section 1.1 of this chapter explores the justification of export control measures under international law, particularly under regimes of the World Trade Organization ("WTO") and the United Nations ("UN"). Section 1.2 explores the domestic legislative and policy considerations underlying export control measures of China, with a focus on Export Control Law of China ("ECL") and China White Paper of Export Controls ("White Paper").

[1] A similar definition of the term is "an export control regime can be defined as a framework designed to regulate the international trade and transfer of sensitive and critical goods/items and related technologies". See Achilleas, P. (2017). Introduction to Export Control. In D. Tamada, & P. Achilleas (eds.), *Theory and Practice of Export Control: Balancing International Security and International Economic Relations* (p. 3). Springer.

D. Zhao, *Contemporary Export Control Law of China*, Modern China and International Economic Law, https://doi.org/10.1007/978-981-99-9825-8_1

1.1 Justification of Export Controls Under WTO and UN

1.1.1 Export Control Under WTO Regime

Classified as trade control measures, export controls, if maintained by WTO Members, may have the effect of distorting the global market and result in violation of one or more commitments under WTO agreements including the commitments made in their WTO accession process by such members.[2] Although the sovereign right of each State to dispose of its wealth and its natural resources has been well-established in contemporary international law,[3] the onset and maintenance of export controls may face legality challenges under the WTO regime.[4]

Though some scholars have admitted that export control is an "under-regulated" area under the WTO regime,[5] three main disciplines of the General Agreement on Tariffs and Trade ("GATT") 1994 can be explored to test the legality or non-justification of export control measures.

1.1.1.1 Article XI of GATT 1994: Quantitative Restrictions

Generally, a ban or limit, either de facto or *de jury*, on the quantity of goods to be exported, whether made effective through quotas, licenses or other measures other than duties, taxes, or other charges, constitutes quantitative restrictions under Article XI:1 of GATT 1994.[6] To establish that an export control measure is inconsistent with Article XI:1, the complaining Member State must literally demonstrate the following

[2] Such commitment can be found in a Report of the Working Party containing a summary of proceedings and conditions of entry, a Protocol of Accession, and Schedules of market access commitments in goods and services agreed between the acceding government and WTO Members. Retrieved September 18, 2023, from https://www.wto.org/english/thewto_e/acc_e/acces_e.htm.

[3] Permanent Sovereignty over Natural Resources, General Assembly Resolution 1803 (XVII) of 14 December 1962.

[4] Disputes related to export control handled by the Dispute Settlement Body ("DSB") include but are not limited to DS155, *Argentina—Measures Affecting the Export of Bovine Hides and the Import of Finished Leather*; DS194, *United States—Measures Treating Export Restraints as Subsidies*; DS394/395/398, *China—Measures Related to the Exportation of Various Raw Materials*; DS431/432/433, *China—Measures Related to the Exportation of Rare Earths, Tungsten, and Molybdenum*; DS590, *Japan—Measures Related to the Exportation of Products and Technology to Korea*. We also noted that on 12 December 2022, China officially launched a dispute settlement mechanism against the United States (U.S.) regarding the export controls affecting the export of certain advanced computing and semiconductor manufacturing items.

[5] Karapinar, B. (2011). Export Restrictions and the WTO Law: How to Reform the "Regulatory Deficiency". *Journal of World Trade*, 45, 1139.

[6] Article XI:1 of GATT 1994: No prohibitions or restrictions other than duties, taxes, or other charges, whether made effective through quotas, import or export licenses or other measures, shall be instituted or maintained by any contracting party on the importation of any product of the territory of any other contracting party or on the exportation or sale for export of any product destined for the territory of any other contracting party.

two elements: (i) the measure falls within the scope of the phrase "quotas, licenses or other measures"; and (ii) the measure constitutes a prohibition or restriction on the exportation or sale for export of any product.[7]

Concerning the first element, as the Panel pointed out in *India—Quantitative Restrictions*, the wording of Article XI:1 is comprehensive and very broad in scope as covers all measures instituted or maintained by a member prohibiting or restricting the importation, exportation, or sale for export of products, other than measures that take the form of duties, taxes, or other charges.[8]

Regarding the second element, it would suffice that the export control maintained by a Member State aims at prohibiting or restricting the export of controlled items to certain destinations. In this context, "prohibition" means a legal ban on the trade or export of a specified commodity, while "restriction" is defined as a thing that restricts someone or something, a limitation on action, a limiting condition or regulation, and thus refers generally to something that has a limiting effect.[9]

The "export control" as defined and discussed in this book very likely constitutes the quantitative restriction inconsistent with Article XI:1 of GATT 1994, provided the export control is direct to quantitative effects.[10]

Notwithstanding the general quantitative prohibition in Article XI:1, Article XI:2 of GATT 1994[11] permits two instances of carving out or exceptions to justify some deviations from the regular export, which include: (i) export prohibitions or restrictions temporarily applied to prevent or relieve critical shortages of foodstuffs or other products essential to the exporting contracting party; and (ii) import and export prohibitions or restrictions necessary to the application of standards or regulations for the classification, grading or marketing of commodities in international trade. As an instance, during the Ukraine-Russia war affair, many countries adopted a food export embargo or restriction, arguing a severe emergency of its domestic food

---

[7] WT/DS476/R, *European Union and its Member States—Certain Measures Relating to the Energy Sector*, 10 August 2018, para 7.243; WT/DS438/AB/R, WT/DS444/AB/R, WT/DS445/AB/R, *Argentina—Measures Affecting the Importation of Goods*, 15 January 2015, paras. 5.216–5.218.

[8] WT/DS90/R, *India—Quantitative Restrictions on Imports of Agricultural, Textile and Industrial Products*—Status Report by India, para 5.129.

[9] WT/DS394/AB/R, WT/DS395/AB/R, WT/DS398/AB/R, *China—Measures Related to the Exportation of Various Raw Materials*, 30 January 2012, paras. 319–320.

[10] For example, on 11 September 2019, Korea requested consultations with Japan regarding certain measures, including licensing policies and procedures, adopted by Japan allegedly restricting exports of fluorinated polyimide, resist polymers and hydrogen fluoride, and their related technologies destined for Korea. Those products are used primarily in the production of smartphones, TV displays, and semiconductors. Korea claimed that the measures appear to be inconsistent with Article XI:1 of the GATT. Retrieved September 18, 2023, from https://www.wto.org/english/tratop_e/dispu_e/cases_e/ds590_e.htm.

[11] Article XI:2 of the GATT 1994: The provisions of paragraph 1 of this Article shall not extend to the following: (a) export prohibitions or restrictions temporarily applied to prevent or relieve critical shortages of foodstuffs or other products essential to the exporting contracting party; (b) import and export prohibitions or restrictions necessary to the application of standards or regulations for the classification, grading or marketing of commodities in international trade; (c) import restrictions on any agricultural or fisheries product, imported in any form,* necessary to the enforcement of governmental measures which operate…

shortage to substantiate such embargo or restriction.[12] Under such circumstances, WTO Members are required to notify WTO of such new embargo or restrictive trade measures and WTO shall process and publish these in a timely manner.[13] As an example, Ukraine notified WTO that it has imposed quantitative restrictions on the export of personal protective equipment, including protective suits, gloves, protective masks, and alcoholic products to produce disinfectants on 26 March 2020, at the beginning of Covid-19 Pandemic.[14]

Apparently, the exception set forth in Article XI:2(a) is more likely to justify the temporary (instead of indefinite) export control policy for food products, raw materials or personal protective equipment adopted during certain abnormal periods of shortage in supplies. However, the standard of proof in such a case may be demanding as the Appellate Body ruled in the well-known case *China—Raw Materials* that the quantitative restrictions to be applied must be absolutely indispensable or necessary for the exporting state and there must be a critical shortage.[15] Furthermore, the shortage of supply must be at the level of reaching a decisive turning point, which can cause a serious crisis in the exporting State.[16] Such a rationale may well explain why export restrictions of China were held as in violation of Article XI:1 in *China—Raw Materials* and *China—Rare Earths*.

1.1.1.2 Article XX of GATT 1994: General Exceptions

Even if the violation of Article XI has been established, a Member State may still argue consistency of export-restricting measures with commitments under WTO by

[12] Glauber, J., Laborde, D., & Mamun, A. (2022, April 13). From bad to worse: How Russia-Ukraine war-related export restrictions exacerbate global food insecurity. Retrieved September 18, 2023, from https://www.ifpri.org/blog/bad-worse-how-export-restrictions-exacerbate-global-food-security.

[13] Last paragraph of Article XI:2 of GATT 1994: Any contracting party applying restrictions on the importation of any product pursuant to subparagraph (c) of this paragraph shall give public notice of the total quantity or value of the product permitted to be imported during a specified future period and of any change in such quantity or value. Moreover, any restrictions applied under (i) above shall not be such as will reduce the total of imports relative to the total of domestic production, as compared with the proportion which might reasonably be expected to rule between the two in the absence of restrictions. In determining this proportion, the contracting party shall pay due regard to the proportion prevailing during a previous representative period and to any special factors* which may have affected or may be affecting the trade in the product concerned.

[14] World Trade Organization.COVID-19 and world trade. Retrieved September 18, 2023, from https://www.wto.org/english/tratop_e/covid19_e/covid19_e.htm.

[15] WT/DS394/AB/R, WT/DS395/AB/R, WT/DS398/AB/R, *China—Measures Related to the Exportation of Various Raw Materials*, 30 January 2012, para. 326.

[16] Yüksel Ripley, B., & Halatçı Ulusoy, Ü. (2022). COVID-19 Related Export Bans and Restrictions Under WTO Law and the Determination of Their Legal Effects on International Sale of Goods Contracts Between Parties Located in WTO Member States: Interplay Between Public and Private International Law. In P. Sooksripaisarnkit, & D. Prasad (eds.), *Blurry Boundaries of Public and Private International Law: Towards Convergence or Divergent Still?* Springer.

virtue of Article XX of GATT 1994 if certain conditions are met.[17] The chapeau of Article XX requires that a given measure adopted shall not constitute a means of arbitrary or unjustifiable discrimination between countries.[18] Otherwise, a given export control is permissible under paragraphs (a) to (j) of Article XX if qualified in a list of exceptions which are necessary or relating to protection of given values, morals, or interests.[19]

In applying Article XX, a "two-tier test" is crucial, i.e., the exception paragraphs run first, followed by the chapeau.[20] In other words, Member States if invoking Article XX to justify its export control measures must first prove that the measures are "necessary" to protect one of the exceptions and that no alternative measures are otherwise "reasonably available" to tackle the then-current issue in a less-trade restrictive manner,[21] which also means that such measures are required to end or

---

[17] World Trade Organization. (2020, April 23). *Information Note: Export Prohibitions and Restrictions* (p. 4). Retrieved September 19, 2023, from https://www.wto.org/english/tratop_e/covid19_e/export_prohibitions_report_e.pdf.

[18] Chapeau of Article XX of GATT 1994: Subject to the requirement that such measures are not applied in a manner which would constitute a means of arbitrary or unjustifiable discrimination between countries where the same conditions prevail, or a disguised restriction on international trade, nothing in this agreement shall be construed to prevent the adoption or enforcement by any contracting party of measures.

[19] Paragraphs (a)–(j) of Article XX of GATT 1994: (a) necessary to protect public morals; (b) necessary to protect human, animal or plant life or health; (c) relating to the importations or exportations of gold or silver; (d) necessary to secure compliance with laws or regulations which are not inconsistent with the provisions of this agreement, including those relating to customs enforcement, the enforcement of monopolies operated under paragraph 4 of Article II and Article XVII, the protection of patents, trademarks and copyrights, and the prevention of deceptive practices; (e) relating to the products of prison labor; (f) imposed for the protection of national treasures of artistic, historic or archaeological value; (g) relating to the conservation of exhaustible natural resources if such measures are made effective in conjunction with restrictions on domestic production or consumption; (h) undertaken in pursuance of obligations under any intergovernmental commodity agreement which conforms to criteria submitted to the contracting parties and not disapproved by them or which is itself so submitted and not so disapproved; (i) involving restrictions on exports of domestic materials necessary to ensure essential quantities of such materials to a domestic processing industry during periods when the domestic price of such materials is held below the world price as part of a governmental stabilization plan; Provided that such restrictions shall not operate to increase the exports of or the protection afforded to such domestic industry, and shall not depart from the provisions of this agreement relating to non-discrimination; (j) essential to the acquisition or distribution of products in general or local short supply; provided that any such measures shall be consistent with the principle that all contracting parties are entitled to an equitable share of the international supply of such products, and that any such measures, which are inconsistent with the other provisions of the agreement shall be discontinued as soon as the conditions giving rise to them have ceased to exist. The contracting parties shall review the need for this sub-paragraph not later than 30 June 1960.

[20] WT/DS2/AB/R, *United States—Standards for Reformulated and Conventional Gasoline*, 29 April 1996, p. 22; WT/DS302/AB/R, *Dominican Republic—Measures Affecting the Importation and the Internal Sale of Cigarettes*, 25 April 2005, para. 64; WT/DS332/AB/R, *Brazil—Measures Affecting Imports of Retreaded Tyres*, 3 December 2007, para. 139.

[21] WT/DS161/R, WT/DS169/R, *Korea—Measures Affecting Imports of Fresh, Chilled and Frozen Beef*, 31 July 2000, para. 659.

modify if there is a change in the circumstances giving rise to adoption of the same measures.[22] Then, the measures need to fulfill the requirements in the chapeau of Article XX, which is aimed at the prevention of abuse of the exceptions by Member States.

China—Rare Earths is a case where the Respondent relies on Article XX as a justifiable reason for its export control measures. In this case, China sought to invoke Article XX(b) as necessary to protect human, animal, or plant life or health and Article XX(g) as relating to the conservation of exhaustible natural resources to justify its export duties and export quotas on rare earths, tungsten, and molybdenum as well as trading limitations on business operators permitted to export the materials, which had been applied in a manner allegedly inconsistent with the Accession Protocol of China and Article XI of GATT 1994 as complained by the U.S., the EU, and Japan.[23]

In presenting the defense under Article XX(b), China asserted that the export duties were necessary to protect human, animal, and plant life and health from the grave harm arising from the mining and production of the products in question. However, in the Panel's view, there was no link between export duties and the pollution reduction objective under the comprehensive environmental policy of China. Instead, the Panel tended to believe that the export duties at issue were designed and structured to promote increased domestic production of high-value-added downstream products that use the raw materials as inputs in this dispute.[24]

Concerning the defense under Article XX(g), China mainly asserted that the export quotas were justifiable for relating to the conservation of an exhaustible natural resource, and the term "conservation" signified the use and management of those resources in line with a State Member's sustainable economic development. The Panel did not agree on this point and found that the export quotas of China were designed to achieve industrial policy goals and control the international market for natural resource rather than conservation.[25] The Appellate Body upheld the Panel's findings on Article XX(g).[26]

Indeed, the precedents where defenses under Article XX were upheld are quite limited.[27] One of the reasons may be that the measure can be justified only if and

---

[22] Akbari, S. (2021). The Relationship Between Freedom of Transit and General and Security Exceptions Under WTO Rules. *The WTO Transit Regime for Landlocked Countries and its Impacts on Members' Regional Transit Agreements: The Case of Afghanistan's Transit Trade with Pakistan* (p. 169). Springer.

[23] The summary of this dispute can be found at: https://www.wto.org/english/tratop_e/dispu_e/cases_e/ds431_e.htm.

[24] WT/DS431/R, WT/DS432/R, WT/DS433/R, *China—Measures Related to the Exportation of Rare Earths, Tungsten, and Molybdenum*, 26 March 2014, paras. 7.149–7.171.

[25] Ibid., paras. 7.362–7.680.

[26] WT/DS431/AB/R, WT/DS432/AB/R, WT/DS433/AB/R, *China—Measures Related to the Exportation of Rare Earths, Tungsten, and Molybdenum*, 7 August 2014, para. 5.252. Please note that China did not appeal to the Appellate Body with respect to Article XX(b) of the GATT 1994.

[27] 2015 Report on Compliance by Major Trading Partners with Trade Agreements—WTO, FTA/EPA and IIA (p. 329). Retrieved September 22, 2023, from https://www.meti.go.jp/english/report/data/2016WTO/pdf/02_06.pdf.

when the measure is "necessary" to achieve the policy objectives. The "necessity" threshold is difficult to overcome in practice if a State Member seeks to invoke Article XX, which has been construed as "inevitable or indispensable necessity"[28] or "non-existence of alternative measures less inconsistent with the agreement".[29] It would not be a wise strategy if a Member State solely relies on Article XX to justify its export control measures.

1.1.1.3 Article XXI of GATT 1994: Security Exceptions

Compared with the general exceptions, "security exceptions" can be more effective and powerful to the invoking State. Article XXI allows States to take an action or prevent a measure that is necessary for their "essential security interests" or for international peace and security.[30] Among three paragraphs, paragraph (b) of Article XXI is the most often quoted paragraph that affords three categories of "essential security interests". Respectively, Category A refers to fissionable materials or the materials from which they are derived. Category B relates to the traffic in arms, ammunition, and implements of war and to such traffic in other goods and materials as is carried on directly or indirectly for the purpose of supplying a military establishment. Category C deals with such measures as taken in times of war or *other emergencies in international relations.*

The term "essential security interests", which is evidently a narrower concept than "security interests", may generally refer to those interests relating to the quintessential functions of the State, namely the protection of its territory and its population from external threats, and the maintenance of law and public order internally,[31] though whether Article XXI is justiciable as an exception has been controversial through the whole history from GATT 1947 to GATT 1994.

During the Geneva discussions of the Preparatory Committee in 1949, it was stated that every country must be the judge in the last resort on questions relating to its own security,[32] implying that the State that invokes the security exception is

[28] WT/DS161/AB/R, WT/DS169/AB/R, *Korea—Measures Affecting Imports of Fresh, Chilled and Frozen Beef*, 11 December 2000, para. 161.

[29] DS10/R—37S/200, *Thailand—Restrictions on Importation of and Internal Taxes on Cigarettes*, 5 October 1990, para. 75.

[30] Article XXI of GATT 1994, nothing in this agreement shall be construed (a) to require any contracting party to furnish any information the disclosure of which it considers contrary to its essential security interests; or (b) to prevent any contracting party from taking any action which it considers necessary for the protection of its essential security interests (i) relating to fissionable materials or the materials from which they are derived; (ii) relating to the traffic in arms, ammunition and implements of war and to such traffic in other goods and materials as is carried on directly or indirectly for the purpose of supplying a military establishment; (iii) taken in time of war or other emergency in international relations; or (c) to prevent any contracting party from taking any action in pursuance of its obligations under the United Nations Charter for the maintenance of international peace and security.

[31] WT/DS512/R, *Russia—Measures Concerning Traffic in Transit*, 5 April 2019, para. 7.130.

[32] GATT/CP.3/SR.22, Corr. 1.

the party to determine its own ingredients of essential security interests.[33] On the other hand, every contracting party shall be cautious not to take any step which might have the effect of undermining GATT,[34] which actually requires a certain degree of restraint on the discretion of Member State in making its determination upon relying Article XXI.

The landmark case *Russia—Traffic in Transit* is the first case in WTO history where the Panel makes the ruling on Article XXI. This dispute concerns the imposition, publication and administration of measures taken by the Russian Federation restricting international transit cargo by road and rail from Ukraine destined for the Republic of Kazakhstan or the Kyrgyz Republic, and banning such transit cargo in terms of certain categories of goods.[35] To respond to Ukraine's claims,[36] Russia asserted that the measures are among those that it considered necessary for protection of its essential security interests, which it took in response to *such emergency in international relations* as occurred in 2014 as presenting threats to the Russian Federation's essential security interests. Russia, therefore, invoked the provisions of Article XXI(b)(iii) of GATT 1994, arguing that, as a result, the Panel lacked jurisdiction to further address the matter.[37]

The first issue in the case is whether Article XXI(b) is justifiable by way of self-judging on the part of the invoking State since the chapeau of Article XXI(b) opens a door to the invoking State with the wording "which it considers". The Panel started its analysis in accordance with the customary rules of interpretation of public international law, especially those codified in Articles 31 & 32 of the Vienna Convention on the Law of Treaties.[38] In the Panel's view, although the chapeau of Article XXI(b) allows a Member State to go through this door "which it considers necessary" for the protection of its essential security interests, such discretion is only limited to circumstances that objectively fall within the scope of the three categories of Article XXI(b). It follows that Article XXI(b) of GATT 1994 is not completely "self-judging" in the manner asserted by Russia, and Russia's argument that the Panel lacks jurisdiction to review Russia's invocation of Article XXI(b) must fail.[39]

[33] Halatçı Ulusoy, Ü. (2021). Covid-19 Salgını Sonrası Med˙ıkal Ürünlere Uygulanan ˙ Ihracat Kısıtlamalarının Dünya T˙ıcaret Örgüt¨ u Kuralları Kapsamında De˘ gerlend˙ır˙ılmes˙ı. *Banka Ve Ticaret Hukuku Dergisi*, XXXVI I(2), 90.

[34] WTO Analytical Index on Article XXI of GATT.

[35] The identified transit restrictions include (1) the 2016 Belarus Transit Requirements, (2) the 2016 Transit Bans on Non-Zero Duty and Resolution No. 778 Goods, and (3) the 2014 Belarus-Russia Bans on Transit of Resolution No. 778 Goods.

[36] Ukraine claimed those measures maintained by Russia violated Articles V:2, V:3, V:4, V:5, X:1, X:2, X:3(a), XI:1, XVI:4 of GATT 1994; and Paragraph 2 of Part I of the Russian Federation's Accession Protocol (to the extent that it incorporates paragraphs 1161, 1426 (first sentence), 1427 (first and third sentences) and 1428 of the Report of the Working Party on the Accession of the Russian Federation).

[37] WT/DS512/R, *Russia—Measures Concerning Traffic in Transit*, 5 April 2019, paras. 7.3–7.4.

[38] Ibid., para. 7.59.

[39] Ibid., paras. 7.102–7.104.

The second issue concerns the extent of review by the Panel of Russia's measures under Article XXI(b)(iii). The Panel acknowledged that it is left, in general, to every State Member to define what it considers to be its essential security interests.[40] However, the obligation of good faith must be in play so that WTO panels may review (i) whether there was any evidence to suggest that the State Member's designation of the issue as its essential security interests was not made in good faith, and (ii) whether the challenged measures taken by such State Member were "not implausible" as measures to protect those essential security interests.[41]

Therefore, a State Member may succeed in invoking Article XXI to justify its export control measures, though it may face the challenge of good faith from the applicant State Member in a dispute.

1.1.2 Export Control Under UN Regime

A State may adopt export control measures to implement multilateral sanctions imposed by the Security Council of the UN. Such multilateral sanctions include export control or embargo measures adopted by the Security Council. Apart from such multilateral sanctions, this section will also explore the national implementation mechanism on those multinational export controls, taking China as an example.[42]

1.1.2.1 UN Export Embargo

As the authority in determining the existence of a threat to the peace or act of aggression, the Security Council of the UN calls upon State parties to a dispute to settle it by peaceful means and recommends methods of adjustment or terms of settlement and even imposes sanctions in some cases.[43]

The springboard for our discussion on embargo measures under UN regime is Article 41 of the UN Charter, which gives the Security Council the authority to use a variety of measures to enforce its decisions.

> The Security Council may decide what **measures NOT involving the use of armed force** are to be employed to give effect to its decisions, and it may call upon the Members of the United Nations to apply such measures. These may include complete or partial interruption of economic relations and of rail, sea, air, postal, telegraphic, radio, and other means of communication, and the severance of diplomatic relations.

Generally, the non-military measures referred to in Article 41 are sanctions or economic sanctions, although the term "sanctions" is not explicitly appeared in that

[40] Ibid., para. 7.131.

[41] Ibid., paras. 7.132–7.135 & 7.138–7.139.

[42] In this section, we do not strictly distinguish the term "export control" from the term "embargo".

[43] United Nations Security Council. Retrieved September 27, 2023, from https://www.un.org/securitycouncil/.

Article. Since the feasibility of certain measures, e.g., interrupting postal, telegraphic, and radio communications is quite challenging,[44] the most frequently adopted sanctions in practice by the Security Council include export and import embargo, services prohibition, prohibition of movement of funds, the freeze of funds and assets, prohibition of air, sea and land communications, severance or reduction of diplomatic and other official relations, and restrictions on the movement of persons. Those sanctions are generally supported by Committees or Panels/Groups of Experts or other mechanisms, to monitor the implementation of the sanctions.[45]

The multilateral sanctions as may adopted by the Security Council may take the form of export embargoes, which prohibits certain exports (including their shipping) from the Member States to the targeted countries, entities or individuals covered by the sanctions. Export embargoes under resolutions of the General Security are often taking the form of selective or targeted export embargo, rather than comprehensive export embargo. Selective or targeted export embargoes mean items only explicitly enlisted on the resolution are prohibited from being exported to the sanctioned destinations.[46] In this regard, North Korea ("DPRK") and Iran may serve as examples of the selective embargo against a targeted country or destination.

A. **Selective embargoes against DPRK**

To condemn DPRK's withdrawal from the Treaty on Non-Proliferation of Nuclear Weapons in 2003 and the nuclear test proclaimed by DPRK on 9 October 2006, the Security Council, acting under Chap. VII of the UN Charter, adopted a series of resolutions to impose sanction measures.[47] The direct or indirect export, supply, sale, or transfer of the following items to DPRK is prohibited.

---

[44] Gowlland-Debbas, V. (2004). Sanctions Regimes under Article 41 of the UN Charter. In V. Gowlland-Debbas (ed.), *National implementation of United Nations sanctions: a comparative study*. Martinus Nijhoff.

[45] United Nations Security Council. Sanctions and Other Committees. Retrieved September 27, 2023, from https://www.un.org/securitycouncil/content/repertoire/sanctions-and-other-committees.

[46] As for comprehensive embargos, there were a few Resolutions containing a comprehensive ban on the import of all commodities and products originating in sanctioned destinations as follows, Southern Rhodesia, S/RES/253 (1968); Iraq and Kuwait, S/RES/661 (1990); the Federal Republic of Yugoslavia (Serbia and Montenegro), S/RES/757 (1992). Notably, S/RES/917 (1994) bans both the import of into Member States' territories of all commodities and products originating in Haiti and the export by their nationals or from their territories or using their flag vessels or aircraft of any commodities or products, whether or not originating in their territories, to any person or body in Haiti or to any person or body for the purpose of any business carried on in, or operated from, Haiti, and any activities by their nationals or in their territories which promote such sale or supply of such commodities or products.

[47] DPRK-related Resolutions adopted after 2006 include, but are not limited to: S/RES/1718 (2006), S/RES/1874 (2009), S/RES/1887 (2009), S/RES/2087 (2013), S/RES/2094 (2013), S/RES/2270 (2016), S/RES/2321 (2016), S/RES/2345 (2017), S/RES/2356 (2017), S/RES/2371 (2017), S/RES/2375 (2017), S/RES/2397 (2017), S/RES/2407 (2018), S/RES/2464 (2019), S/RES/2515 (2020), S/RES/2569 (2021), S/RES/2627 (2022).

Resolution No	Items subject to export embargo
S/RES/1718 (2006)	i. Any battle tanks, armored combat vehicles, large caliber artillery systems, combat aircraft, attack helicopters, warships, missiles or missile systems as defined for the purpose of the United Nations Register on Conventional Arms, or related materiel including spare parts, or items as determined by the Security Council or the Committee established by paragraph 12 below (the Committee) ii. All items, materials, equipment, goods, and technology as set out in the lists in documents S/2006/814 and S/2006/815 iii. Luxury goods
S/RES/1874 (2009)	All arms and related material
S/RES/2087 (2013)	Items in INFCIRC/254/Rev.11/Part 1 & INFCIRC/254/Rev.8/Part 2 and S/2012/947[48]
S/RES/2094 (2013)	i. Nuclear items (including Perfluorinated Lubricants & UF6 Corrosion Resistant Bellow-sealed Valves) ii. Missile items iii. Chemical weapons iv. Luxury goods
S/RES/2270 (2016)	i. Any item, except food or medicine, if the State Member determines that such item could directly contribute to the development of DPRK's operational capabilities of its armed forces, or to exports that support or enhance the operational capabilities of armed forces of another Member State outside DPRK ii. Luxury goods
S/RES/2321 (2016)	i. Nuclear- and/or missile-usable items ii. Chemical/Biological weapons-usable items iii. Luxury goods
S/RES/2375 (2017)	i. All condensates and natural gas liquids ii. All refined petroleum products
S/RES/2397 (2017)	i. All crude oil ii. All refined petroleum products iii. All industrial machinery (HS codes 84 and 85), transportation vehicles (HS codes 86 through 89), and iron, steel, and other metals (HS codes 72 through 83)

[48] INFCIRC/254/Rev.11/Part 1 is the Trigger List of nuclear items. INFCIRC/254/Rev.8/Part 2 is the List of nuclear-related dual-use equipment, materials, software, and related technology. Items in S/2012/947 are those items, materials, equipment, goods, and technology related to ballistic missile programs.

B. Selective embargoes against iran

The Security Council has also adopted certain Resolutions on Iran as a response to all aspects of Iran's nuclear programs.[49] As summarized, the direct or indirect export, supply, sale, or transfer of the following items to Iran is prohibited.

Resolution No	Items subject to export embargo
S/RES/1737 (2006)	All items, materials, equipment, goods, and technology which could contribute to Iran's enrichment-related, reprocessing or heavy water-related activities, or to the development of nuclear weapon delivery systems, namely: i. Those set out in sections B.2, B.3, B.4, B.5, B.6 and B.7 of INFCIRC/254/Rev.8/Part 1 in document S/2006/814 ii. Those set out in sections A.1 and B.1 of INFCIRC/254/Rev.8/Part 1 in document S/2006/814, with certain exceptions iii. Those set out in document S/2006/815, except the supply, sale or transfer of items covered by 19.A.3 of Category II iv. Any additional items, materials, equipment, goods, and technology, determined as necessary by the Security Council or the Committee established by paragraph 18 below (herein "the Committee"), which could contribute to enrichment-related, or reprocessing, or heavy water-related activities, or to the development of nuclear weapon delivery systems The following items, materials, equipment, goods, and technology: i. Those set out in INFCIRC/254/Rev.7/Part2 of document S/2006/814 if the Member State determines that they would contribute to enrichment-related, reprocessing or heavy water-related activities ii. Any other items not listed in documents S/2006/814 or S/2006/815 if the Member State determines that they would contribute to enrichment-related, reprocessing or heavy water-related activities, or to the development of nuclear weapon delivery systems iii. Any further items if the Member State determines that they would contribute to the pursuit of activities related to other topics about which the IAEA has expressed concerns or identified as outstanding
S/RES/1803 (2008)	i. All items, materials, equipment, goods, and technology set out in INFCIRC/254/Rev.7/Part 2 of document S/2006/814, with certain exceptions ii. All items, materials, equipment, goods, and technology set out in 19.A.3 of Category II of document S/2006/815
S/RES/1929 (2010)	Any battle tanks, armored combat vehicles, large caliber artillery systems, combat aircraft, attack helicopters, warships, missiles or missile systems as defined for the purpose of the United Nations Register of Conventional Arms, or related materiel, including spare parts, or items as determined by the Security Council or the Committee established pursuant to resolution 1737 (2006)

[49] Iran-related Resolutions mainly include but are not limited to: S/RES/1696 (2006), S/RES/1737 (2006), S/RES/1747 (2007), S/RES/1803 (2008), S/RES/1835 (2008), S/RES/1929 (2010), S/RES/2015 (2013).

1.1.2.2 The Implementation of UN Export Embargoes by China

It is generally recognized that the decisions adopted by the Security Council are mandatory, and Member States are therefore obliged to carry out or implement these decisions. Such binding effect is derived from Article 25 of the Charter and further crowned by Articles 48 and 49 of the UN Charter. Though a Member State which has contracted valid international obligations is bound to make in its legislation such modifications as may be necessary to fulfill the obligations as undertaken,[50] the specific implementing mechanism is an issue of national law.

As some scholars summarized, there are mainly three types of tools Member States may use to implement sanctions measures of the Security Council. Namely, the Member State may implement UN export embargo through (i) prior enabling legislation, (ii) pre-existing legislation not uniquely designed for sanctions legislation, or (iii) ad hoc legislation.[51]

Before the enactment of PRC's *Foreign Relations Law*,[52] China does not have specific laws or administrative regulations on implementing UN sanctions, but only with pre-existing legislation in China, e.g., the *Foreign Trade Law* of the PRC as the tool (ii), which authorizes the administrative powers to regulate international trade relations in particular circumstances.[53]

Specifically, under the *Foreign Trade Law* of the PRC, the Ministry of Commerce of China ("MOFCOM"), the General Administration of Customs of China ("GAC"),

---

[50] *Exchange of Greek and Turkish Populations*, Advisory Opinion, P. C. I. J., Series B, No. 10, February 21, 1925, p. 10.

[51] Prior enabling legislation refers to an existence of a general law adopted as framework legislation expressly enabling the executive branch to implement by decree the UN Security Council decisions. Pre-existing legislation not designed for sanctions refers to existing laws or statutes not directly related to decisions of international organizations for the implementation of Security Council sanctions of a traditional type, such as trade sanctions, arms embargoes, restrictions on transfer of capital (the freezing of funds has been more problematic, being seen as seizure of private property), ban on air traffic and restriction of movement of persons. Ad hoc legislation means the parliamentary process for the adoption, on a case-by-case basis, of particular sanctions law.

See Gowlland-Debbas, V. (2004). Implementing Sanctions Resolutions in Domestic Law. In V. Gowlland-Debbas (ed.), *National implementation of United Nations sanctions: a comparative study* (pp. 41–44). Martinus Nijhoff.

[52] Article 35 of the *Foreign Relations Law* prescribes that the State takes measures to implement binding resolutions on sanctions and related measures of the United Nations Security Council in accordance with Chapter VII of the Charter of the United Nations. The implementation of the sanction resolutions and measures mentioned in the preceding paragraph shall be notified and announced by the Ministry of Foreign Affairs. The departments concerned of the State and the people's governments of the provinces, autonomous regions, or municipalities directly under the central government shall take measures for the implementation thereof within the scope of their respective functions and powers. All the organizations and individuals within the territory of China shall abide by the announcement of the Ministry of Foreign Affairs and the relevant measures of all departments and regions concerned and shall not engage in any act in violation of the aforesaid sanction resolutions and measures.

[53] Note, with the enactment of ECL, in the future, the legal basis for China to implement the UN's export embargo may also include ECL.

or the Ministry of Transport has issued several announcements to ban the export of items prohibitive under related resolutions adopted by the Security Council.

Taking DPRK as an example, to implement S/RES/2375 (2017), MOFCOM, together with GAC, issued Announcement No. 52 of 2017 on 22 September 2017 to ban the export of condensates and natural gas liquids as well as restrict the export of refined petroleum products to DPRK. The announcement made it clear that it was based on the Foreign Trade Law of China.

Similarly, with a view to implementing S/RES/2397 (2017), MOFCOM and GAC issued Announcement No. 4 of 2018 on 5 January 2018 to ban the export of industrial machinery, transportation vehicles, and iron, steel, and other metals as well as restrict the export of crude oil and refined petroleum products to DPRK, also invoking the *Foreign Trade Law* of China as its predominant domestic law basis. Besides, the Ministry of Transport issued Announcement No. 19 of 2018 on 29 January 2018 to forbid Chinese citizens and freighters from facilitating such carriage.

However, there were times when only the Ministry of Foreign Affairs of the PRC issued a notification of sanctions or embargoes adopted by the Security Council. According to a circular issued by the Ministry of Foreign Affairs, it has been the position of China to abide by the sanctions by the Security Council "automatically" without the need to enact an implementing domestic law or regulation no matter whether China has abstained from voting for the sanctions or embargoes.[54]

For the procedures of the implementation of the UN embargo, there is a reporting and monitoring mechanism under the UN. This book will not elaborate on this topic. Suffice it to say that China supports the multilateral trade embargo scheme of the Security Council and has been among the first countries to submit its national report on implementation of the resolutions of Security Council.[55]

1.2 Export Control in China: Legislative and Policy Background

Section 1.2 outlines the legislative and policy background of export controls of China. We will first review the legal structure of export controls of China, including laws, regulations, and normative documents, then analyze Export Control Law of China ("ECL") adopted in 2020 and then, introduce the policy considerations of ECL according to China White Paper of Export Controls ("White Paper").

[54] For example, China abstained in the vote regarding the extension of sanctions against South Sudan, while Resolution S/RES/2683(2023) was still adopted by the Security Council at its 9332nd meeting on 30 May 2023. Subsequently, the Ministry of Foreign Affairs published an announcement implementing this resolution on its official website on 9 June 2023.

[55] Annex to the letter dated 4 December 2007 from the representative of China to the Chairman of the Security Council Committee established pursuant to resolution 1540 (2004). Retrieved September 27, 2023, from https://www.un.org/en/sc/1540/documents/ChinaReport4Dec2007.pdf.

1.2.1 Legal Structure of Export Controls of China

1.2.1.1 Laws

ECL is the fundamental law as far as export control is concerned under Chinese law, the concrete rules of which will be introduced in Sect. 1.2.2.

Before the enactment of ECL, the *Foreign Trade Law* of the PRC was treated as the basic law of export control, which was originally enacted in 1994 and has been amended respectively in 2004, 2016 and 2022.[56] As manifested in its general provisions, this law is formulated with a view to more opening to the outside world, developing foreign trade, maintaining foreign trade order, protecting the legitimate rights and interests of foreign trade business operators and promoting the development of the socialist market economy.[57] Understandably from such general provisions, the same law fails to address sufficiently the operational export controls based on national security and non-proliferation of WMD consideration.

The *Foreign Trade Law* consists of 11 chapters, with Chap. 3 (Articles 13–22) regulating import and export of goods and technologies. As a principle, the State shall allow the free import and export of goods and technologies, except otherwise provided for by other laws and administrative regulations.[58] On this basis, Article 15 carves out the export and import restrictive measures for reasons such as severe disruption in domestic export order.[59] Moreover, the State can also take necessary

---

[56] The latest amendment of 2022 deleted the previous Article 9 of the Law, which prescribes that foreign business operators engaged in the import and export of goods or technologies shall apply for a record registration with the competent department for foreign trade under the State Council or with an organization entrusted by the competent department for foreign trade under the State Council, except for those cases where a record registration is not required under the laws, administrative regulations, and the provisions. The specific measures for record registration shall be prescribed by the competent department for foreign trade under the State Council. Where a foreign business operator fails to register for the record, the Customs department shall not carry out customs clearance of imported or exported goods.

[57] Article 1 of the *Foreign Trade Law* of the PRC.

[58] Ibid., Article 13.

[59] Article 15 of the *Foreign Trade Law* of the PRC, the State may restrict or ban the import or export of goods or technologies due to the following reasons: (1) being necessary to restrict or ban the import or export for national security, public interests or public morals, (2) being necessary to restrict or ban the import or export for protecting the health or safety of the people, life or health of animals and plants and the ecological environment, (3) being necessary to restrict or ban the import or export for implementing measures on import and export of gold or silver, (4) being necessary to restrict or ban the export because of shortage of supplies domestically or as important natural resources that are of danger of depletion, (5) being necessary to restrict the export as the limited market in the importing countries or regions, (6) being necessary to restrict the export due to the severe disruption in domestic export order, (7) being necessary to restrict the import to establish or accelerate to establish certain domestic industries, (8) being necessary to restrict the import for agricultural, animal husbandry and fishery products in any form, (9) being necessary to restrict the import for maintaining the international financial position or ensuring a balance of international payments, (10) being necessary to restrict or ban the import or export due to other reasons in accordance with

measures concerning the import and export of goods and technologies at wartime or to maintain international peace and security.[60]

Under this law, it is required to publish and amend the catalogues of goods and technologies subject to export control or embargo.[61] Accordingly, the quota or license administration may be imposed under the *Foreign Trade Law* and its implementing regulations,[62] which is markedly not the same considerations underlying the control of dual-use items, nuclear and military items under ECL.

Other export-control-related laws mainly include *National Security Law*, *Data Security Law*, *Nuclear Safety Law*, *Biosecurity Law*, *Cryptography Law*, *Customs Law*, *Administrative Licensing Law*, *Administrative Punishment Law*, and *Criminal Law*.

1.2.1.2 Administrative Regulations

In China, administrative regulations are those enacted by the State Council in accordance with the Constitution and any law, prescribing any of the matters mentioned below: (i) matters that demand the enactment of an administrative regulation for the purpose of implementing a law; and (ii) matters subject to the administration of the State Council under Article 89 of the Constitution.[63] Administrative regulations are normally called "regulations" or "provisions" in practice.[64]

The major existing effective export control regulations are enlisted as follows:

Subject matter	Name of regulations
Biologics	Regulations on Export Control of Dual-use Biological Items and Related Equipment and Technologies (2002)
Controlled chemicals	Regulations on Administration of Controlled Chemicals (Revised in 2011)
Cryptographies	Regulations on Administration of Commercial Cryptography (Revise)
Military items	Administrative Regulations on Export of Military Items (Revised in 2002)
Missile-related items	Regulations on Export Control of Missiles and Missile-related Items and Technologies (2002)

(continued)

laws and administrative rules; and (11) being necessary to restrict or ban the import or export in accordance with international treaties or agreements to which the PRC has signed or entered.

[60] Article 16 of the *Foreign Trade Law* of the PRC.

[61] Ibid., Article 17(1).

[62] Ibid., Article 18.

[63] Article 72 of *Legislative Law* of the PRC. (Amended in 2023).

[64] Article 5 of *Regulations on Procedures for the Formulation of Administrative Regulations* of the PRC. (Revised in 2017).

(continued)

Subject matter	Name of regulations
Nuclear	Regulations on Export Control of Nuclear (Revised in 2006)
Nuclear-related dual-use items and technologies	Regulations on Export Control of Nuclear-Related Dual-use Items and Technologies (2007)
Precursor chemicals	Regulations on Administration of Precursor Chemicals (2005)
Radiation	Regulations on Safety and Protection of Radioisotope and Radiation Devices (Revised in 2019)

Most of the above regulations were enacted prior to ECL with the policy to control WMD proliferation relevant to nuclear, biological, and chemical weapons as well as their delivery vehicles, e.g., missiles of a certain delivery range. Accordingly, regulatory conciliation with ECL is necessary and desirable. On 22 April 2022, MOFCOM issued the Draft Regulations on Export Control of Dual-use Items for public comment (the "Dual-use Draft Regulations"), which aims at consolidating the existing regulations and streamlining export controls.[65] The Draft Regulations if officially adopted will replace the *Regulations on Export Control of Nuclear-Related Dual-use Items and Technologies, Regulations on Export Control of Missiles and Missile-related Items and Technologies, Regulations on Export Control of Dual-use Biological Items and Related Equipment and Technologies & Measures on Export Control of Certain Chemicals and Related Equipment and Technologies.*[66]

1.2.1.3 Normative Documents

Administrative normative documents are official documents formulated and published by administrative or quasi-administrative organs or organizations in accordance with legal authority and procedures.[67] Those normative documents are normally titled as "measures", "announcements", or "orders" in practice.

The major existing effective export control normative documents are enlisted as follows, and some of these normative documents may be replaced after enactment of the Dual-use Regulations:

[65] Article 1 of the Draft Regulation on the Export Control of Dual-use Items (for public comments).

[66] Ibid., Article 60.

[67] Chapeau of Notice of the General Office of the State Council on Strengthening the Formulation and Supervision of Administrative Normative Documents (Guo Ban Fa [2018] No. 37), 16 May 2018.

Subject matter	Name of the normative documents
Certain chemicals	Measures on Export Control of Certain Chemicals and Related Equipment and Technologies (2002) Announcement on Export Control of Potassium Perchlorate (2021)
Dual-use items and technologies (Comprehensive)	Administration Measures on Import and Export License of Dual-use Items and Technologies (2006) Administration Measures on General License of Exports of Dual-use Items and Technologies (2009) Guidance of MOFCOM on Establishment of Internal Compliance Mechanism of Dual-use Item to Exporting Business Operators (2021)
Missile-related items	Administration Measures on Export Classification of Components and Parts of Civil Aviation (2006) Notice on Export Control Work of Components and Parts of Civil Aviation (2013)
Nuclear	Administration Measures on Nuclear Product Transshipment and Transit Transportation Approval (Trial Implementation) (2000)
Nuclear dual-use items	Announcement on Temporary Export Control on Tributyl Phosphate (2003) Announcement on Temporary Export Control on Graphite-Related Products (2006)
Others	Announcement on Export Control on Hydro Cannon Products (2022)
Precursor chemicals	Administration Provisions on International Verification of Import and Export of Precursor Chemicals (2006) Administration Provisions on Import and Export of Precursor Chemicals (2006) Announcement on Export of Precursor Chemicals by Export Operators to Myanmar and Laos (2006) Announcement on Detailed Provisions on Import and Export of Mixtures Containing Precursor Chemicals (2007) Interim Administration Provisions on Export of Precursor Chemicals to Particular Countries (Regions) (2015) Interim Measures on Verification of Exporters of Ephedrine Precursor Chemicals (2015)
Sensitive items and technologies	Administration Measures on Business Registration for Exports of Sensitive Items and Technologies[68] (2015)

[68] According to Article 2 of the *Administration Measures on Business Registration for Exports of Sensitive Items and Technologies*, "sensitive items and technologies" under these Measures are those enlisted on the lists annexed to the *Regulations on Export Control of Nuclear-Related Dual-use Items and Technologies, Regulations on Export Control of Missiles and Missile-related Items and Technologies, Regulations on Export Control of Dual-use Biological Items and Related Equipment and Technologies & Measures on Export Control of Certain Chemicals and Related Equipment and Technologies.*

1.2.2 *Export Control Law of China*

On 17 October 2020, ECL was approved by the Standing Committee of the National People's Congress and came into effect on 1 December 2020. ECL has abandoned the fragmental regulatory approach to export controls and established a consolidated and comprehensive legal framework on the export of dual-use items, military items, nuclear items, and other items that relate to the policy of maintenance of national security and interests, as well as to fulfillment of non-proliferation and other international obligations. Such items subject to ECL include goods, technologies inclusive of software and services.

ECL apparently borrows some export control concepts from the Export Administrative Regulations ("EAR") issued by the Department of Commerce of the U.S. But the mindset behind ECL compared to that of EAR is far from identical. Facing the threat of foreign abuse of export controls and economic sanctions, ECL emphasizes national security and interests, apart from non-proliferation commitments. Nevertheless, as further elaborated in this book, the unilateral export control list under ECL is much shorter than that of EAR, and ECL does not seem to control foreign-made products though the same may control China-origin contents or be made by using China-origin technology.

1.2.2.1 Legislative Process of ECL

Pursuant to "State Council Legislative Work Plan 2016"[69] and "State Council Legislative Work Plan 2017",[70] MOFCOM initiated the drafting work and released the draft version of ECL (for public comment) in 2017.

The staged process of ECL is summarized as follows[71]:

Time	Enacting body	ECL agenda
16 June 2017	MOFCOM	Release of draft version (for public comment)
23 December 2019	The 15th Session of the Standing Committee of the 13th National People's Congress (NPC)	First deliberation of the draft version (for public comments)

(continued)

[69] The drafting of the ECL was positioned as one of the legislative projects related to adapting to the requirements of the new normal of economic development, promoting sustainable and healthy economic development and opening up to the outside world in the 2016 plan. In other words, the legislation of the ECL was only suggested (to conduct surveys on the necessity and feasibility) in 2016.

[70] The drafting of the ECL was positioned as one of the legislative projects urgently needed for comprehensive deepening reform in the 2017 plan, which means the drafting work should be finished in a timely manner.

[71] Details of the legislative process of the ECL can be found at: http://www.npc.gov.cn/npc/c1773/c1848/c21114/ckgzlf/.

(continued)

Time	Enacting body	ECL agenda
28 December 2019	The Standing Committee of the NPC	Release of the First Reading Draft
28 June 2020	The 20th Session of the Standing Committee of the 13th NPC	Second deliberation of the First Reading Draft
3 July 2020	The Standing Committee of the NPC	Release of the Second Reading Draft
13 October 2020	The 22nd Session of the Standing Committee of the 13th NPC	Third deliberation of the Second Reading Draft
17 October 2020	The 22nd Session of the Standing Committee of the 13th NPC	Passing of ECL (effective date: 1 December 2020)

1.2.2.2 Export Control Patterns

ECL consists of five chapters, including general provisions (this chapter), control policies, control lists and control measures (Chap. 2), supervision and regulation (Chap. 3), legal liabilities (Chap. 4), and supplementary provisions (Chap. 5), with 49 Articles in total. With the objectives of national security and WMD non-proliferation considerations, ECL adopts the export control patterns as follows:

A. **Controlled activities**

The first thing the legislature needs to consider control under ECL is what activities are to be controlled to avoid risks of national security or WMD proliferation. For the business community, you need to determine whether there are any controlled activities that may occur within your organization. If the answer is positive, your organization may run export control risks and you will need to further examine the items in such activities as well as end-use and end-users of such items to identify if there are any real risks under ECL.

(a) Export/cross-border transfer

Obviously, the cross-border transfer or transmission of items subject to ECL is the most common manifestation of the national security or WMD proliferation risks. Under ECL, "export" activities under control are not merely confined to shipment of commodities out of the customs territory of China, but signifying a wide range of transfer or transmission of items subject to ECL from the customs territory of mainland China to overseas.[72] Similar to the definition under EAR, it is reasonable that "export" under ECL includes an actual shipment or transmission out of China or the sending or taking of an item subject to ECL out of China, in any manner, no matter whether it is a tangible commodities or intangible technology or personal belongings, whether it is cleared through the customs authority in China or not.

[72] Article 2(3) of the ECL.

In practice, it may occur that the items subject to ECL may be transferred or transmitted into the free trade zones from other parts of China. Such transfer or transmission is not treated under ECL as "export" under ECL and no export license is necessary for such transfer or transmission of items subject to ECL. However, if the same item is transferred or transmitted overseas or to the Hong Kong Special Administrative Region, the Macau Special Administrative Region, or the Taiwan region, it will be treated as an "export" activity under ECL as these regions are outside the customs territory of China.

(b) Deemed export

Though cross-border transfer is controlled, it may occur to the legislature that the risks still exist when there are no cross-border activities regarding items subject to ECL. If a foreign national in China has access to an item subject to ECL, any sensitive information engraved in his/her mind will be taken outside China; thus, it is a risk that needs control. The legislature uses the term "deemed export" to tackle such risk.

"Deemed export" is an extraction of the concept of export under ECL, which means the provision of controlled items by any Chinese citizen or incorporated or non-incorporated organization of China to any foreign organization or individual, no matter whether such provision occurs within or outside China. In such a case, an export license is required before such provision.[73]

Generally, such "provision" may occur under the following circumstances, (i) allowing a visual inspection of technical data or plans; (ii) providing technical assistance or guidance on the use of the technology; or (iii) having an oral exchange about the technology.[74] However, the deemed export is not limited to technology or source code of software, it also covers provision of or even access to a commodity subject to ECL even within China. Accordingly, it would seem dangerous for a foreign citizen in China to form a visual image of the appearance of such a commodity. If the legislature does not so intend, it needs to make an interpretation.

(c) Re-export

The activity of re-export as an extension of the concept "export" is also subject to control under ECL.[75] This control is a supplementary measure to remedy an export control failure in end-use or end-user controls. If an export license is duly obtained for export from China with approved end-user in a foreign country, but eventually the end-user turns out to be in a third country, the "re-export" then may apply, which means such re-export activity is not permissible unless otherwise approved by MOFCOM in advance. Interestingly, ECL only has one provision in which the term "re-export" appears, which generally provides that such re-export is controlled according to "relevant provisions" of ECL, though such "relevant provisions" are difficult to locate.

---

[73] Ibid.

[74] O'Rourke, J. (2014). The deemed export rule, *Orange County Lawyer*, 56(2), 20–22.

[75] Article 45 of the ECL.

In the draft version of ECL (2017), it was once proposed that the re-export control applies to foreign products containing more than a *de minimis* proportion of controlled items of China origin.[76] This "foreign product rule" has been removed in the subsequent draft versions and does not appear in the final version of ECL. Therefore, it is inferred that re-export control under ECL only applies to items of China origin from an importing foreign country or region to a third country or region.

(d) In-country transfer

In-country transfer means a change of end-use or end-user in the importing country of an item subject to ECL. Such control is based on a covenant between the importer and end-user that the end-use and end-use must conform to what has been promised to MOFCOM in applying for the export license. Such information about the importer, end-use and end-user is indicated in the export license. If there is any change in such end-use or end-user, an approval by MOFCOM in advance must be obtained.

B. **Items subject to ECL**

If any of the controlled activities may occur in your organization, you need then to identify whether such activities may involve any items subject to ECL. Items subject to ECL include dual-use items, military items, nuclear items, and other items that relate to maintenance of national security or interests or fulfillment of non-proliferation and other international obligations.[77] The cross-border transfer, deemed export or re-export or in-country transfer of such controlled items are subject to export controls under ECL. Such export controls may be (i) "list control items", (ii) "temporary control items", and (iii) "catch-all control items".

The "dual-use items" refer to items that can be used for civil purposes as well as for military purposes or for helping improve military potentials, especially those goods, technologies, and services that can be used for the design, development, production, or use of WMD.[78] "Military items" refer to equipment, special production facilities, and other related goods, technologies, and services that are used for military purposes.[79] "Nuclear" refers to nuclear materials, nuclear equipment, non-nuclear materials used for nuclear reactors and the related technologies and services.[80]

Please note that the term "controlled items" under ECL includes the data[81] such as technical information and so forth related to such items.[82] If an item is indeed subject to ECL, the technical information of the item may also constitute controlled item.

---

[76] Article 64 of the draft version of the ECL (for public comments) (2017).

[77] Article 2(1) of the ECL.

[78] Ibid., Article 2(4).

[79] Ibid., Article 2(5).

[80] Ibid., Article 2(6).

[81] According to Article 3(1) of the *Data Security Law of the PRC*, data shall refer to any record of information in electronic or other form.

[82] Article 2(2) of ECL.

(a) List control items

The State may implement the export control through control lists, checklists, or catalogues,[83] and the State's export control administrative departments shall, in conjunction with relevant departments, formulate and adjust export control lists for controlled items, and shall publish such lists in a timely manner.[84]

For instance, China released the Military Item List in 2002. The export of military items explicitly enlisted on this list, without obtaining licenses in advance, is prohibited. For dual-use items, China normally amends and releases such control catalogue (consolidated) on an annual basis.

(b) Temporary control items

Pursuant to the need to safeguard national security or interests, or fulfill non-proliferation and other international obligations, upon the approval of the State Council or both the State Council and the Central Military Commission ("CMC"), the State's export control administrative departments may exercise temporary control over any goods, technologies, and services not included in the export control lists as presumably released annually and make an announcement of such controls.[85]

As an example, on 3 July 2023, MOFCOM and GAC jointly issued *Announcement No. 23 of 2023 on Export Controls over Items Related to Gallium and Germanium* to impose export controls on certain gallium-related items including gallium metal (monomer), gallium nitride, gallium oxide, gallium phosphide, and so forth and germanium-related items including germanium metal (monomer), district fused germanium ingots, zinc phosphor germanium, germanium dioxide, and so forth.

(c) Catch-all control items

For items that are not on the export control lists or not subject to temporary control, if an exporter knows or ought to know or is notified by one of the State export control authorities that any relevant goods, technologies, or services outside the control lists that are to be exported by it may pose any of the following risks, the same items are controlled items as well and the exporter must apply to the State export control authorities for a license: (i) endangerment to national security or interest; (ii) they are used to design, develop, produce or use any WMD or its delivery vehicle; or (iii) they are used for terrorist purposes.[86] The difficulty in complying with the catch-all controls is how an exporter or re-exporter ought to know the given export may endanger the national security or interest. This difficulty will be illustrated in the pertaining subsequent chapter.

Catch-all control has been well developed in other jurisdictions and multilateral export control regimes, and functions as a supplement to traditional list controls when the item not covered by the controlling list is for restrictive or prohibitive usage. For instance, the export of items in connection with the development, production,

[83] Ibid., Article 4.

[84] Ibid., Article 9(1).

[85] Ibid., Article 9(2).

[86] Ibid., Article 12(3).

handling, operation, maintenance, storage, detection, identification or dissemination of chemical, biological or nuclear weapons or other nuclear explosive devices or the development, production, maintenance, or storage of missiles capable of delivering such weapons cybersurveillance items shall be subject to authorization under EU law, even though the items are not listed on Annex I of Regulation (EU) 2021/821.[87] Such catch-all control is essentially based on the end-use control, and the exporter who knows or ought to know such prohibitive usages before or at the time of export will be liable under ECL if the same item is exported without export license.

(d) Other controls by reason of maintenance of national security and interests

By virtue of Article 2 of ECL, if an item is prohibited or restricted from export by reason of maintenance of national security or interests under a separate law or regulation, the violation of the same law or regulation may result in the imposition of penalties under ECL on the violating party, even when the item is not a controlled item under ECL. As explained in the preceding paragraph, catch-all control is essentially a control of end-use, but the control under this paragraph depends on the pure national security and interest policy, rather than controls of the actual end-use.

C. **Parties subject to export control**

Assuming there is a controlled activity concerning an item subject to ECL, in other words, as long as the export, deemed export, re-export, or in-country transfer concerns a controlled item, it remains an issue as to who is obligated to apply for licenses and to be liable for violations under ECL.

(a) Exporting business operators ("EBO")

ECL prescribes EBO as the party who is to apply for an export license and be liable for violations. However, such EBO is not clearly defined and may be easily misunderstood as only referring to an exporting company with a proper export business license. Given the essence of ECL is to avoid cross-border transfer (export) or deemed cross-border transfer (deemed export) and retransfer to a third country (re-export) of controlled items, any entity or individual who as a matter of fact effects any unauthorized transfer will bear the consequences of violation of ECL. Very likely EBO will be broadly construed as to include such entity and individual, no matter whether the same party has the export business license or has any business at all. In line with this thought, the author believes the term "EBO" may include any citizen, legal person, or unincorporated organization conducting the controlled activities, whether it is a Chinese or foreign national or organization.[88]

(b) Service providers

Any organization or individual shall not provide agency, freight, delivery, customs clearance, third-party e-commerce trading platforms, finance, and other services for

---

[87] Articles 4 & 5 of Regulation (EU) 2021/821 of the European Parliament and the Council of 20 May 2021 Setting Up a Union Regime for the Control of Exports, Brokering, Technical Assistance, Transit and Transfer of Dual-use Items.

[88] Article 2(3) of ECL.

exporting business operators engaging in violations of export control.[89] Such service providers is not confined to Chinese companies or individuals.

(c) Foreign importers

Importers presumably in a foreign country who discover that end-users or end-uses are likely to change shall immediately report it to the State's export control administrative departments.[90] In addition, the importer is also subject to re-export and in-country transfer controls. The importers if breaching the requirements of end-users or end-uses, posing a potential danger to national security or interests, or using any controlled item for any terrorist purpose is subject to designation onto the List of Controlled Parties.[91]

(d) Foreign end-users

End-users of controlled items shall covenant that, without the approval of the State's export control administrative departments, they are subject to in-country transfer and re-export controls and shall not alter the end-uses of relevant controlled items or transfer them to any third party.[92] Foreign end-users who breach requirements of end-users or end-uses, pose a potential danger to national security and interests, or use any controlled item for any terrorist purpose is subject to designation onto the List of Controlled Parties.[93]

(e) Re-exporters

Article 45 of ECL is the provision where the term re-export appears. Article 45 only sets out that *relevant provisions* of ECL shall apply to the re-export of controlled items and it is difficult to derive the obligations and liabilities of a re-exporter from such a general provision. It is likely that in practice "relevant provisions of ECL" may be construed as those provisions prescribing the obligations and liabilities of EBO, so that the exporter will undertake the same obligations and liabilities of EBO as far as ex-export activities are concerned. Such re-exporter can be the original importer, original end user or even any third party in a foreign country.

D. **Administrative authorities**

Departments under the State Council and departments under the CMC with functions of export control administration shall be responsible for the export control within their respective scope of power.[94] The administrative authorities are illustrated in the table below:

---

[89] Ibid., Article 20.

[90] Ibid., Article 16(2).

[91] Ibid., Article 18(1).

[92] Ibid., Article 16(1).

[93] Ibid., Article 18(1).

[94] Ibid., Article 5(1).

Items	Authorities
Biologics	MOFCOM jointly with Ministry of Agriculture and Rural Affairs and National Health Commission
Certain chemicals	MOFCOM
Commercial cryptography	MOFCOM jointly with State Cryptography Administration
Controlled chemicals	MOFCOM jointly with Ministry of Industry and Information Technology
Missile-related items	MOFCOM jointly with State Administration of Science, Technology and Industry for National Defense and the Equipment Development Department of CMC
Military items	State Administration of Science, Technology and Industry for National Defense, and Equipment Development Department of CMC
Nuclear	China Atomic Energy Authority and MOFCOM in cooperation with other departments
Nuclear-related dual-use items and technologies	MOFCOM jointly with China Atomic Energy Authority

E. **Investigation powers**

ECL empowers the administrative authorities (normally MOFCOM for non-military items) to investigate non-compliance with and violation of ECL.[95] MOFCOM currently does not possess any investigation and imposition of penalties powers other than those under ECL, which are as follows:

(a) Entering the business premises of parties under investigation or other relevant places to carry out the investigation,
(b) Interviewing parties under investigation, interested parties or other relevant entities or individuals, and requesting them to provide explanations related to the investigated matter,
(c) Examining and duplicating relevant vouchers, agreements, accounting books, business correspondence, and other documents and data of the parties under investigation, interested parties, or other relevant organizations or individuals,
(d) Checking the carrying vehicles used for the export, stopping the loading of suspicious items to be exported, and ordering return transport of illegally exported items,
(e) Sealing up and detaining relevant items involved in the investigation, and
(f) Examining the bank accounts of parties under investigation.

Please note that MOFCOM may conduct interviews with such parties if assessed with a certain degree of export control risks. A company without implementing an ICP consistent with MOFCOM's guidelines may be viewed by MOFCOM as a risky

[95] Ibid., Article 28.

entity, which may trigger MOFCOM's interview and even investigation. MOFCOM may also invite customs authorities to join such interviews and investigations. Of course, if the violation involves exported goods, the customs authority may initiate an investigation by itself, which will be further elaborated in Chap. 7.

F. **Liabilities for violations**

The administrative authorities may impose penalties for violations as follows:

(a) Unauthorized exports

An exporter that is engaged in the export of a controlled item without obtaining the export business qualification, or exports a controlled item without licenses, exports a controlled item beyond the scope of licenses, or exports a controlled item prohibited from export, will be subject to a fine between five and ten times the illegal value, subject to a minimum of CNY500,000.[96]

(b) Irregularities in obtaining and using licenses

An exporter who obtains licenses for a controlled item through fraud, bribery or other improper means, or illegally transfers an export license for a controlled item to another person will be subject to a fine between five and ten times the illegal value, subject to a minimum of CNY200,000.[97]

An exporter who forges, alters, or transacts any export license will be subject to a fine between five and ten times the illegal value, subject to a minimum of CNY50,000.[98]

(c) Services to illegal exports

The service provider that knowingly provides agency, freight, delivery, third-party e-commerce trading platform financial or other services to an exporter engaged in any violation of ECL will be subject to a fine between three and five times the illegal value, subject to a minimum of CNY100,000.[99]

The test of "knowingly" is likely to be similar to that under General Prohibition Ten of the EAR administrated by the Bureau of Industry and Security of the U.S. Department of Commerce, which prohibits any third party from proceeding with transactions with the knowledge that a violation has occurred or is about to occur.[100]

---

[96] Ibid., Articles 33 & 34.

[97] Ibid., Article 35(1).

[98] Ibid., Article 35(2).

[99] Ibid., Article 36.

[100] §736.2(b)(10) of the EAR, General Prohibition Ten—*Proceeding with transactions with knowledge that a violation has occurred or is about to occur (Knowledge Violation to Occur).* You may not sell, transfer, export, re-export, finance, order, buy, remove, conceal, store, use, loan, dispose of, transport, forward, or otherwise service, in whole or in part, any item subject to the EAR and exported, reexported, or transferred (in-country) or to be exported, reexported, or transferred (in-country) with knowledge that a violation of the Export Administration Regulations, the Export Control Reform Act of 2018, or any order, license, license exception, or other authorization issued thereunder has occurred, is about to occur, or is intended to occur in connection with the item.

Such knowledge not only covers actual knowledge but also constructive knowledge which means the service provider should have known the illegal exports given the circumstance of the case.

(d) Transactions with Controlled Parties

An exporter that trades with importers or end-users who are designated onto the List of Controlled Parties will be subject to a fine between ten and twenty times the illegal value, subject to a minimum of CNY 500,000. In serious cases, there may be an order to suspend business for rectification up to the revocation of export business qualifications for the relevant controlled items.[101]

(e) Obstruction of enforcement measures

An exporter who resists or obstructs any supervision or inspection by the administrative authorities will be subject to a fine between CNY 100,000 and CNY 300,000. In serious cases, there may be an order to suspend business for rectification up to the revocation of export business qualification for the relevant controlled items.[102]

(f) Personal liabilities

The persons in charge of export control matters of an entity in violation may be banned from engaging in relevant export businesses for five years or prohibited from engaging in relevant export business activities for life if criminally liable.[103]

1.2.3 China White Paper of Export Controls

On 19 December 2021, the State Council Information Office of China released the first edition of the White Paper, which explains export control policies and position of China.

Apart from the preamble and conclusion, the White Paper includes four parts, respectively, (i) basic position of China on export controls, (ii) ongoing improvements to the legal and regulatory system for export controls, (iii) modernizing export control system, and (iv) promoting international exchanges and cooperation.

Nor may you rely upon any license or license exception after notice to you of the suspension or revocation of that license or exception. There are no-license exceptions to this General Prohibition Ten in part 740 of the EAR.

[101] Article 37 of the ECL.

[102] Ibid., Article 38.

[103] Ibid., Article 39.

1.2.3.1 Basic Position of China on Export Controls

(a) Maintaining a holistic approach of national security

A holistic approach of national security[104] provides fundamental guidelines and direction for the attitude of China on export controls. Over the past years, the Chinese government has coordinated the relationship between development and security, opening up and security, traditional security and non-traditional security, and China's own security and the security of other countries.

(b) Honoring international obligations and commitments

It is the solemn commitment of China to maintain international peace, and to honor non-proliferation and other international obligations. Therefore, the Chinese government actively draws useful experience from international standard practices and employs that experience to strengthen and improve its export control system. For the participation of China in the multilateral export control regime, please refer to Chap. 2.

(c) Promoting international cooperation and coordination

China advocates that all countries must firmly uphold the international system with the United Nations at its core and the international order based on international law, effectively safeguard the authority of international treaties and mechanisms consistent with genuine multilateralism and establish a common, comprehensive, cooperative, and sustainable concept of global security.

(d) Opposing the abuse of export control measures

China believes that export controls shall be fair, reasonable, and non-discriminatory. They shall not undermine the legitimate right of other countries to the peaceful use of controlled items, interfere with normal international science and technology exchanges and economic and trade cooperation, or obstruct the secure and smooth operation of global industrial and supply chains.[105]

---

[104] The concept of "a holistic approach of national security" was put forward by President Xi Jinping in the First Meeting of the Central National Security Committee on 15 April 2014. Five key elements of this concept are (a) people's security, (b) political security, (c) economic security, (d) military, scientific and technological, cultural and social security, and (d) international security.

[105] Both MOFCOM and the Ministry of Foreign Affairs of the PRC have repeatedly opposed certain export controls maintained by the U.S. government. For example, On April 8, the U.S. Department of Commerce announced to add seven Chinese institutions to its "entity list" for their "support to the military modernization of China". Hereto, MOFCOM spokesman responded as follows, "China firmly opposes the U.S.'s adding the seven Chinese institutions to its export control "entity list". Under the pretext of "national security" and "support to the military modernization of China", the U.S. has repetitively abused export control measures and wielded state power against businesses and institutions of other countries. This severely disrupts international economic and trade order and poses critical threats to the security of global industrial and supply chains. It does not benefit China, the U.S., or the whole world. China urges the U.S. to stop its erroneous moves. We will take necessary countermeasures to protect the lawful rights and interests of its enterprises". Retrieved September 27, 2023, from http://english.mofcom.gov.cn/article/newsrelease/significantnews/202104/20210403052997.shtml.

1.2.3.2 Ongoing Improvements to the Legal and Regulatory System for Export Controls

(a) Establishing and improving export control legal systems

With the enactment of ECL in 2020, China has formed an effective and well-coordinated legal system of export controls including laws, administrative regulations and administrative normative documents. The comprehensive analysis of legal structure of export controls of China can be found in Sect. 1.2.1.

(b) Building an efficient and coordinated export control regime

Export controls involve multiple departments of the State Council and the Central Military Commission. China has established a sound working mechanism on dual-use items export control, military items export control, and nuclear export control, respectively.

1.2.3.3 Modernizing the Export Control System

(a) Improving license management.

China widely adopts internationally accepted practices in export controls such as license management, end-user and end-use certificates, and multiple licensing. An interagency consultation mechanism for prudent and accurate review has been established. To facilitate license applications, China maintains a two-tiered (MOFCOM and Provincial government departments) management model.

(b) Strengthening enforcement capability

China continues to reinforce its export control enforcement mechanism by expanding methods and sharpening capabilities. An authoritative and efficient system has gradually taken shape with consistent rights and responsibilities, which plays an important role in tackling violations and ensuring complete, accurate and strict implementation of relevant laws and regulations.

(c) Developing export control compliance systems

China is committed to developing export control compliance systems. In 2021, MOFCOM revised and issued the Guidance of MOFCOM on the Establishment of Internal Compliance Mechanism of Dual-use Item Exporting Business Operators, which serves as a "soft law" for EBOs. For a detailed analysis of compliance measures, please see Chap. 8.

(d) Complying with international obligations

China consistently advocates the complete prohibition and thorough destruction of WMD, including nuclear, biological and chemical weapons, and resolutely opposes the proliferation of such weapons and their means of delivery. China firmly upholds the authority and efficacy of all relevant international treaties, strictly complies with its international obligations, and safeguards international and regional peace and stability.

1.2.3.4 Promoting International Exchanges and Cooperation

(a) Bilateral exchanges and cooperation

For intergovernmental bilateral cooperation, China has established intergovernmental mechanisms with various countries and regions to share experiences and practices through government-to-government consultations and discussions and dialogues with the business community. For example, China has signed bilateral agreements with Russia and several other countries for mutual issuing of end-user and end-use certificates.[106]

For non-governmental bilateral cooperations, Chinese institutions such as the Chinese Academy of International Trade and Economic Cooperation of the Ministry of Commerce, the China Arms Control and Disarmament Association, the China Institute of Contemporary International Relations, and the China Nuclear Energy Association, have held non-governmental exchanges, conducted academic research, and engaged in international interactions with research institutions of other countries through symposiums, forums and on-site visits.

(b) Multilateral exchanges and cooperation

China is willing to work with the international community to ensure that multilateral export control mechanisms are just and open, and to increase the diversity and breadth of representation in their membership. For example, since its accession to the Nuclear Suppliers Group in 2004, China has actively taken part in policy consultations, list formulation, information sharing, and other Group matters.

Besides, China has maintained communication and exchanges with the organization which it has not joined yet. For example, China has been involved in six rounds of consultation with the Australia Group on biological and chemical non-proliferation.

[106] According to MOFCOM's end-user and end-use certificate statement online, China issues end-user and end-use certificates (for sensitive items and technologies) for Chinese importers to the following 23 countries or regions, namely Australia, Belarus, Belgium, Canada, Denmark, France, Germany, Greece, Italy, Japan, Kazakhstan, Luxembourg, Netherlands, Norway, Portugal, Russia, Spain, Switzerland, Turkey, Ukraine, United Kingdom, United States of America, Hongkong of China. Retrieved September 27, 2023, from http://zzyhzm.mofcom.gov.cn/.

Chapter 2
Multilateral Non-proliferation Export Controls

As far as policies are concerned, a given State controls exports for the purpose of non-proliferation, national security, anti-terrorism, and sometimes human right protection. For export controls based on non-proliferation considerations, national laws of a given State normally adopt the control mechanism and control lists of such multinational non-proliferation regimes. The multilateral non-proliferation regime is the core of the non-proliferation, but the non-proliferation regime also comprises national and bilateral non-proliferation laws and agreements.[1]

In the context of multilateral export control, non-proliferation means to prevent the proliferation of WMD which includes nuclear, biological and chemical weapons, and their delivering vehicles.[2] Non-proliferation is conducive to the preservation of international and regional peace and security, and the international community has gradually developed a multilateral non-proliferation regime. China has either acceded to or factually adopted the multinational non-proliferation treaties or arrangements, which reflects its adherence to multinational controls over WMD proliferation.

This chapter introduces the prevailing multilateral non-proliferation regimes and the participation of China in or attitude toward such regimes. Section 2.1 analyzes the commitments of China to non-proliferation regimes established by international conventions, including the Treaty on the Non-Proliferation of Nuclear Weapons ("NPT"), the Nuclear Suppliers Group ("NSG", which is not an international convention but interprets and implements the NPT), the Convention on the Prohibition of the Development, Production and Stockpiling of Bacteriological (Biological) and Toxin Weapons and on their Destruction ("BTWC"), and the Convention on the Prohibition of the Development, Production, Stockpiling, and Use of Chemical Weapons and on their Destruction ("CWC"). This chapter also introduces the Arms Trade Treaty

[1] Oxford Research Group. (1993). Strengthening the Non-Proliferation Regime: 1995 and Beyond. *Current Decision Report,* No. 13, 11.

[2] China Atomic Energy Authority. (2023, December 3). Full text of China white paper on non-proliferation policy and measures. Retrieved October 20, 2023, from https://www.caea.gov.cn/english/n6759377/c6792767/content.html.

D. Zhao, *Contemporary Export Control Law of China*, Modern China and International Economic Law, https://doi.org/10.1007/978-981-99-9825-8_2

("ATT") that focuses on the export control of arms, which is an indispensable part of international export control endeavors. China acceded to these regimes and has maintained an export control administration that is in conformity with such regimes. Section 2.1 also summarizes the export control requirements of these regimes and the fulfillment of China of its commitments, especially related export control lists and policies of China. Section 2.2 focuses on multilateral non-proliferation arrangements that China has not acceded to, including the Australia Group, the Missile Technology Control Regime ("MTCR"), and the Wassenaar Arrangement. Section 2.2 further explores reasons why China has not been a member of such regimes and the attitude of China toward them, especially the connection between export control policies of China and those of these regimes.

2.1 Commitments of China to International Conventions

Maintaining international peace and security is one of the purposes of the United Nations. According to Chapter VII of the UN Charter, the Security Council may take measures to maintain or restore international peace and security.[3] Preventing the proliferation of WMD and their means of delivery is an international challenge and is crucial to international peace, security and stability. The UN has played a central and leading role in multilateral cooperations regarding non-proliferation. In April 2004, the UN Security Council unanimously adopted Resolution 1540 ("UNSCR 1540") and affirmed that the proliferation of nuclear, chemical, and biological weapons, as well as their means of delivery, constituted a threat to international peace and security and all countries shall take and enforce effective measures to establish domestic management and export control of WMD and relevant materials and technologies and to prevent and combat the proliferation of such items among non-State actors.[4] In addition, over the past decades, UN General Assembly has adopted a series of non-proliferation conventions, including the NPT, BTWC, CWC, and ATT.

As a part of the effort to promote world peace and regional security, China prioritizes communication and consultation on global issues and emergencies via the UN and related multilateral export control mechanisms.[5] Over the years, China has participated extensively in the construction of multilateral non-proliferation regimes

---

[3] United Nations. United Nations Charter, Chapter VII. Retrieved October 20, 2023, from https://www.un.org/en/about-us/un-charter/full-text.

[4] Security Council. (2004, April 28). Resolution 1540 Adopted by the Security Council at its 4956th meeting, on 28 April 2004. United Nations. Retrieved October 20, 2023, from http://unscr.com/files/2004/01540.pdf.

[5] The China White Paper of Export Controls.

under relevant UN frameworks and actively promoted their constant improvement and development. China has signed major international treaties related to non-proliferation and joined most of the relevant international organizations.[6]

2.1.1 Treaty on the Non-proliferation of Nuclear Weapons

2.1.1.1 Overview of the NPT

The guiding principle of nuclear non-proliferation is that countries possessing nuclear weapons shall not assist other countries in their capability to acquire nuclear weapons, and countries that do not possess nuclear weapons shall renounce acquiring nuclear weapons.[7] The first half of the twentieth century witnessed the worldwide rapid development of nuclear technology as well as its disastrous and irretrievable consequences. Since its entry into force, the NPT has been the core international legal framework by which nations have worked to steer the use of nuclear science and technology toward peace and development, away from developing nuclear weapons.[8] The NPT is regarded as the cornerstone of the global nuclear non-proliferation regime, and it represents the only binding commitment in a multilateral treaty to the goal of disarmament by the nuclear-weapon States.[9]

Opened for signature in 1968, the NPT entered into force in 1970. In 1995, the parties of the NPT decided that it shall continue in force indefinitely. By December 2022, a total of 191 States have joined the NPT, including the five nuclear-weapon States, i.e., the United States, the Russian Federation (successor State to the Soviet Union), the UK, France, and China.[10]

The objectives of the NPT are twofold: one is to prevent the spread of nuclear weapons and related technologies; the other is to promote cooperation in peaceful uses of nuclear energy and technologies. The NPT groups State parties into two categories: nuclear-weapon States[11] and non-nuclear-weapon States, and it prescribes

[6] China Atomic Energy Authority. (2003, December 3). Full text of China white paper on non-proliferation policy and measures. Retrieved October 20, 2023, from https://www.caea.gov.cn/english/n6759377/c6792767/content.html.

[7] Chen, X. L. (2000). Analysis of the Nuclear Non-Proliferation Regime: A Case Study of the International Security Regime. *International Politics and Security*, No. 8, 36.

[8] Grossi, R. M. (2021, December). The NPT and the IAEA's critical role in steering nuclear toward peaceful uses. Retrieved October 20, 2023, from https://www.iaea.org/bulletin/the-npt-and-the-iaeas-critical-role-in-steering-nuclear-towards-peaceful-uses.

[9] Office for Disarmament Affairs. (n.d.). Treaty on the Non-Proliferation of Nuclear Weapons (NPT). United Nations. Retrieved October 20, 2023, from https://www.un.org/disarmament/wmd/nuclear/npt/.

[10] Office for Disarmament Affairs. (n.d.). Treaty on the Non-Proliferation of Nuclear Weapons (NPT). United Nations. Retrieved October 20, 2023, from https://www.un.org/disarmament/wmd/nuclear/npt/.

[11] Article 9 of the NPT defines "a nuclear-weapon State": For the purposes of this Treaty, a nuclear-weapon State is one which has manufactured and exploded a nuclear weapon or other nuclear

different obligations for each category to control proliferation from both the exporting parties and the receiving parties.

The operation of the NPT is subject to a review every five years.[12] Theoretically, parties to the NPT meet every five years to adopt action plans. However, the recent two NPT Review Conferences closed without any substantive consensus.

2.1.1.2 Obligations Under the NPT

The nuclear-weapon States according to the NPT must not export such weapons or help non-nuclear-weapon States develop the weapons. This obligation is elaborated under Article I of the NPT that each nuclear-weapon State undertakes not to "transfer to any recipient whatsoever nuclear weapons or other nuclear explosive devices or control over such weapons or explosive devices directly, or indirectly; and not in any way assist, encourage, or induce any non-nuclear-weapon State to manufacture or otherwise acquire nuclear weapons or other nuclear explosive devices, or control over such weapons or explosive devices".[13] Accordingly, each non-nuclear-weapon State undertakes not to receive or develop nuclear weapons or other nuclear explosive devices, as stipulated in Article 2 of the NPT.[14]

Despite of the above-mentioned restraints, the NPT State parties undertake that peaceful uses of nuclear-related materials are permissible under the NPT if certain preconditions are satisfied. The NPT emphasizes the inalienable right of all State parties to develop research, production and use of nuclear energy for peaceful purposes.[15] All State parties also undertake to facilitate and have the right to participate in, the exchange of equipment, materials and scientific and technological information for the peaceful uses of nuclear energy.[16] According to Article 3 of the NPT, subject to the safeguards system, State parties of the NPT may provide source or special fissionable material and related equipment or material to non-nuclear-weapon States for peaceful purposes.[17]

Although regarded as an essential foundation for the pursuit of nuclear disarmament, the NPT does not stipulate specific restraints on the nuclear-weapon State parties. Most of the constraints apply to the non-nuclear-weapon States, and the NPT itself does not delineate export control implementing practices or regulations.[18]

---

explosive device prior to 1 January 1967. See Treaty on the Non-Proliferation of Nuclear Weapons (NPT), https://disarmament.unoda.org/wmd/nuclear/npt/text.

[12] Article 9 of the NPT.

[13] Article 1 of the NPT.

[14] Article 2 of the NPT.

[15] Article 4(1) of the NPT.

[16] Article 4(2) of the NPT.

[17] Article 3 of the NPT.

[18] Frieman, W. (2004). *China, Arms Control, and Nonproliferation* (p. 12). RoutledgeCurzon.

2.1.1.3 Control Mechanism of the NPT

A. Safeguards system under the responsibility of IAEA

In 1957, the International Atomic Energy Agency ("IAEA") was created in response to the deep anxiety and peaceful expectation generated by the discoveries and diverse uses of nuclear technology.[19] IAEA is explicitly entrusted with key nuclear verification responsibilities by the NPT.[20] To further the goal of non-proliferation and as a confidence-building measure between State parties, the NPT establishes a safeguards system, under which IAEA conducts inspections to verify compliance with the NPT by its State parties,[21] especially non-nuclear-weapon State parties.

According to Article 3 of the NPT, each non-nuclear-weapon State party shall accept safeguards that are applied on all source or special fissionable material, for the exclusive purpose of verification of the fulfillment of its obligations assumed under the NPT with a view to preventing the diversion of nuclear energy from peaceful uses to nuclear weapons or other nuclear explosive devices.[22] As of 3 May 2023, the IAEA has concluded comprehensive safeguards agreements with 182 States.[23]

For both nuclear-weapon States and non-nuclear-weapon States, according to Article 3(2) of the NPT, unless the source or special fissionable material is subject to the safeguards, they cannot be provided to any non-nuclear-weapon State even for peaceful purposes.[24]

Safeguard measures include examining the design of specialized equipment and facilities inclusive of nuclear reactors, requiring the maintenance and production of operating records, sending inspectors and so forth.[25]

B. Zangger Committee and Trigger List

As a framework international convention, the NPT does not define the scope of "nuclear weapons", "nuclear explosive devices", "source or special fissionable material", or "equipment or material especially designed or prepared for the processing, use or production of special fissionable material", which are the subject matters of the NPT. To harmonize the interpretation of nuclear export control policies for NPT State parties, named after its first Chairman Prof. Claude Zangger, Zangger

[19] International Atomic Energy Agency. (n.d.). History of IAEA. Retrieved October 20, 2023, from https://www.iaea.org/about/overview/history.

[20] Article 3 of the NPT.

[21] Office for Disarmament Affairs. (n.d.). Treaty on the Non-Proliferation of Nuclear Weapons (NPT). United Nations. Retrieved October 20, 2023, from https://www.un.org/disarmament/wmd/nuclear/npt/

[22] Article 3(1) of the NPT.

[23] International Atomic Energy Agency. (n.d.). Safeguards agreements. Retrieved October 20, 2023, from https://www.iaea.org/topics/safeguards-agreements.

[24] Article 3(2) of the NPT.

[25] Article 12 Agency Safeguards of the Statute of the IAEA. Retrieved October 31, 2023, from https://www.iaea.org/sites/default/files/statute.pdf.

Committee was established in 1971 to serve as the "faithful interpreter" of Article 3(2) of the NPT.[26]

Also known as the "NPT Exporters Committee", Zangger Committee focuses on materials that trigger IAEA safeguards as a condition of supply to non-nuclear-weapon States, as provided in Article 3(2) of the NPT. Zangger Committee drafted and constantly amends the designation of items of equipment or material especially designed or prepared for the processing, use or production of special fissionable material, which is commonly referred to as the "trigger list".[27] The trigger list contains nuclear-related strategic goods that can assist the NPT State parties in identifying equipment and materials subject to export controls.[28]

Apart from the trigger list, Zangger Committee establishes three conditions for the supply of such items: a non-explosive-use assurance, an IAEA Safeguards requirement, and a re-transfer/re-export provision that required the receiving State to apply the same conditions when re-exporting these items.[29]

By the end of 2022, Zangger Committee has 39 members, including China and other nuclear-weapon States. The European Union stands only as a permanent observer of the committee.[30]

The trigger list made the NPT commitments more explicit, but Zangger Committee is not an international export control regime. Instead, it is an agreement to use shared

---

[26] Zangger Committee. (n.d.). Retrieved October 31, 2023, from http://zanggercommittee.org/

[27] IAEA Information Circular, Communication dated 18 February 2020 received from the Permanent Mission of Denmark regarding the Export of Nuclear Material and of Certain Categories of Equipment and Other Material, Retrieved October 31, 2023, from http://zanggercommittee.org/download/18.6a32cf891717bf4c02d11/1588579969571/infcirc209r5.pdf.

According to the Communication dated 18 February 2020 received from the Permanent Mission of Denmark regarding the Export of Nuclear Material and of Certain Categories of Equipment and Other Material, the latest trigger list contains the following:

- nuclear reactors and especially designed or prepared equipment and components therefor;
- non-nuclear materials for reactors;
- plants for the reprocessing of irradiated fuel elements, and equipment especially designed or prepared therefor;
- plants for the fabrication of nuclear reactor fuel elements, and equipment especially designed or prepared therefor;
- plants for the separation of isotopes of natural uranium, depleted uranium or special fissionable material and equipment, other than analytical instruments, especially designed or prepared therefor;
- plants for the production or concentration of heavy water, deuterium and deuterium compounds and equipment especially designed or prepared therefor;
- plants for the conversion of uranium and plutonium for use in the fabrication of fuel elements and the separation of uranium isotopes, and equipment especially designed or prepared therefor.

[28] Zangger Committee. (n.d.). Retrieved October 31, 2023, from http://zanggercommittee.org/

[29] Information Circular. (2000, April). Communication Received from the Permanent Mission of the Netherlands on Behalf of the Member States of the Nuclear Suppliers Group. International Atomic Energy Agency. Retrieved October 20, 2023, from https://www.iaea.org/sites/default/files/infcirc539r1.pdf.

[30] Zangger Committee. (n.d.). Our mission. Retrieved October 31, 2023, from http://zanggercommittee.org/our-mission.html.

definitions to implement national export control systems and, on occasion, to share information among the signing parties.[31]

2.1.1.4 Commitments of China to the NPT

The evolution of the support of China for the nuclear non-proliferation regime is one of the most important developments in the short history of the association of China with the world of arms control and international security affairs.[32] Before the 1980s, China remained at the margin or outside the global arms control and non-proliferation regime. China criticized and declined to join the NPT, viewing it as discriminatory against non-nuclear-weapon States.[33] In the 1980s, due to the dramatical change in international environment and the reform and open policies of China, China re-evaluated its participation strategy in multilateral non-proliferation regime.[34] In terms of nuclear non-proliferation, China has switched from criticizing and resisting the regimes to actively participating in the regimes, and from unilateral compliance with nuclear non-proliferation norms to formal accession to almost all multilateral international non-proliferation treaties and arrangements.[35] In the latest NPT Review Conference, China views the NPT as the cornerstone of non-proliferation regime and believes that the international community shall apply joint efforts to firmly oppose and eliminate all forms of nuclear proliferation, properly handle the hotspot issues, and enhance common and universal security of all countries.[36]

Before joining the NPT, China had joined the IAEA in 1984 and signed the agreement between the People's Republic of China and the International Atomic Energy Agency for the Application of Safeguards in China in 1988, voluntarily placing civilian nuclear facilities of China under Agency safeguards. In November 1991, the Chinese government announced that it would notify the IAEA on a continuous basis of its exports to, or imports from, non-nuclear-weapon States of any nuclear material greater than one effective kilogram.[37]

---

[31] Frieman, W. (2004). China, Arms Control, and Nonproliferation (pp. 20–21). RoutledgeCurzon.

[32] Medeiros, E. S. (2007). *Reluctant Restraint: The Evolution of China's Nonproliferation Policies and Practices, 1980–2004* (p. 30). Stanford University Press.

[33] Xinhua News Service, "Envoy Tells IAEA of PRC Nuclear Stand", *FBIS Daily Report: China,* November 13, 1984, p. A3.

[34] Frieman, W. (2004). China, Arms Control, and Nonproliferation (p. 1). RoutledgeCurzon.

[35] Wang, J. (2002). Analysis of China's Post-Cold War Shift in Non-proliferation Policies and its Causes. *Pacific Journal*, No. 4, 62.

[36] Permanent Mission of the People's Republic of China to the UN. (2022, August 8). Statement by the H. E. Amb. Li Song on Nuclear Non-Proliferation at the Tenth NPT Review Conference. Retrieved October 20, 2023, from http://un.china-mission.gov.cn/eng/chinaandun/disarmament_armscontrol/npt/202208/t20220810_10738604.htm.

[37] Permanent Mission of the People's Republic of China to the UN. (2005, May 18). Report of China on the Implementation of NPT, New York, 2–27 May 2005. Retrieved October 20, 2023, from http://un.china-mission.gov.cn/eng/chinaandun/disarmament_armscontrol/npt/200505/t20050518_8412390.htm.

China acceded to the NPT in 1992. China has actively and comprehensively fulfilled its obligations under the NPT. In July 1993 after acceding to the NPT, China formally committed to notify the IAEA of all imports and exports of nuclear material as well as exports of nuclear equipment and related non-nuclear material.[38]

In May 1996, China pledged not to provide any assistance to nuclear facilities in other countries that are not under the IAEA safeguards, including nuclear exports, personnel and technology exchanges and cooperation with them. In October 1997, China joined the Zangger Committee[39] and harmonized its nuclear export control policies and controlled items accordingly.

In 1998, China signed the Additional Protocol aimed at strengthening the IAEA safeguard system, and formally completed the domestic legal procedures necessary for the entry into force of the Additional Protocol in early 2002, thus becoming the first nuclear-weapon State to complete the relevant procedures.[40]

2.1.1.5 The Nuclear Export Control Regime of China

In conformity with the NPT, the exports of nuclear items in China are carried out in strict accordance with three principles—that nuclear items must be exported for peaceful purposes only, that they must be under the supervision and safeguard of the IAEA, and that they must not be transferred to third countries without the permission of the Chinese government.[41]

Pursuant to the commitment of China to the NPT, the IAEA, and the Zangger Committee, the Chinese government has promulgated a series of legally binding laws and regulations on the export control of nuclear items, nuclear dual-use items, and related technologies, established a complete system of laws and regulations on nuclear export control, which has legalized export control activities of China.[42] Competent authorities carry out rigorous reviews of nuclear exports and impose severe penalties on violators.

In September 1997, the Chinese government promulgated the Regulations on the Export Control of Nuclear,[43] which stipulate that no assistance shall be provided to nuclear facilities not under IAEA safeguards; that the nuclear export shall be

[38] Permanent Mission of the People's Republic of China to the UN. (2005, May 18). Report of China on the Implementation of NPT, New York, 2–27 May 2005. Retrieved October 20, 2023, from http://un.china-mission.gov.cn/eng/chinaandun/disarmament_armscontrol/npt/200505/t20050518_8412390.htm.

[39] Permanent Mission of the People's Republic of China to the UN. (2005, May 18). Report of China on the Implementation of NPT, New York, 2–27 May 2005. Retrieved October 20, 2023, from http://un.china-mission.gov.cn/eng/chinaandun/disarmament_armscontrol/npt/200505/t20050518_8412390.htm.

[40] China White Paper of Export Controls.

[41] China White Paper of Export Controls.

[42] Wang, J. (2002). Analysis of China's Post-Cold War Shift in Non-proliferation Policies and its Causes. *Pacific Journal*, No. 4, 62.

[43] The Regulations on the Export Control of Nuclear were revised in November 2006.

exclusively conducted by such entities designated by the State Council; and that China implements a licensing system for nuclear exports.[44] The Nuclear Export Control List of China has included all items in the trigger list of the Zangger Committee.

The amendment to the Criminal Law adopted in December 2001 criminalizes the illegal manufacture, trade and transport of radioactive substances and imposes criminal penalties.[45]

In February 2002, the Chinese government promulgated the Provisions on Supervision and Administration of Nuclear Import and Export and Foreign Nuclear Cooperation Safeguards.[46] The provisions require that key clauses that shall be included in export agreements, guarantee documents that receivers shall provide, control requirements for re-export, and related administrative measures.[47]

On 3 December 2003, the Chinese government published a white paper entitled "the Non-Proliferation Policy and Measures of China", which comprehensively presents non-proliferation supervision policies of China, including nuclear non-proliferation measures, export control system and regulation, coordinating mechanism among export control departments, and investigation of violation cases.[48]

2.1.2 *Nuclear Suppliers Group and Export Control*

2.1.2.1 Overview of the NSG

After the NPT entered into force in 1970, there had been multilateral consultations on nuclear export controls to reach common understandings on how to implement Article 3(2) of the NPT, or in other words, how to determine the transfer of items

---

[44] Permanent Mission of the People's Republic of China to the UN. (2005, May 18). Report of China on the Implementation of NPT, New York, 2–27 May 2005. Retrieved October 20, 2023, from http://un.china-mission.gov.cn/eng/chinaandun/disarmament_armscontrol/npt/200505/t20050518_8412390.htm.

[45] Permanent Mission of the People's Republic of China to the UN. (2005, May 18). Report of China on the Implementation of NPT, New York, 2–27 May 2005. Retrieved October 20, 2023, from http://un.china-mission.gov.cn/eng/chinaandun/disarmament_armscontrol/npt/200505/t20050518_8412390.htm.

[46] Permanent Mission of the People's Republic of China to the UN. (2005, May 18). Report of China on the Implementation of NPT, New York, 2–27 May 2005. Retrieved October 20, 2023, from http://un.china-mission.gov.cn/eng/chinaandun/disarmament_armscontrol/npt/200505/t20050518_8412390.htm.

[47] Order of the Commission for Science, Technology and Industry for National Defense, the Ministry of Foreign Affairs and the Ministry of Foreign Trade and Economic Cooperation, Provisions on Supervision and Administration of Nuclear Import and Export and Foreign Nuclear Cooperation Safeguards, Article 18–25.

[48] Permanent Mission of the People's Republic of China to the UN. (2005, May 18). Report of China on the Implementation of NPT, New York, 2–27 May 2005. Retrieved October 20, 2023, from http://un.china-mission.gov.cn/eng/chinaandun/disarmament_armscontrol/npt/200505/t20050518_8412390.htm.

that may trigger IAEA safeguards. As analyzed above, Zangger Committee is the first mechanism that institutionalized such understandings by establishing the trigger list and related guidelines. The NSG is the other important multilateral mechanism dealing with nuclear export/transfer control.

Following the explosion in 1974 of a nuclear device by a non-nuclear-weapon State, which demonstrated that nuclear technology transferred for peaceful purposes could be misused, the NSG was established in 1975. The NSG brought together major suppliers of nuclear items that are NPT parties as well as States that are not parties to the NPT.[49] By 2022, there are 48 participating States of the NSG. China acceded to the NSG in 2004.

NSG utilizes its guidelines to exercise nuclear export control. The NSG Guidelines were published in 1978 as IAEA Document INFCIRC/254 (subsequently amended) to apply to nuclear transfers for peaceful purposes to help ensure that such transfers would not be diverted to an unsafeguarded nuclear fuel-cycle or nuclear explosive activities.[50]

2.1.2.2 NSG Guidelines and Zangger Committee Trigger List

The significance and specialty of the NSG lie in its two sets of guidelines for nuclear exports and nuclear-related exports: one is Guidelines for Nuclear Transfers ("Part 1 Guidelines") and the other is Guidelines for Transfers of Nuclear-related Dual-use Equipment, Materials, Software, and Related Technology ("Part 2 Guidelines").[51] The NSG Guidelines are supplemented by two control lists called "Technical Annexes": one is the Trigger List (annexed to the Part 1 Guidelines) and the other is the Dual-Use List (annexed to the Part 2 Guidelines).

In Part 1 Guidelines, the NSG adopted the original Zangger Committee's trigger list as the annex and elaborated on the three original conditions of supply.[52] In addition to covering equipment and material, Part 1 Guidelines also cover the technology for the development, production and use of the items on the list.[53]

---

[49] Information Circular. (2000, April). Communication Received from the Permanent Mission of the Netherlands on Behalf of the Member States of the Nuclear Suppliers Group. International Atomic Energy Agency. Retrieved October 20, 2023, from https://www.iaea.org/sites/default/files/infcirc539r1.pdf.

[50] Nuclear Suppliers Group. (n.d.). Retrieved October 31, 2023, from https://www.nuclearsuppliersgroup.org/en/about-nsg.

[51] Nuclear Suppliers Group. (n.d.). Retrieved October 31, 2023, from https://www.nuclearsuppliersgroup.org/en/about-nsg.

[52] Nuclear Suppliers Group. (n.d.). Why was the NSG created? What are its origins? Retrieved October 20, 2023, from https://nsg-online.org/en/27-faq/197-why-was-the-nsg-created-what-are-its-origins.

[53] Information Circular. (2000, April). Communication Received from the Permanent Mission of the Netherlands on Behalf of the Member States of the Nuclear Suppliers Group. International Atomic Energy Agency. Retrieved October 20, 2023, from https://www.iaea.org/sites/default/files/infcirc539r1.pdf.

Since the 1990s, dual-use items not covered by the NSG have been transferred and used to build items listed in Part 1 Guidelines. To ensure the non-explosive use of dual-use items, Part 2 Guidelines of NSG was created to cover exports of dual-use items not covered by the trigger list of Zangger Committee and falling outside the committee's mandate. The dual-use items listed have both nuclear and non-nuclear applications that may potentially and significantly lead to an unsafeguarded nuclear fuel-cycle or nuclear explosive activity. Such dual-use items consist of the following categories[54]:

- industrial equipment;
- materials;
- uranium isotope separation equipment and components (other than trigger list items);
- heavy water production plant-related equipment (other than trigger list items);
- test and measurement equipment for the development of nuclear explosive devices; and
- components for nuclear explosive devices.

The control of the dual-use items has been recognized as making an important contribution to nuclear non-proliferation.[55]

2.1.2.3 Control Mechanism of the NSG

Specifying items subject to export control, NSG Guidelines also establish a control mechanism with concrete control requirements and measures.

The NSG Part 1 Guidelines function as the control mechanism of transfers for peaceful purposes to any non-nuclear-weapon State and, in the case of controls on re-transfer, to transfers to any State.[56] According to the NSG Part 1 Guidelines, the exporting and importing governments shall provide formal government assurances that the nuclear transfer is for peaceful purposes. The importing government is to provide assurance that it will not re-transfer items, material or technology that it has received to a third government without the exporting government's prior consent.[57]

The Part 2 Guidelines impose conditions on the transfer of dual-use items. Specifically, before authorizing the transfer, the supplier must obtain: (a) a statement from the end-user specifying the uses and end-use locations of the proposed transfers, and (b) an assurance explicitly stating that the proposed transfer or any replica thereof

---

[54] Nuclear Suppliers Group. (n.d.). NSG Guidelines. Retrieved October 20, 2023, from https://nuclearsuppliersgroup.org/en/guidelines.

[55] Id.

[56] Information Circular. (2000, April). Communication Received from the Permanent Mission of the Netherlands on Behalf of the Member States of the Nuclear Suppliers Group. International Atomic Energy Agency. Retrieved October 20, 2023, from https://www.iaea.org/sites/default/files/infcirc539r1.pdf.

[57] Nuclear Suppliers Group. (n.d.). How Does the NSG Achieve Its Aims Through the Guidelines? Retrieved October 20, 2023, from https://nuclearsuppliersgroup.org/en/nsg-faq.

will not be used in any "nuclear explosive activity" or "unsafeguarded nuclear fuel cycle activity".[58] In particular, the Part 2 Guidelines apply the "catch-all" control. Suppliers shall ensure that their national legislation requires an authorization for the transfer of items not listed in the dual-use items list if the items in question are or may be intended, in their entirety or in part, for use in connection with a "nuclear explosive activity".[59]

Although NSG Guidelines are not legally binding, NSG participating governments undertake to apply those guidelines via their national legislation.

2.1.2.4 Commitments of China to the NSG

In June 2004, China joined the NSG and has since taken an active part in the NSG while fulfilling the relevant rights and obligations.[60]

Before joining the NSG, in June 1998, the Chinese government had already promulgated the Regulations on the Export Control of Nuclear-Related Dual-use Items and Technologies,[61] which impose strict controls on the export of nuclear dual-use goods and related technologies and implemented a licensing system for the relevant exports. The regulations also establish a registration system for export operators, export approval procedures and penalties for non-compliance.[62]

After joining the NSG, in accordance with the NSG Guidelines, China has accordingly amended the Regulations on the Export Control of Nuclear and the Regulations on the Export Control of Nuclear-Related Dual-use Items and Technologies, making the acceptance of the full-scope safeguards by the importing country a condition for nuclear exports, and introducing the principle of catch-all control.[63]

With respect to the scope of control, China also amended the export control lists of nuclear and nuclear dual-use items after joining the NSG. The Nuclear Export Control List of China and Nuclear Dual-Use Goods and Related Technologies Export Control

[58] Information Circular. (2022, July 29). Guidelines for Transfers of Nuclear-Related Dual-Use Equipment, Materials, Software, and Related Technology, Para 6. Retrieved October 20, 2023, from https://www.iaea.org/sites/default/files/publications/documents/infcircs/1978/infcirc254r12p2.pdf.

[59] Id, para 5.

[60] China White Paper of Export Controls.

[61] Regulations on the Export Control of Nuclear-Related Dual-use Items and Technologies were revised in January 2007.

[62] Permanent Mission of the People's Republic of China to the UN. (2005, May 18). Report of China on the Implementation of NPT, New York, 2–27 May 2005. Retrieved October 20, 2023, from http://un.china-mission.gov.cn/eng/chinaandun/disarmament_armscontrol/npt/200505/t20050518_8412390.htm.

[63] The Ministry of Foreign Affairs of the People's Republic of China. (2011, April 7). Nuclear Suppliers Group. Retrieved October 20, 2023, from https://www.mfa.gov.cn/web/wjb_673085/zfxxgk_674865/gknrlb/tywj/zcwj/200705/t20070521_9869104.shtml.

List have encompassed all items and technologies on the Zangger Committee and NSG control lists.[64]

2.1.3 Convention on the Prohibition of the Development, Production, and Stockpiling of Bacteriological (Biological) and Toxin Weapons and on Their Destruction

2.1.3.1 Overview of the BTWC

Biological weapons disseminate disease-causing organisms or toxins to harm or kill humans, animals or plants. Deliberate releasing biological weapons can trigger catastrophic consequences, and the diseases caused may spread across the borders of a given State. In addition to the tragic loss of lives, such events may cause food shortages, environmental catastrophes, devastating economic loss, and widespread illness, panic and mistrust among the public.[65]

To address risks related to the development, production, and stockpiling of biological and toxin weapons, the BTWC was negotiated in Geneva, Switzerland, within the Eighteen Nation Committee on Disarmament and the Conference of the Committee on Disarmament from 1969 until 1971.[66] BTWC opened for signature on 10 April 1972 and entered into force on 26 March 1975.[67]

BTWC is a significant milestone in the development of multilateral non-proliferation regimes. It is the first multilateral disarmament treaty banning an entire category of WMD,[68] and is the first measure reached since World War II involving the destruction of existing weapons.[69]

---

[64] Permanent Mission of the People's Republic of China to the UN. (2005, May 18). Report of China on the Implementation of NPT, New York, 2–27 May 2005. Retrieved October 20, 2023, from http://un.china-mission.gov.cn/eng/chinaandun/disarmament_armscontrol/npt/200505/t20050518_8412390.htm.

[65] Office for Disarmament Affairs. (n.d.). Biological Weapons Convention. United Nations. Retrieved October 20, 2023, from https://www.un.org/disarmament/biological-weapons.

[66] Office for Disarmament Affairs. (n.d.). History of the Biological Weapons Convention. United Nations. Retrieved October 20, 2023, from https://www.un.org/disarmament/biological-weapons/about/history/

[67] Office for Disarmament Affairs. (n.d.). Biological Weapons Convention. United Nations. Retrieved October 20, 2023, from https://www.un.org/disarmament/biological-weapons.

[68] Office for Disarmament Affairs. (n.d.). Biological Weapons Convention. United Nations. Retrieved October 20, 2023, from https://www.un.org/disarmament/biological-weapons.

[69] Statement by the Minister of State for Foreign and Commonwealth Affairs, the Rt Hon David Hedley Ennals MP at the ceremony marking the entry into force of the Biological Weapons Convention in London on Wednesday 26 March 1975. Retrieved October 20, 2023, from https://front.un-arm.org/wp-content/uploads/2020/12/Ennalsstatement.pdf.

BTWC has effectively prohibited the development, production, acquisition, transfer, stockpiling, and use of biological and toxin weapons. The review conferences of BTWC State parties have been held every five years since 1980 to review its operation, with a view to assuring that the purposes of BTWC are realized.[70]

By the end of 2022, BTWC has reached almost universal membership with 184 States Parties and four Signatory States. China acceded to the BTWC in 1984.[71]

2.1.3.2 Main Commitments of the BTWC

With only 15 articles, BTWC formulates a framework of international commitments to prevent the proliferation of biological weapons and destroy them.

A. Prevention of proliferation of biological weapons

State parties of BTWC undertake never in any circumstances to develop, produce, stockpile, or otherwise acquire or retain: (a) microbial or other biological agents, or toxins whatever their origin or method of production, of types and in quantities that have no justification for prophylactic, protective or other peaceful purposes; and (b) weapons, equipment, or means of delivery designed to use such agents or toxins for hostile purposes or in armed conflict.[72]

As to the export control of biological weapons, State parties undertake not to transfer to any recipient whatsoever, directly or indirectly, and not in any way to assist, encourage, or induce anyone to manufacture or otherwise acquire biological weapons.[73]

B. Biological weapon destruction

State parties of BTWC undertake to destroy biological weapons or divert them to peaceful purposes.[74]

2.1.3.3 Control Mechanism of the BTWC

Article IV of BTWC requires State parties to take any national measures necessary to prohibit and prevent the development, production, stockpiling, acquisition, or retention of biological weapons within a State's territory, under its jurisdiction, or under its control.[75] BTWC does not stipulate concrete or standard implementing

---

[70] Article XII of BTWC. Retrieved October 20, 2023, from https://front.un-arm.org/wp-content/uploads/2020/12/BWC-text-English-1.pdf.

[71] Office for Disarmament Affairs. (n.d.). Lists of States Parties, Signatory States and Non-Signatory States. United Nations. Retrieved October 20, 2023, from https://www.un.org/disarmament/biological-weapons/about/membership-and-regional-groups.

[72] Article I of BTWC.

[73] Article III of BTWC.

[74] Article II of BTWC.

[75] Article IV of BTWC.

measures that State parties shall take. These necessary measures depend on the circumstances and legal systems of each State party, and as such there can be different national approaches to implementing the provisions of BTWC.[76]

The BTWC has not yet established a list of items that shall be subject to control under Article III and other provisions. Therefore, as regards the export control of biological weapons and related items, States must, at their discretion, take necessary measures to prevent the transfer of items that are biological weapons or can manufacture biological weapons.

2.1.3.4 Commitments of China to the BTWC

Since it became a State party of the BTWC, China has been fully involved in the BTWC reviews, and actively proposed multilateral initiatives on regulating biological scientific research exercises, biological technology, and global resource allocation. China calls for positive outcomes in the BTWC reviews, particularly regarding the negotiations for a legally binding verification protocol to maximize the effectiveness of the BTWC.[77]

China has formulated and strictly enforced relevant laws and regulations to ensure the effective implementation of the BTWC.

As to the manufacture and development of biological weapons-related items, in December 2001, the Standing Committee of the National People's Congress of China adopted Amendment (III) to the Criminal Law, which criminalizes and punishes acts that endanger public security, such as the illegal manufacture, trade, transport, storage or release of toxic substances and infectious disease pathogens. On 15 April 2021, the Biosecurity Law came into force, further enhancing the political commitment of China to fulfill its obligations under related international conventions, including the BTWC. The Biosecurity Law addresses both the prohibition of the development, manufacture, or other acquisition, stockpiling, possession and use of biological weapons, and the prevention of biological terrorism, as well as participation in and strengthening of international cooperation in biosecurity.[78]

As to the export control of items related to biological weapons, China is firmly opposed to the proliferation of biological weapons and related technologies, and it has continuously strengthened export controls on biological dual-use items and technologies. In December 2002, China promulgated and implemented the Regulations on Export Control of Dual-use Biological Agents and Related Equipment and

[76] Office for Disarmament Affairs. (n.d.). National Implementation of the Biological Weapons Convention. United Nations. Retrieved October 20, 2023, from https://www.un.org/disarmament/biological-weapons/national-implementation.

[77] China White Paper of Export Controls.

[78] The Ministry of Foreign Affairs of the People's Republic of China. Convention on the Prohibition of the Development, Production and Stockpiling of Bacteriological (Biological) and Toxin Weapons and on their Destruction. Retrieved October 20, 2023, from http://russiaembassy.fmprc.gov.cn/wjb_673085/zzjg_673183/jks_674633/zclc_674645/hwhsh_674653/200802/t20080229_7669102.shtml.

Technologies and its control list, and China revised the control list in July 2006. The export control system, control measures, and international cooperation are specified as well in the regulations.[79]

At the international level, as analyzed above, the BTWC does not have specific rules and arrangements regarding the export control of items related to biological weapons. The Australia Group does maintain control lists of biological and chemical weapons, but it is an informal arrangement with much fewer State parties than the BTWC, and China is not yet a member of the Australia Group. In view of this, during the review conference of the BTWC in 2016, China proposed to establish a "non-proliferation export control and international cooperation mechanism" within the framework of the BTWC, a mechanism with uniform rules and compliance measures that are universally observed by all countries, including list control, end-user certificate system and so forth. China advocates that the rights and obligations of States shall be reciprocal in the multilateral mechanism, which may remove the existing discrimination and promote international cooperation.[80]

2.1.4 Convention on the Prohibition of the Development, Production, Stockpiling, and Use of Chemical Weapons and on Their Destruction

2.1.4.1 Overview of the CWC

Chemical weapons are munitions and other devices that use the toxic effects of chemicals on living organisms to cause death or other harm.[81] As a category of WMD, chemical weapons have caused more than one million casualties globally since World War I. Although chemical weapons have reportedly been used in only a few cases since World War II, the Cold War period saw significant development, manufacture and stockpiling of chemical weapons.[82]

---

[79] Id.

[80] The Ministry of Foreign Affairs of the People's Republic of China. (2016, November 7). Working Paper on the Establishment of a Non-proliferation Export Control and International Cooperation Mechanism for the Convention on the Prohibition of the Development, Production and Stockpiling of Bacteriological (Biological) and Toxin Weapons and on their Destruction. Retrieved October 20, 2023, from https://www.fmprc.gov.cn/wjb_673085/zzjg_673183/jks_674633/fywj_674643/201709/t20170915_7668691.shtml.

[81] Convention on the Prohibition of the Development, Production, Stockpiling, and Use of Chemical Weapons and on their Destruction, 1. Chemical Weapons—their Characteristics and Properties. Retrieved October 20, 2023, from https://legal.un.org/avl/ha/cpdpsucw/cpdpsucw.html.

[82] Office for Disarmament Affairs. (n.d.). Chemical Weapons. United Nations. Retrieved October 20, 2023, from https://www.un.org/disarmament/wmd/chemical/.

The CWC was adopted by the Conference on Disarmament in Geneva on 3 September 1992.[83] It opened for signature in Paris on 13 January 1993 and entered into force on 29 April 1997. By the end of 2022, 193 States have committed to the CWC. China acceded to the CWC in 1997.

The purpose of the CWC is to prohibit the development, production, acquisition, stockpiling, retention, transfer or use of chemical weapons by States Parties. To achieve the purpose, State parties are required to take necessary steps to enforce such prohibitions within their jurisdiction.[84]

Unlike the NPT and the BTWC, the CWC allows for the stringent verification of compliance by State parties. In addition, the CWC has explicitly listed schedules of toxic chemicals and their precursors that shall be controlled by State parties.

2.1.4.2 Main Commitments Under the CWC

The CWC prohibits chemical weapons[85] and fixes obligations on its State parties mainly from the following aspects:

(a) The arms control obligation: State parties undertake never under any circumstances to develop, produce, otherwise acquire, stockpile or retain chemical weapons, or transfer, directly or indirectly, chemical weapons to anyone.[86]
(b) The disarmament obligation: State parties undertake to destroy chemical weapons in the possession of a State party, abandoned chemical weapons and chemical weapons production facilities.[87]
(c) The prohibition in armed conflicts: States undertake not to use chemical weapons, including not to use riot control agents as a method of warfare.[88]

---

[83] Office for Disarmament Affairs. (n.d.). Chemical Weapons. United Nations. Retrieved October 20, 2023, from https://www.un.org/disarmament/wmd/chemical/.

[84] Office for Disarmament Affairs. (n.d.). Chemical Weapons. United Nations. Retrieved October 20, 2023, from https://www.un.org/disarmament/wmd/chemical/.

[85] Convention on the Prohibition of the Development, Production, Stockpiling, and Use of Chemical Weapons and on Their Destruction. Retrieved October 20, 2023, from https://www.opcw.org/sites/default/files/documents/CWC/CWC_en.pdf. According to Article II (1) of the CWC, "Chemical Weapons" means the following, together or separately:

(a) toxic chemicals and their precursors, except where intended for purposes not prohibited under this Convention, as long as the types and quantities are consistent with such purposes;

(b) munitions and devices, specifically designed to cause death or other harm through the toxic properties of those toxic chemicals specified in subparagraph (a), which would be released as a result of the employment of such munitions and devices;

(c) any equipment specifically designed for use directly in connection with the employment of munitions and devices specified in subparagraph (b).

[86] Article I (1) of CWC.

[87] Article I (2), (3) and (4) of the CWC.

[88] Article I (5) of the CWC.

The arms control obligation requires States to control the export of items related to the development, production, acquisition, stockpiling, retention, transfer, or use of chemical weapons.

2.1.4.3 Control Mechanism of the CWC

The control mechanism of the CWC is administered by the Organization for the Prohibition of Chemical Weapons ("OPCW"), which was established upon the entry into force of the CWC. The OPCW's mission is to implement the provisions of the CWC and to ensure a credible, transparent regime to verify the fulfillment of State parties' obligations.[89]

The export control mechanism of chemicals under the CWC comprises the following elements:

- routine verification of the non-proliferation of chemicals;
- national measures to implement the CWC;
- challenge inspection in cases of doubt about the compliance of State parties.

In practice, all chemicals that can be used to produce chemical weapons have beneficial civilian uses. To control the diversion of chemicals from such civilian uses to military purposes, the OPCW designates inspectors and inspection assistants to conduct on-site verifications.[90]

As to national measures to implement the CWC, the CWC requires State parties to adopt necessary measures in accordance with their constitutional processes, and to inform the OPCW of the national legislative and administrative measures. The CWC does not specify concrete measures States shall take, but it provides a general obligation for States to prohibit natural and legal persons under their jurisdiction from undertaking any activity prohibited under the CWC (including transferring controlled chemicals).[91]

A unique feature of the CWC is the mechanism of "challenge inspection" as a complement to the routine verification procedures. If a State party has doubts about compliance by any other State party, it may ask for clarification. It may also request an on-site challenge inspection of the location where the doubtful activities allegedly take place.[92] Under the "challenge inspection" procedure, State parties have committed themselves to the principle of "anytime, anywhere" inspections with no right of refusal.[93]

---

[89] Office for Disarmament Affairs. (n.d.). Chemical Weapons. United Nations. Retrieved October 20, 2023, from https://www.un.org/disarmament/wmd/chemical/.

[90] Annex on Implementation and Verification of the CWC.

[91] Article VII of the CWC.

[92] Article IX of the CWC.

[93] Organization for the Prohibition of Chemical Weapons. (n.d.). Chemical Weapons Convention. Retrieved October 20, 2023, from https://www.opcw.org/chemical-weapons-convention.

2.1.4.4 Commitments of China to the CWC

China made a positive contribution to the conclusion of the CWC, which it signed in January 1993. In April 1997, China deposited its instrument of ratification, becoming an original State party of the CWC. Since the CWC entered into force, China has set up agencies dedicated to compliance, submitted annual declarations in full and on time, and firmly committed itself to the inspections by the OPCW. By September 2022, China has accepted 599 inspections of OPCW.[94]

China has adopted a series of regulations implementing the CWC, which include the Regulations on the Administration of the Controlled Chemicals (1995, revised in 2011, "Regulations on Controlled Chemicals") and corresponding control lists, and thus has established a set of management systems controlling the production, operation, use, storage and import of listed chemicals.[95] To further fulfill the commitment of China to the CWC, the Chinese government has also promulgated and implemented the Measures on Export Control of Certain Chemicals and Related Equipment and Technologies (with the export control list, 2002) ("Measures on Certain Chemicals"), further enhancing the export control of relevant chemicals and dual-use chemical equipment and technologies.[96] With a view to preventing and penalizing the use of toxic chemicals and other acts to commit terrorist activities, the Standing Committee of the National People's Congress of China adopted Amendment (III) to the Criminal Law of the PRC in December 2001, which explicitly criminalizes the illegal manufacture, transport, storage or delivery of toxic substances and other acts that endanger public security.[97]

As to chemical-weapon-related items subject to export control, the Catalogue of Export License for Dual-use Items and Technologies includes the items on the control lists associated with the Regulations on Controlled Chemicals and the Measures on Certain Chemicals. The export of such items is also regulated by ECL and other rules applicable to the export of dual use items. China has modified such catalogue according to the Schedules of Chemicals of the CWC.[98]

[94] The Ministry of Foreign Affairs of the People's Republic of China. The Convention on the Prohibition of the Development, Production, Stockpiling, and Use of Chemical Weapons and on their Destruction. Retrieved October 20, 2023, from http://russiaembassy.fmprc.gov.cn/wjb_673085/zzjg_673183/jks_674633/zclc_674645/hwhsh_674653/200802/t20080229_7669104.shtml.

[95] According to Article 3 of the Regulations on Controlled Chemicals, "controlled chemicals" refer to chemicals of the following four categories: chemical weapons; chemicals precursors for chemical weapons; common chemicals that could also be used as raw materials for producing chemical weapons; discrete organic chemicals other than explosives and pure hydrocarbons.

[96] The concept of "certain chemicals" is not specifically defined under the Measures on Certain Chemicals. For details of "certain chemicals" under export control, see Chap. 3, Sect. 3.2.1.5 Certain Chemicals and Related Equipment and Technologies Export Control List.

[97] The State Council of the People's Republic of China. (2007, April 28). Review of the Tenth Anniversary of China's Fulfilment of the CWC. Retrieved October 20, 2023, from http://www.gov.cn/jrzg/2007-04/28/content_599649.htm.

[98] China White Paper of Export Controls.

2.1.5 Arms Trade Treaty

2.1.5.1 Overview of the ATT

The ATT was adopted by the UN General Assembly to regulate international trade in conventional arms by establishing the highest international standards and to prevent and eradicate illicit trade and diversion of conventional arms.[99] The ATT contributes to international and regional peace, security and stability, reducing human suffering, and promoting cooperation, transparency and responsible action among the international community.[100] The object of the ATT is to establish common international standards for regulating the international trade in conventional arms and to prevent and eradicate the illicit trade in conventional arms and prevent their diversion.[101]

The ATT opened for signature on 3 June 2013, and entered into force on 24 December 2014. By December 2022, the ATT has 113 State parties, and 28 signatories (including the US) that have not yet ratified, approved, acceded, or accepted it. China acceded to the ATT in 2020.[102]

2.1.5.2 Main Commitments of the ATT

The ATT applies to all categories of conventional arms, including battle tanks, armored combat vehicles, large-caliber artillery systems, combat aircraft, attack helicopters, warships, missiles and missile launchers, and small arms and light weapons.[103] In relation to the conventional arms, the ATT also requires State parties to establish and maintain a national control system to regulate the export of ammunition/munitions fired, launched or delivered by the conventional arms as well as parts and components that capable to assemble the conventional arms.[104]

The activities of international trade under the ATT are defined as "transfer", including the export, import, transit, transshipment, and brokering.[105]

To implement the export control of conventional arms, State parties undertake to prohibit or conduct export assessment of conventional arms or items.

As to prohibitions, State parties shall not authorize any transfer of conventional arms controlled under the ATT if the transfer would violate their obligations under measures adopted by the UN Security Council (in particular, arms embargoes), the transfer would violate their obligations under international agreements, or the State

---

[99] The Arms Trade Treaty, Article 13. Retrieved October 20, 2023, from https://thearmstradetreaty.org/hyper-images/file/ATT_English/ATT_English.pdf?templateId=137253.

[100] Article 1 of the ATT.

[101] Ibid.

[102] The Arms Trade Treaty, Status of Participation. Retrieved October 17, 2023, from https://thearmstradetreaty.org/treaty-status.html?templateId=209883.

[103] Article 2 of the ATT.

[104] Article 3 and 4 of the ATT.

[105] Article 2(2) of the ATT.

parties have knowledge at the time of authorizing the transfer that the arms or items would be used in severe crimes, including the commission of genocide, crimes against humanity and war crimes.[106]

If the export is not prohibited, State parties of the ATT shall conduct the export assessment of the conventional arms or items to identify risks of endangering international peace and security or violating other international obligations. State parties shall not authorize exports that are not prohibited but have an overriding risk.[107]

2.1.5.3 Control Mechanism of the ATT

The control (including export control) of arms under the ATT is substantiated through the national implementation. State parties are required to maintain a national control list of conventional arms covered by the ATT and to designate competent national authorities to secure an effective and transparent national control system.[108]

Each State party of the ATT shall submit an annual report to the Secretariat of ATT concerning authorized or actual exports and imports of conventional arms covered under the ATT.[109]

2.1.5.4 Commitments of China to the ATT

China actively participated in the negotiations on the ATT and made a significant contribution to the conclusion of the ATT. China announced that it would initiate the domestic legal procedures to join the ATT in September 2019 and formally acceded to the Treaty in July 2020. As a State party, the attitude of China toward the AAT is that it firmly supports the ATT's purposes and objectives through full compliance with its obligations, and China stands ready to work with other States Parties to regulate the trade in conventional arms, promote the universality and effectiveness of the Treaty, and improve global governance of the arms trade.[110]

As to the export control of arms, China promulgated the Regulations on Export Control of Military Items in 2002 and maintained the Military Items Export Control List. The Military Items Export Control List covers more than the conventional arms regulated under Article 2 of the ATT. This is in conformity with Article 5 of the ATT which encourages State parties to apply the ATT to the broadest range of conventional arms.[111]

---

[106] Article 6 of the ATT.

[107] Article 7 of the ATT.

[108] Article 5 of the ATT.

[109] Article 13 of the ATT.

[110] China White Paper of Export Controls.

[111] Article 5(3) of the ATT states as follows: Each State Party is encouraged to apply the provisions of this Treaty to the broadest range of conventional arms. National definitions of any of the categories covered under Article 2 (1) (a)–(g) shall not cover less than the descriptions used in the United

2.1.6 *Summary of Multilateral Commitments of China*

2.1.6.1 Attitudes of China Toward Non-proliferation

After some years of international isolation due to embargoes by the Coordinating Committee for Multilateral Export Controls ("COCOM"),[112] Chinese participation in non-proliferation regimes since the 1980s implies a positive shift in Chinese policy from the Cold War notions of self-reliance, toward the increased cooperation with the international community on security matters.[113]

Entering the 1990s, China experienced rapid economic growth, including vast increases in imports, exports, and foreign inbound investment. In the meanwhile, the participation of China in arms control and non-proliferation regimes has increased unprecedently and rapidly.[114] Non-proliferation commitments have since been consistent with the new, outward-looking landscape of economic policies of China.[115] Shouldering its international non-proliferation obligations is of great benefit to building the international image of China as a responsible power and the economic development of China.

2.1.6.2 Roles of China in Multinational Non-proliferation Regimes

China believes in multilateralism in that the international society shall follow the purposes and principles of the UN Charter, strengthen the collective security mechanism with the UN at its core, and uphold the authority of the Security Council.[116] In line with the consistent policies of China on international affairs, China advocates that as the most representative international organization, the UN should and must play a central role in seeking and finding the balance between non-proliferation and peaceful uses, and in safeguarding the legitimate rights of developing countries to peaceful uses of technological advances.[117] Accordingly, China tends to participate in regimes if administrated by the UN, with broad participation involving developing countries, and in formal definitions for compliance or verification.[118]

Nations Register of Conventional Arms at the time of entry into force of this Treaty. For the category covered under Article 2 (1) (h), national definitions shall not cover less than the descriptions used in relevant United Nations instruments at the time of entry into force of this Treaty.

[112] De Bruin, E. (2022). Export Control Regimes—Present-Day Challenges and Opportunities. In R. Beeres, R. Bertrand, J. Klomp, J. Timmermans, & J. Voetelink (Eds.), *NL ARMS Netherlands Annual Review of Military Studies 2021*. (1st ed., p. 34). T.M.C. ASSER PRESS.

[113] Frieman, W. (2004). *China, Arms Control, and Nonproliferation* (p.182). RoutledgeCurzon.

[114] Id., at 1.

[115] Id., at 2.

[116] MOFCOM. (2022, June 17). *China Calls for Genuine Multilateralism to Address Non-Proliferation Issues*. China Export Control Information. Retrieved October 17, 2023, from http://exportcontrol.mofcom.gov.cn/article/gndt/202206/662.html.

[117] China White Paper of Export Controls.

[118] Frieman, W. (2004). China, Arms Control, and Nonproliferation. (p. 3). RoutledgeCurzon.

As one of the major powers, the acceptance and participation of China in international non-proliferation regimes enhance the influence and effectiveness of such regimes. China has actively played a constructive role in the multilateral non-proliferation regime. According to its White Paper, China firmly upholds the authority and efficacy of all relevant international conventions, strictly complies with its international obligations, and safeguards international and regional peace and stability.[119] As to export control, China strives to promote such international export controls as fair, reasonable, and non-discriminatory. In the author's view, fairness means non-selfishness; reasonableness means non-abuse of unilateral controls, and non-discrimination means the same control treatment to all members of the international community.

2.1.6.3 Export Controls of China and Its International Commitments

Since the mid-1990s, China has gradually formulated a set of non-proliferation policies implemented within a legal framework of non-proliferation and export control,[120] which has paved the way for further acceptance of international non-proliferation regime.[121] Thus far, China has established a comprehensive legal system for export control of nuclear, biological, chemical, missile, and other related items and technologies, as well as all military items.[122] Export controls of China have adopted internationally accepted practices such as the export operator registration system, end-user and end-use certification, licensing system, list control, and catch-all control.[123]

2.2 China and Multilateral Non-proliferation Arrangements

As regards international export control regimes, apart from international conventions, there have been multilateral non-proliferation arrangements coordinating international export control activities. The Australia Group, MTCR, and the Wassenaar Arrangement are the most influential international arrangements addressing such export control activities.

[119] China White Paper of Export Controls.

[120] Full text of China white paper on non-proliferation policy and measures. Retrieved October 17, 2023, from https://www.caea.gov.cn/english/n6759377/c6792767/content.html.

[121] Ibid.

[122] The State Council Information Office of the People's Republic of China. (2005, September). *China's Arms Control, Disarmament and Non-proliferation Efforts*. Retrieved October 17, 2023, from https://www.gov.cn/zwgk/2005-09/01/content_28157.htm.

[123] Gao, W. (2012). Analysis of the Practice Process of China's Participation in the Nuclear Non-proliferation Regime. *International Forum*, 14(3), 46–50.

2.2.1 *The Australia Group*

2.2.1.1 Overview of the Australia Group

In the 1980s, the BTWC entered into force and some States exercised export control over certain biological and chemical items that may be transferred and utilized to produce related weapons. These controls suffered from a lack of uniformity, and it soon became apparent that attempts were being made to circumvent them.[124] In view of such circumstances, the Australia Group was established in 1985, with an aim at enabling exporting or transshipping countries to minimize the risk of assisting chemical and biological weapon proliferation through a harmonized export licensing system. Members of the Australia Group meet annually to discuss ways of increasing the effectiveness of participating countries' national export licensing measures to prevent the potential proliferators from obtaining materials for chemical and biological weapon programs.[125]

The Australia Group is an informal arrangement, in which the State participants do not undertake any legally binding obligations. The effectiveness of the arrangement depends on national measures taken by its members to control the export of certain items. By December 2022, the Australia Group has 43 participants, with 42 States and the European Union.

As a multilateral arrangement focusing on the export control of biological and chemical weapons, all States participating in the Australia Group are parties to the BTWC and the CWC.[126] The Australia Group believes that the national export licensing mechanisms it promotes serve to strengthen the non-proliferation goals of the BTWC and the CWC.

2.2.1.2 Control Mechanism of the Australia Group

The principal objective of Australia Group is to use licensing measures to ensure that exports of certain chemicals, biological agents, and dual-use chemical and biological manufacturing facilities and equipment, do not contribute to the spread of chemical and biological weapons. The Australia Group achieves this by harmonizing the participants' national export licensing measures.[127]

[124] The Origins of the Australia Group, The Australia Group. Retrieved October 17, 2023, from https://www.dfat.gov.au/publications/minisite/theaustraliagroupnet/site/en/origins.html.

[125] The Australia Group: An Introduction, The Australia Group. Retrieved October 17, 2023, from https://www.dfat.gov.au/publications/minisite/theaustraliagroupnet/site/en/introduction.html.

[126] Ibid.

[127] Objectives of the Group, The Australia Group. Retrieved October 17, 2023, from https://www.dfat.gov.au/publications/minisite/theaustraliagroupnet/site/en/objectives.html.

The Australia Group maintains control lists of the following items,[128] as a basis for the harmonized national export licensing measures:

- chemical weapons precursors;
- dual-use chemical manufacturing facilities and equipment and related technology and software;
- dual-use biological equipment and related technology and software;
- human and animal pathogens and toxins; and
- Plant pathogens.

According to the guidelines of the Australia Group, as an underlying principle, participants shall control the transfer of items in the control lists by their sovereign judgment, and participants shall deny transfers in which the controlled items are intended to be used in a chemical weapons or biological weapons program, or for related terrorism, or that a significant risk of diversion exists.[129] Participants shall implement national export control legislation, including enforcement and sanctions for violations.[130]

The guidelines of Australia Group provide a non-exhaustive list of factors for participants to evaluate export applications of controlled items, including the capabilities and objectives of the chemical and biological activities of the recipient State, the role of distributors, brokers or other intermediaries in the transfer, the end-use of the transfer, the extent and effectiveness of the export control system in the recipient State as well as any intermediary States and so forth.[131]

Regarding the re-export of items controlled by the Australia Group, a participant must, before authorizing a transfer, either (a) satisfy itself that goods are not intended for re-export; (b) satisfy itself that, if re-exported, the goods would be controlled by the recipient government pursuant to these guidelines; or (c) obtain satisfactory assurances that its consent will be secured prior to any re-transfer to a third country.[132]

The Australia Group also applies the "catch-all" control, requiring participants not to authorize the transfer of non-listed items if such items may be intended, in their entirety or part, for use in connection with chemical or biological weapons activities.[133] Participants are encouraged to share information on export control measures on a regular basis, and to exchange information on catch-all denials.

[128] Australia Group Common Control Lists, The Australia Group. Retrieved October 17, 2023, from https://www.dfat.gov.au/publications/minisite/theaustraliagroupnet/site/en/controllists.html.

[129] Guidelines for Transfers of Sensitive Chemical or Biological Items, paragraph 2, The Australia Group. Retrieved October 17, 2023, from https://www.dfat.gov.au/publications/minisite/theaustraliagroupnet/site/en/guidelines.html.

[130] Id., paragraph 3.

[131] Id., paragraph 4.

[132] Id., paragraph 5.

[133] Id., paragraph 7.

2.2.1.3 Concept of Toxins

The BTWC neither specifies the definition of toxins nor explicitly lists toxins controlled by the BTWC since it has not established a list of items subject to control.

OPCW, however, does illustrate the definition and scope of controlled toxins in the context of CWC. According to OPCW, toxins are toxic chemicals produced by living organisms or synthesized in laboratories without harvesting the organisms that produce them in nature. Toxins are considered as *both chemical and biological weapons* when used in violation of the CWC. The development, production, and stockpiling of toxins for purposes of warfare are prohibited under both CWC and the BTWC. There are two toxins explicitly listed in Schedule 1 of the CWC, namely ricin (produced in nature in the seeds of the castor bean plant) and saxitoxin (produced in nature by cyanobacteria).[134]

Currently, 21 toxins and subunits thereof[135] are listed in the List of Human and Animal Pathogens and Toxins for Export Control of the Australia Group, and the list does not distinguish between toxins controlled under CWC and those controlled under the BTWC.

As to toxins controlled by China, the Catalogue of Dual-use Items and Technologies Subject to Export License ("Consolidated Catalogue") has included ricin (tariff code: 3002499020) and saxitoxin (tariff code: 2939801000) in the Controlled Chemicals List as chemicals that can be used as chemical weapons. Ricin (tariff code: 3002499020) and saxitoxin (tariff code: 3002499020) are also listed in the Biological Dual-use Items and Related Equipment and Technologies Export Control List.[136] Other toxins are controlled under the Biological Dual-use Items and Related Equipment and Technologies Export Control List, and such toxins are similar to the toxins listed by the Australia Group.

---

134 Organisation for the Prohibition of Chemical Weapons. What is a Chemical Weapon?. Retrieved November 27, 2023, from https://www.opcw.org/our-work/what-chemical-weapon.

135 Such toxins are: Abrin, Aflatoxins, Botulinum toxins, Clostridium perfringens alpha, beta 1, beta 2, epsilon and iota toxins, Conotoxins, Diacetoxyscirpenol, HT-2 toxin, Microcystins (Cyanoginosins), Modeccin, Ricin, Saxitoxin, Shiga toxins (shiga-like toxins, verotoxins, and verocytotoxins), Staphylococcus aureus enterotoxins, hemolysin alpha toxin, and toxic shock syndrome toxin (formerly known as Staphylococcus enterotoxin F), T-2 toxin, Tetrodotoxin, Viscumin (Viscum album lectin 1), Volkensin, Brevetoxins, Gonyautoxins, Nodularins, and Palytoxin. See List of Human and Animal Pathogens and Toxins for Export Control, The Australia Group. Retrieved November 27, 2023, from https://www.dfat.gov.au/publications/minisite/theaustraliagroupnet/site/en/human_animal_pathogens.html.

136 Announcement No. 42 of 2022 of the MOFCOM and the GAC, 30 December 2022.

2.2.1.4 China and the Australia Group

China has been involved in six rounds of consultation with the Australia Group on biological and chemical non-proliferation, implementation of the CWC and the BTWC, and operation of the Australia Group.[137]

Although China is not yet a participant, China's export control of biological dual-use items and chemical items is largely consistent with the regulatory patterns established by the Australia Group. China also implements national measures, including but not limited to the licensing system, end-use control, catch-all control through ECL and related regulations. As export control lists of China, when determining chemical and biological items subject to export control,[138] China does derive controlled items from the control lists of Australia Group, including the chemical weapons precursors list, dual-use chemical manufacturing facilities and equipment and related technology and software list, and dual-use biological equipment and related technology and software list.

2.2.2 Missile Technology Control Regime

2.2.2.1 Overview of the MTCR

Established in 1987, the MTCR is an informal and voluntary association of countries that share the goals of non-proliferation of systems capable of delivering WMD (other than manned aircraft) and which seek to coordinate national export licensing efforts for non-proliferation.[139] The goals of the MTCR are to restrict the proliferation of missiles, complete rocket systems, unmanned air vehicles, and related technology for those systems capable of carrying a 500-kg payload at least 300 km, as well as systems intended for the delivery of WMD.[140] As an export control regime involving multiple countries focusing on missiles and missile technology, MTCR has played a positive role in containing the proliferation of missiles and related items and technologies.[141]

By December 2022, MTCR has 35 Member States.

---

[137] China White Paper of Export Controls.

[138] Biological Dual-use Items and Related Equipment and Technologies Export Control List, Controlled Chemicals List, and Certain Chemicals and Related Equipment and Technologies Export Control List.

[139] Missile Technology Control Regime. (2017). *Introduction.* MTCR Annex Handbook—2017. Retrieved October 17, 2023, from https://mtcr.info/wordpress/wp-content/uploads/2017/10/MTCR-Handbook-2017-INDEXED-FINAL-Digital.pdf.

[140] What are the main objectives of the MTCR. Frequently Asked Questions (FAQ). Retrieved October 17, 2023, from https://www.mtcr.info/en/faq.

[141] MOFCOM. (2021, December 30). *Missile Technology Control Regime.* China Export Control Information. Retrieved October 18, 2023, from http://exportcontrol.mofcom.gov.cn/article/zcfg/gwzcfg/202111/476.html.

2.2.2.2 Control Mechanism of the MTCR

The export control mechanism under the MTCR is established through participating States' adherence to two fundamental documents: (a) Guidelines for Sensitive Missile-Relevant Transfers, the common export policy guidelines, and (b) MTCR Equipment, Software, and Technology Annex ("ESTA"), an integral common list of controlled items.

The MTCR does not take export licensing decisions as a group. Participating States are responsible for implementing the guidelines and the control list as a matter of sovereign discretion and in accordance with national legislation and practice. The participating States regularly exchange information about relevant national missile non-proliferation export licensing issues.[142]

The ESTA has listed both military and dual-use controlled items—including virtually all key equipment, materials, software, and technology needed for the development, production, and operation of systems capable of delivering WMD. The ESTA is divided into "Category I" and "Category II" items.[143] Category I items are those items of greatest sensitivity. As required by the guidelines, restraint will be exercised in considering Category I transfers regardless of their purpose, and there will be a strong presumption to deny such transfers; restraint will also be exercised in considering transfers of any items in Category II of the ESTA, or of any missiles (whether or not listed), if the participating States find that they are intended to be used for the delivery of WMD after evaluation on a case-by-case basis.[144] The guidelines provide general factors to be considered when evaluating the transfer of such items, including the capabilities and objectives of the missile and space programs of the recipient State, the assessment of the end-use of the transfers, the risk of controlled items falling into the hands of terrorist groups and individuals and so forth.[145]

---

[142] How does the MTCR achieve its objectives. Frequently Asked Questions (FAQ). Retrieved October 18, 2023, from https://www.mtcr.info/en/faq.

[143] Category I items include complete rocket systems (including ballistic missiles, space launch vehicles and sounding rockets) and unmanned air vehicle systems (including cruise missiles systems, target and reconnaissance drones) with capabilities exceeding a 300 km/500 kg range/payload threshold; production facilities for such systems; and major sub-systems including rocket stages, re-entry vehicles, rocket engines, guidance systems and warhead mechanisms. Category II items include complete rocket systems (including ballistic missiles systems, space launch vehicles and sounding rockets) and unmanned air vehicles (including cruise missile systems, target drones, and reconnaissance drones) not covered in item I, capable of a maximum range equal to or greater than, 300 km. Also included are a wide range of equipment, material, and technologies, most of which have uses other than for missiles capable of delivering WMD. See MTCR Guidelines and the Equipment, Software and Technology Annex. Retrieved October 18, 2023, from https://www.mtcr.info/en/mtcr-guidelines.

[144] Missile Technology Control Regime. (2017). *Appendix I—Guidelines for Sensitive Missile-Relevant Transfers.* MTCR Annex Handbook—2017. (paragraph 2). Retrieved October 20, 2023, from https://mtcr.info/wordpress/wp-content/uploads/2017/10/MTCR-Handbook-2017-INDEXED-FINAL-Digital.pdf.

[145] Id., paragraph 3.

For non-listed items, participating States may decide whether to authorize the export of non-listed items with different degrees of risks that the items may be intended, in their entirety or part, for use in connection with delivery systems for WMD.[146]

2.2.2.3 China and the MTCR

China applied to join the MTCR in 2004 and has since maintained communication and exchanges, with five rounds of dialogue focusing on the accession of China and issues regarding control systems, lists, and the enforcement of missile export controls. Although China has not participated in the MTCR, China referred to the MTCR Guidelines and ESTA when formulating its missile export control regulations and control list.[147] The missile export control mechanism of China is in line with that of the MTCR. Missiles and their related items and technologies are controlled separately as military items and dual-use items, and the end-use control and catch-all control are also imposed in missile export controls.[148]

China supports international efforts to prevent the proliferation of missiles, and missile-related items and technologies, and adopts a positive and open attitude to international proposals designed to strengthen the mechanisms for non-proliferation. China promulgated and implemented the Regulations on Export Control of Missiles and Missile-related Items and Technologies in 2002, which provide the legal basis for its export of missile-related items and technologies.[149]

2.2.3 Wassenaar Arrangement

2.2.3.1 Origin of Wassenaar Arrangement

The origin of Wassenaar Arrangement is the COCOM, which was established by the US, the UK, France, Italy, Netherland and Belgium in 1950. COCOM coordinated the national controls that industrialized countries had applied over the export of strategic materials and technology to the communist world.[150]

The COCOM maintained three export control lists: (1) the International Industrial List, (2) the International Munitions List, and (3) the International Atomic Energy

[146] Id., paragraph 7.

[147] China White Paper of Export Controls.

[148] Article 6 and 16 of Regulations on Export Control of Missiles and Missile-related Items and Technologies.

[149] China White Paper of Export Controls.

[150] Office of Technology Assessment. (1979). CHAPTER VIII Multilateral Export Control Policy: The Coordinating Committee (COCOM). In *Technology and East–West Trade* (p.153). United States. Congress. Office of Technology Assessment. Retrieved October 20, 2023, from https://www.princeton.edu/~ota/disk3/1979/7918/791810.PDF.

List. Members of the COCOM may request to export certain items in the COCOM lists, and such requests are subject to review by all COCOM members. Such exports can only be exercised when all the Member States make a unanimous approval decision.[151]

The force that initially brought COCOM into being and held it together through its formative years was the enormous economic leverage the US could exert on its Western allies in the immediate aftermath of World War II and the early years of the Cold War.[152] With the drastic changes in the international political and economic situation and the rapid development of science and technology, Western European countries engaged in heated discussions with the US in the late 1980s, demanding revision and reduction of embargoed items for the economic interests of Western Europe. In 1990, COCOM significantly eased restrictions on exports of high-technology products to the Soviet Union and Eastern European countries.[153]

2.2.3.2 Overview of the Wassenaar Arrangement

At the end of the Cold War, members of the COCOM recognized that the East–West focus was no longer the appropriate basis for export controls, and they established a new arrangement in 1994 focusing on the export control of conventional weapons and dual-use goods and technologies—Wassenaar Arrangement.[154] In 1994, COCOM collapsed before emergence of Wassenaar Arrangement, which exhibits the divergent interests as between the US and Western Europe.

Wassenaar Arrangement was established to contribute to regional and international security and stability, by promoting transparency and greater responsibility in transfers of conventional arms and dual-use goods and technologies.

By December 2022, Wassenaar Arrangement has 42 participating States, most of which are developed countries.[155]

---

[151] Id., at 157.

[152] Id., at 154.

[153] MOFCOM. (2021, December 30). *From COCOM to Wassenaar Arrangement, the Unchanged Control of Semiconductor Substrates*. China Export Control Information. Retrieved October 20, 2023, from http://exportcontrol.mofcom.gov.cn/article/zjsj/202111/529.html.

[154] Origins, Wassenaar Arrangement. Retrieved October 20, 2023, from https://www.wassenaar.org/about-us/.

[155] About Us, Wassenaar Arrangement. Retrieved October 20, 2023, from https://www.wassenaar.org/about-us/.

2.2.3.3 Control Mechanism of the Wassenaar Arrangement

The Wassenaar Arrangement maintains a Munitions List and a List of Dual-Use Goods and Technologies with 9 Categories[156]:

Category 1 Special Materials and Related Equipment
Category 2 Materials Processing
Category 3 Electronics
Category 4 Computers
Category 5—Part 1 Telecommunications,
Category 5—Part 2 Information Security
Category 6 Sensors and Lasers
Category 7 Navigation and Avionics
Category 8 Marine
Category 9 Aerospace and Propulsion.

Participating States of Wassenaar Arrangement apply export controls to all items set forth in the above control lists pursuant to their national policies and legislations, with the objective of preventing unauthorized transfers or re-transfers of those items.[157]

Participating States are required to report twice a year arms transfers and transfers/denials of certain dual-use goods and technologies to non-participants of Wassenaar Arrangement. In some cases, especially for more sensitive items, shorter reporting timeframes apply.[158] Additionally, within 60 days, participating States are requested to notify Wassenaar Secretariat of any export license approvals of transactions that are "essentially identical" to transactions that another Wassenaar member denied within the past three years.[159] Owing to such notification obligation, for certain items whose export has once been denied by Wassenaar members, the export of the same items from other participating States of Wassenaar Arrangement would be subject to strict examination.

2.2.3.4 China and the Wassenaar Arrangement

Though not a participating State, according to its White Paper, China has maintained communication and exchanges with Wassenaar Arrangement. The two sides

---

[156] List of Dual-Use Goods and Technologies and Munitions List. Retrieved October 20, 2023, from https://www.wassenaar.org/app/uploads/2021/12/Public-Docs-Vol-II-2021-List-of-DU-Goods-and-Technologies-and-Munitions-List-Dec-2021.pdf.

[157] About Us, Wassenaar Arrangement. Retrieved October 20, 2023, from https://www.wassenaar.org/about-us/

[158] Guidelines and Procedures, including the Initial Elements, p. 7. Retrieved October 20, 2023, from https://www.wassenaar.org/app/uploads/2021/12/Public-Docs-Vol-I-Founding-Documents.pdf.

[159] Id., at 5.

have held five rounds of in-depth dialogue on control principles, lists, and best practices pertaining to the export of conventional arms and relevant dual-use items and technologies.[160]

Regarding items in the control lists, the items controlled by Wassenaar Arrangement differ substantially from those of China. China does not adopt the dual-use control lists under Wassenaar Arrangement as China views the arrangement as discriminative and over-reaching. The unilateral dual-use control list of China is much shorter and more concise than that of Wassenaar Arrangement.

2.2.4 Summary of Multilateral Non-proliferation Arrangements

2.2.4.1 Nature of Multilateral Non-proliferation Arrangements

The Australia Group, the MTCR, and Wassenaar Arrangement have established separate export control regimes on chemical and biological items, missiles and related items, and conventional arms and dual-use items. Unlike export control regimes built by international conventions, these export control regimes set out more specific control lists of controlled items and cover a wider scope, thus posing more strict and concrete compliance requirements on their participating members.

These export control regimes are informal arrangements that have no binding force on their members. The implementation of these regimes depends on the implementation of domestic export control regulations by members. However, these regimes emphasize on enhancing the transparency and information exchange of members' export control activities, which can effectively coordinate member's export control practices.[161]

Most participating States of the regimes above, especially the leading participants, are Western developed countries. With a Western perspective, such export control regimes are utilized by the participants to secure and promote their national and foreign policy interests. While export control regimes built by international conventions try to strike a balance between non-proliferation and peaceful utilization and sharing of sensitive items and technologies, these export regimes focus more on restricting proliferation, maintaining stability and securing strategic advantages of the exporters.

---

[160] China White Paper of Export Controls.

[161] Wang, J. (2005). An Analysis of the Transition of the Relationship between China and Multilateral Export Control Regimes and the Reasons. *Journal of Liaoning University (Philosophy and Social Sciences)*, 33(2), 78.

2.2.4.2 Attitudes of China Toward Multilateral Non-proliferation Arrangements

China has not formally participated in the Western-led export control arrangements. Compared with subjective unilateral standards formed by relatively small export control cartels, the Chinese government is more receptive to and attaches greater importance to objective, internationally agreed-upon rules formed by global or multilateral agreements.[162] As analyzed above, for instance, in the review conference of the BTWC in 2016, China has proposed to establish a mechanism with uniform rules and compliance measures that are universally observed by all Member States of BTWC. This reveals that China believes States shall follow uniform standards and take measures pursuant to the binding treaty, instead of imposing separate standards and rules.

From the perspective of developing countries, China differs from these voluntary export control regimes in terms of export control objectives. China upholds solidarity and opposes discriminatory approaches, insisting that the rights of developing countries to peacefully utilize and share dual-use items and technologies shall be secured under the premise of non-proliferation.[163] In December 2021, the 76th Session of the UN General Assembly adopted the China-initiated resolution "Promoting International Cooperation on Peaceful Uses in the Context of International Security", which emphasizes the significance of international cooperation in science and technology for peaceful purposes, in facilitating economic and social development, and urges all Member States, without prejudice to their non-proliferation obligations, to lift unnecessary restrictions on peaceful use in developing countries.[164]

Although China has not participated in these arrangements and maintains a somewhat skeptical attitude, China has paid close attention to the control mechanisms of these arrangements. China has made references to related control lists and control measures. The scope and practice of export controls of China in the nuclear, biological, chemical, and missile fields are largely consistent with the above-mentioned arrangements. Table 2.1 shows export control lists of China and its connection with international regimes with China as a member and other non-proliferation arrangements. According to the current policy stand of China, China will continue to strengthen dialogue and exchange with existing export control mechanisms and continuously improve respective export controls.[165]

---

[162] Frieman, W. (2004). China, Arms Control, and Nonproliferation (p. 177). RoutledgeCurzon.

[163] Full text of China white paper on non-proliferation policy and measures. Retrieved October 20, 2023, from https://www.caea.gov.cn/english/n6759377/c6792767/content.html.

[164] China White Paper of Export Controls.

[165] The Ministry of Foreign Affairs of the People's Republic of China. (2023 July). China's Relationship with Non-proliferation Export Control Regimes of Multiple Countries. Retrieved October 20, 2023, from http://russiaembassy.fmprc.gov.cn/wjb_673085/zzjg_673183/jks_674633/zclc_674645/fkswtjks_674649/200802/t20080229_7669063.shtml.

Controlled items	Control lists of China	Relevance to conventions or arrangements
Military items	Military items export control list	ATT; *Wassenaar Arrangement
Nuclear	Nuclear export control list	NPT; Zangger Committee; NSG
Nuclear dual-use items	Nuclear dual-use items and related technologies export control list	NPT; NSG
Biological dual-use items	Biological dual-use items and related equipment and technologies export control list	BTWC; *AG
Controlled chemicals	Controlled chemicals list	CWC *AG
Certain chemicals	Certain chemicals and related equipment and technologies export control list	CWC *AG
Missile and missile-related items	Missile and missile-related items and technologies export control list	*MTCR
Precursor chemical	Precursor chemical (I) and (II)	United Nations Convention against Illicit Traffic in Narcotic Drugs and Psychotropic Substances (falls outside the non-proliferation regime)
Certain dual-use items and technologies list		Control lists of items unilaterally controlled by China
Special civil items and technologies list		
Commercial cryptography export control list		

Note "*" means the arrangements in which China has not participated

Chapter 3
Export Control of Dual-Use Items

This chapter discusses the regulations, rules, and practices of export control of dual-use items[1] (including nuclear items) under ECL. Section 3.1 analyzes the Chinese legal framework of dual-use items export controls, the current decentralized regulations and rules which will be replaced by the *Regulations on the Export Control of Dual-use Items* (currently under enactment) in the near future. Section 3.2 introduces the consolidated catalogue of dual-use items released by MOFCOM jointly with GAC at the end of each calendar year. Section 3.3 then presents a brief conclusion.

3.1 The Legal Framework

Dual-use items are defined in a similar way in the major export control jurisdictions and are normally controlled through dual-use item lists.[2] Under ECL, "dual-use items" are defined as items that can be used for civil purposes, as well as for military

[1] Please note that in China, given that the nuclear items are also enlisted in the Catalogue of Dual-use Items and Technologies Subject to Export License, nuclear items are, therefore, treated as part of dual-use items in this Chapter.

[2] For example, the U.S. has maintained a complex and fluid regulation entitled "*Export Administration Regulations*" ("EAR") and formulated a "Commercial Control list" which mainly includes dual-use items of sensitive use; the EU has updated "*Regulation (EU) 2021/821 of the European Parliament and of the Council of 20 May 2021 setting up a union regime for the control of exports, brokering, technical assistance, transit and transfer of dual-use items*", Annex I of which is the List of Dual-use Items subject to control; Japan has promulgated "*Export Trade Control Order*" (Cabinet Order No. 378 of Showa 24), Attached Table 1 of which is the List of controlled military items and dual-use items. Similarly, the Wassenaar Arrangement has also formulated a List of Dual-use Goods and Technologies, last updated on 1 December 2022.

D. Zhao, *Contemporary Export Control Law of China*, Modern China and International Economic Law, https://doi.org/10.1007/978-981-99-9825-8_3

purposes or for substantiating military potentials, especially those goods, technologies, and services that can be used for design, development, production, or use of WMD.[3]

3.1.1 Decentralized Regulations and Rules

Given that the dual-use items China controls are mostly originating from multilateral export control regimes, with a small portion of a unilateral nature, it has been a practice to regulate different categories of export controls through separate State regulations or departmental rules, which include: (i) *Regulations on Export Control of Nuclear Dual-use Items and Technologies*, (ii) *Regulations on Export Control of Missiles and Missile-related Items and Technologies*, (iii) *Regulations on Export Control of Dual-use Biological Items and Related Equipment and Technologies*, (iv) *Regulations on Export Control of Nuclear*, (v) *Regulations on Administration of the Controlled Chemicals*, (vi) *Regulations on Administration of Precursor Chemicals*, (vii) *Regulations on Administration of Commercial Cryptography*, and (viii) *Measures on Export Control of Certain Chemicals and Related Equipment and Technologies*. Please note that the export control lists under each of the regulations or rules have been combined as a consolidated export control catalogue, as further elaborated in Sect. 3.2.

3.1.1.1 Regulations on Export Control of Nuclear Dual-Use Items and Technologies

China promulgated *Regulations on Export Control of Nuclear Dual-use Items and Technologies* in 1998,[4] which strengthened export control of nuclear dual-use items and related technologies to prevent proliferation of nuclear weapons, protect against nuclear terroristic acts, promote international cooperation in the peaceful use of nuclear energy, and safeguard national security and public interests.[5] Items (inclusive of technologies) subject to control under this Regulation are those equipment,

---

[3] Article 2(4) of the ECL; also see Article 2(3) of the *Draft Regulations on the Export Control of Dual-use Items*. The definition of "dual-use items" resembles that under other jurisdictions. For instance, according to § 730.3 of the EAR, a "dual-use" item is one that has civil applications as well as terrorism and military or WMD-related applications. Pursuant to Article 2(1) of Regulation (EU) 2021/821, "dual-use items" means items, including software and technology, which can be used for both civil and military purposes, and includes items which can be used for the design, development, production or use of nuclear, chemical or biological weapons or their means of delivery, including all items which can be used for both non-explosive uses and assisting in any way in the manufacture of nuclear weapons or other nuclear explosive devices.

[4] Order No. 245 of the State Council, 10 June 1998.

[5] Article 1 of the *Regulations on the Export Control of Nuclear Dual-use Items and Related Technologies* (1998).

materials, software, and related technologies listed in "Nuclear Dual-use Items and Related Technologies Export Control List" annexed to this Regulation.[6]

After joining the NSG in 2004, China amended and released a new version of the Regulation in 2007[7] to fulfill the commitments under the NSG, with an adaptation to the international non-proliferation situation.

The new amendments to the Regulation exhibit themselves in the following aspects:

(a) *Purpose of this Regulation*: "Prevention of acts of nuclear terrorism" is added in Article 1 as one of the legislative purposes of this Regulation.
(b) *Definition of controlled nuclear dual-use items and technologies*: Apart from the equipment, material and software, "technologies" is covered comprehensively as related to the equipment, material and software.
(c) *Definition of export*: "Services and transfers by other means" are added as one of the export activities subject to control.
(d) *End-use and user control*: In the 1998 version, the export of nuclear dual-use items and technologies is subject to the following principles: the recipient undertakes (i) not to use the nuclear dual-use items and technologies supplied by China for nuclear explosive purposes; (ii) not to use nuclear dual-use items and technologies supplied by China in nuclear facilities not under IAEA safeguards; and (iii) not transfer nuclear dual-use items and technologies supplied by China to third parties without the permission of the Chinese government. The 2007 version makes a bit revision to the effect that the recipient is to undertake (i) not to use the nuclear dual-use items and technologies, *or any copies thereof* supplied by China, for nuclear explosive purposes *or any purpose other than declared*; (ii) not to use nuclear dual-use items and technologies, *or any copies thereof* supplied by China, *for nuclear fuel cycle activities* not under IAEA safeguards; and (iii) not transfer nuclear dual-use items and technologies, *or any copies thereof* supplied by China, to third parties *other than the stated end-user* without the permission of the Chinese government.
(e) *Catch-all control*: A new Article (Article 19) is inserted prescribing that items and technologies not explicitly enlisted are also subject to control if the exporting business operators ("EBOs") know or should know or are notified by the MOFCOM that there is a risk of nuclear proliferation or the items to be exported may be used for nuclear terrorism purposes.
(f) *Authority of the Customs*: A new Article (Article 16) authorizes the customs the power of inquiry over the export of commodities.
(g) *Authority of MOFCOM*: Two Articles are newly added relating to the power and obligation of MOFCOM. Article 21 requires MOFCOM to organize experts to undertake the work of technical consultation, evaluation, and demonstration of export control of nuclear dual-use items and related technologies. Besides,

[6] Article 2 of the *Regulations on the Export Control of Nuclear Dual-use Items and Related Technologies* (1998 & 2007).

[7] Order No. 484 of 2007 of the State Council, 26 January 2007.

Article 22 is to authorize MOFCOM the power of investigation if there is a potential illegal export.

(h) *Obligations of EBOs*: A new Article (Article 18) imposes obligations on EBOs to set in place an ICP and keep a record of all related documents for at least five years.

(i) *Legal liabilities*: Penalties are more detailed. Under Article 23, anyone who exports nuclear commodities in violation of this Regulation shall be subject to penalties specified in the *Customs Law;* anyone who exports controlled technologies in violation of this Regulation may be subject to a warning by MOFCOM and a fine between one and five times the illegal proceeds with a minimum of CNY50,000 and criminal liabilities may ensue if the violation constitutes a crime.

(j) *Control list adjustment*: The adjustment of the Nuclear Dual-use Items and Related Technologies Export Control List was subject to the approval of the State Council before implementation in the 1998 version. Considering that the NSG modifies its control list from time to time and the obligation of China to amend its domestic controlling list accordingly, the new Regulation (Article 26) prescribes that MOFCOM, together with the State Atomic Energy Agency and related authorities, reserves the right to make any adjustments to the list.

(k) *Transit, transshipment, through transport:* Under a new Article (Article 28) relevant provisions of this Regulation shall apply to the transit, transshipment, through transport of controlled items and technologies or the export of such controlled items from customs special supervision areas such as bonded areas and export processing zones, and bonded supervision places such as export supervision warehouses and bonded logistics centers.

3.1.1.2 Regulations on Export Control of Missiles and Missile-Related Items and Technologies

Regulations on Export Control of Missiles and Missile-related Items and Technologies were promulgated in 2002.[8] Items and technologies subject to control under this Regulation are those missiles, missile-related equipment, materials, and technologies listed in "Missile and Missile-related Items and Technologies Export Control List" annexed to the Regulation.[9]

This List consists of Part I & Part II. Part I of the annexed List shall be subject to the *Administration Regulations on the Export of Military Items* and other relevant provisions, which means items and technologies listed in Part I are regarded as quasi-military items in the exporting practice. Export of items and technologies listed in Part II of the annexed Control List is subject to Dual-use Export License if not used for military purposes. However, if the missile-related items and technologies

[8] Order No. 361 of 2002 of the State Council, 22 August 2002.

[9] Article 2 of the *Regulations on the Export Control of Missiles and Missile-related Items and Technologies.*

listed in Part II are exported for military purposes, they shall also be subject to the *Administration Regulations on the Export of Military Items.*[10]

For items and technologies not explicitly enlisted, they may also be subject to catch-all export control if the EBOs know or should know that the items to be exported may be used for developing missiles and other delivering systems that can be used to deliver WMD.[11]

3.1.1.3 Regulations on Export Control of Dual-Use Biological Items and Related Equipment and Technologies

Regulations on the Export Control of Dual-use Biological Items and Related Equipment and Technologies were promulgated in 2002.[12] Items and technologies subject to control under this Regulation are those explicitly listed in "Biological Dual-use Items and Related Equipment and Technologies Export Control List" annexed to this Regulation.[13]

This Regulation was formulated to strengthen control of the export of dual-use biological items and related equipment and technologies from being used as weapons,[14] although China has not officially joined the Australia Group. For the export of controlled dual-use biological items and related equipment and technologies, a certification guaranteeing that items and related equipment and technologies exported from China will not be used to produce biological weapons and will not be transferred to any third party other than the declared end-user is required.[15]

3.1.1.4 Regulations on Export Control of Nuclear

The background of legislation and the subsequent amendment of the *Regulations on Export Control of Nuclear* is similar to that of the *Regulations on Export Control of Nuclear Dual-use Items and Technologies* mentioned above. China enacted the *Regulations on Export Control of Nuclear* in 1997.[16] After joining the NSG in 2004, China amended and released a new version of the *Regulations on the Export Control of Nuclear* in 2006.[17]

New amendments are summarized as follows:

---

[10] Ibid., Article 5.

[11] Ibid., Article 16.

[12] Order No. 365 of 2002 of the State Council, 14 October 2002.

[13] Article 2 of the *Regulations on the Export Control of Dual-use Biological Items and Related Equipment and Technologies.*

[14] Ibid., Article 4.

[15] Ibid., Article 7.

[16] Order No. 230 of the State Council, 10 September 1997.

[17] Order No. 480 of the State Council, 9 November 2006.

(a) *Purpose of this Regulation*: This Regulation was formulated for the purpose of strengthening control of the export of nuclear, safeguarding national security and public interests, and promoting international cooperation in the peaceful use of nuclear energy in the 1997 version. "Preventing the proliferation of nuclear weapons and acts of nuclear terrorism" is added in Article 1 as one of the legislative purposes in the 2006 version.
(b) *Positions of China on the export of nuclear*: Article 3(2) emphasizes that "the government of the PRC shall strictly restrict the export of uranium enrichment instruments and equipment, irradiating fuel disposal instruments, heavy water production instruments and equipment, the sensitive materials of nuclear diffusion of the related technology and the materials used in the nuclear weapons or the other exploders".
(c) *End-use and user control*: In the 1997 version, export of nuclear is subject to following principles: the recipient undertakes (i) not to use the nuclear materials, nuclear equipment or non-nuclear materials for reactors, and special fissionable material produced through their use, for any nuclear explosive purpose; (ii) to take appropriate physical protection measures for nuclear material and special fissionable material produced through its use; (iii) to have signed a safeguards agreement in force with IAEA and to accept IAEA safeguards on nuclear material, nuclear equipment or non-nuclear material for reactors supplied by China, and special fissionable material produced through their use, under the safeguards agreement; and (iv) not to transfer nuclear material, nuclear equipment or non-nuclear material for reactors and related technologies supplied by China to a third party without the prior written consent of the Chinese National Atomic Energy Agency, and the eligible third party receiving the retransfer shall assume obligations equivalent to those assumed by China in direct supply. On this basis, the 2006 version revises a bit the end-use and user controls so that the recipient undertakes (i) not to use the nuclear materials, nuclear equipment or non-nuclear materials for reactors, and special fissionable material produced through their use, for any nuclear explosive purpose; (ii) to take appropriate physical protection measures for nuclear material and special fissionable material produced through its use; (iii) to have signed an effective comprehensive safeguards agreement with IAEA, *and this requirement is not applied to States with which IAEA has a voluntary safeguards agreement*; (iv) not to transfer nuclear material, nuclear equipment or non-nuclear material for reactors and related technologies supplied by China to a third party without the prior written consent of the Chinese National Atomic Energy Agency, and the eligible third party receiving the retransfer shall assume obligations equivalent to those assumed by China in direct supply; and (v) *not use the uranium enrichment facilities, technology or any facilities based on such technology provided by China to produce enriched uranium above 20% without the consent of the Chinese government.*
(d) *Authority of the Customs*: A new Article (Article 16) is added to authorize the customs the power of inquiry.
(e) *Legal liabilities*: Detailed penalties are specified compared with the 1997 version. For example, according to Article 18 (which is almost identical to

Article 23 of the *Regulations on the Export Control of Nuclear Dual-use Items and Technologies*), anyone who exports nuclear materials, nuclear equipment, or non-nuclear materials for reactors in violation of this Regulation shall be subject to the penalties specified in the Customs Law, and anyone who exports controlled technologies listed in the Nuclear Export Control List in violation of this Regulation may be subject to a warning by MOFCOM and a fine between one and five times the illegal proceeds with a minimum of CNY 50,000. Criminal liabilities may also be imposed if the violation constitutes a crime.

(f) *Control list adjustment*: Pursuant to Article 21, China Atomic Energy Authority, together with the Commission of Science, MOFCOM, the Ministry of Foreign Affairs, and the General Customs, reserves the right to make any adjustments to this list.

(g) *Transit, transshipment, through transport:* A new Article (Article 23) is added prescribing that relevant provisions of this Regulations shall apply to the transit, transshipment, through transport of controlled items and technologies or the export of such controlled items from customs special supervision areas such as bonded warehouses, bonded areas and export processing zones.

3.1.1.5 Regulations on Administration of Controlled Chemicals

Regulations on Administration of Controlled Chemicals were promulgated in 1995[18] and subsequently revised in 2011.[19] Accordingly, the *Implementing Rules of Regulations on Administration of Controlled Chemicals* was promulgated in 1997[20] and further revised in 2018.[21]

Controlled chemicals are classified into four categories (Categories I, II, III, or IV) under this Regulation. Category I refers to chemicals that can be used as chemical weapons. Category II refers to chemicals that can be used as precursors of chemical weapons. Category III refers to chemicals that can be used as the major raw materials to produce chemical weapons. Category IV refers to specially designated organic chemicals other than explosives and pure hydrocarbons.[22] The items of each category are specified in the "Catalogue of Controlled Chemicals", formulated and maintained by the Ministry of Industry and Information Technology.[23]

Please note that the term "controlled chemicals" includes not only their pure form but also industrial products with different concentrations of such chemicals.[24] Furthermore, when controlled chemicals are below a certain concentration threshold,

[18] Order No. 190 of 1995 of the State Council, 27 December 1995.

[19] Order No. 588 of the State Council, 8 January 2011.

[20] Order No. 12 of the Ministry of Chemical Industry, 10 March 1997. Please note that the Ministry of Chemical Industry was abolished on 10 March 1998.

[21] Order No. 48 of the Ministry of Industry and Information Technology, 2 July 2018.

[22] Article 3 of the *Regulations on the Administration of the Controlled Chemicals* (2011).

[23] Order No. 52 of the Ministry of Industry and Information Technology, 3 June 2020.

[24] Article 56 of the *Implementing Rules of Regulations on the Administration of the Controlled Chemicals* (2018).

they could be exempted from requirements of data declaration and import/export license. Pertaining concentration thresholds are to be determined and adjusted by the Ministry of Industry and Information Technology based on actual situations.[25] However, such concentration thresholds have not yet been officially announced. Without a clear indication of concentration thresholds, no exemption is available administratively in practice so that industrial products like detergents containing some minimal content of controlled chemicals are all subject to the export license requirement, which sounds a bit irrational. To address this confusion, for industrial products like detergents, and cosmetics containing triethanolamine, if the triethanolamine is already neutralized and cannot be extracted in monomer, Chinese Customs may take the position that the export of such products is exempted from the Dual-use Export License. Otherwise, a license is still required even if the content of controlled triethanolamine is extremely low.[26]

In China, only EBOs as authorized by the ministry in charge of the chemical industry under the State Council, together with the ministry in charge of foreign economics and trade under the State Council, are entitled to engage in the export of chemicals of Category I and chemicals and related production technology and equipment of Categories II and III. Other EBOs who intend to conduct the above exporting business shall entrust the authorized EBOs as their agent.[27]

For the export of chemicals of Category I and chemicals and related production technology and equipment of Categories II and III, a certification issued by the government or governmental agencies of the importing country that the chemicals and related production technology and equipment to be imported will not be used to produce chemical weapons and will not be transferred to a third country, together with the item name, item quantity, end-use, end-user and the address of the end-user of the controlled chemicals to be exported is required.[28]

3.1.1.6 Measures on Export Control of Certain Chemicals and Related Equipment and Technologies

The so-called certain chemicals and related equipment and technologies are regulated by the "*Measures on Export Control of Certain Chemicals and Related Equipment and Technologies*" which was adopted in 2002.[29] As a typical type of lower-tier administrative normative document, the measures further strengthen the control on

[25] Ibid., Article 57.

[26] Letter of Department of General Operation of the General Administration of Customs on the Clarification of import/export license regulatory requirements of mixtures containing triethanolamine, 28 October 2022.

[27] Article 14 of the *Regulations on the Administration of Controlled Chemicals* (2011).

[28] Article 30 of the *Implementing Rules of Regulations on the Administration of Controlled Chemicals* (2018).

[29] Order No. 33 of 2002 of Ministry of Foreign Trade and Economic Cooperation, State Economic and Trade Commission, and GAC, 18 October 2002.

some listed chemicals that can be used as chemical weapons, in addition to the aforementioned *Regulations on Administration of Controlled Chemicals.*

The concept of "certain chemicals" is actually not specifically defined under the measures but refers to those enlisted in the "Certain Chemicals and Related Equipment and Technologies Export Control List" annexed to the Measures.[30] For the export of certain chemicals, the recipient shall undertake that (i) not to use certain chemicals and related equipment supplied by China for storage, processing, production, handling of chemical weapons or for the production of chemical weapons precursor chemicals; and (ii) not to use certain chemicals and related equipment supplied by China for usages other than the declared end-uses, or to transfer to third parties other than the stated end-users without the permission of the Chinese government.[31]

3.1.1.7 Regulations on Administration of Precursor Chemicals

Regulations on Administration of Precursor Chemicals were first promulgated in 2005,[32] and were subsequently revised in 2014,[33] 2016,[34] and 2018.[35]

Precursor chemicals under this Regulation are classified into three categories (Categories I, II, or III). Category I refers to the main raw materials that can be used to produce drugs, while Categories II and III refer to chemical preparations that can be used to produce drugs.[36]

The export of precursor chemicals is subject to Dual-use Export License, and a certification issued by the government of the importing country that the chemicals will be used legally, or a guarantee document of the legal use by the importing party is required before the license can be issued.[37] For the export of certain key precursor chemicals such as ephedrine, only such EBOs as with a proper ICP[38] that has been verified by competent department of commerce of the State Council in conjunction with other relevant departments of the State Council are entitled to conduct such exporting business,[39] which is further explained and regulated in the *Interim Measures on Verification of Exporters of Ephedrine Precursor Chemicals*

---

[30] Article 2 of the *Measures on Export Control of Certain Chemicals and Related Equipment and Technologies.*

[31] Ibid., Article 6.

[32] Order No. 445 of the State Council, 26 August 2005.

[33] Order No. 653 of the State Council, 29 July 2014.

[34] Order No. 666 of the State Council, 6 February 2016.

[35] Order No. 703 of the State Council, 18 September 2018.

[36] Article 2 of the *Regulations on the Administration of Precursor Chemicals* (2018).

[37] Ibid., Article 26.

[38] Ibid., Article 5.

[39] Ibid., Article 28.

adopted in 2006.[40] The export of precursor chemicals is subject to international verification mechanism, and other control measures relevant to exports of precursor chemicals and chemicals other than those specified in "List of Precursor Chemicals" to countries or regions with serious drug manufacturing or trafficking situations.[41]

To further strengthen the export (as well as import) control of precursor chemicals, the government of the PRC updated in 2015 the *Administrative Provisions on the Import and Export of Precursor Chemicals* in accordance with the *Foreign Trade Law* and the *Regulations on Administration of Precursor Chemicals*,[42] which was previously released in 1999.[43] According to the Administrative Provisions, mixtures containing precursor chemicals shall be reviewed in terms of the pure precursor chemicals notionally converted from the mixtures to determine whether a license is required. However, the notional conversion does not apply to compounded pharmaceutical preparations that contain precursor chemicals.[44] To further define the term "mixtures containing precursor chemicals", MOFCOM particularly issued an announcement entitled *"Announcement on Detailed Provisions on Import and Export of Mixtures Containing Precursor Chemicals"*[45] to define such mixtures as **(i)** goods containing any of the four types of precursor chemicals, namely toluene, acetone, butanone and sulfuric acid, with a proportion higher than 40% (not inclusive) and goods containing hydrochloric acid with a proportion higher than 10% (not inclusive), and **(ii)** goods containing other precursor chemicals in the List of Precursor Chemicals other than the above types, regardless of the content.

3.1.1.8 Regulations on Administration of Commercial Cryptography

Regulations on Administration of Commercial Cryptography were first released in 1999.[46] With the promulgated *Cryptography Law* in 2019[47] and the "Commercial Cryptography Export Control List" released in 2020,[48] China released a new version of *Regulations on the Administration of Commercial Cryptography (Draft*

---

[40] Order No. 9 of 2006 of the MOFCOM, the Ministry of Public Security, the General Administration of Customs, and State Food and Drug Administration, 10 October 2006. Please note that State Food and Drug Administration has been abolished in 2018.

[41] Article 29 of the *Regulations on the Administration of Precursor Chemicals* (2018).

[42] Order No. 2 of 2015 of the MOFCOM, 28 October 2015.

[43] Order No. 4 of 1999 of the Ministry of Foreign Trade and Economic Cooperation, 18 December 1999. Please note the Ministry of Foreign Trade and Economic Cooperation has been abolished in 2003.

[44] Article 7 of the *Administration Provisions on Import and Export of Precursor Chemicals* (2015).

[45] Order No. 23 of 2007 of the MOFCOM, 16 May 2007.

[46] Order No.273 of 1999 of the State Council, 7 October 1999.

[47] Order No.35 of the President of the PRC, 26 October 2019.

[48] Order No. 63 of 2020 of the MOFCOM, the State Cryptography Administration, and the GAC, 26 November 2020.

for Comment) on 20 August 2020. On 27 April 2023, the newly amended Regulations were published, effective as of 1 July 2023.[49]

The new Regulation reiterates that the export of items and technologies listed in Commercial Cryptography Export Control List formulated by competent department of commerce of the State Council jointly with the State Cryptography Administration, and GAC, is subject to Dual-use Export License, with an exemption of commercial cryptography adopted by mass-consumption products.[50] Regarding the definition of commercial cryptography adopted by mass-consumption products, according to the official explanation of State Cryptography Administration, this term refers to products or technologies that can be purchased by the public through regular retail channels without restriction for personal use and the cryptography functions of which cannot be easily changed.[51] Furthermore, similar to other decentralized regulations or rules, under this Regulation, the customs is empowered to make inquiry and product inspection before allowing the release of the items for export.[52] Violations of the export control will result in imposition of penalties by competent department of commerce of the State Council and GAC,[53] and now ECL will probably be the law for assessment of the penalties in practice.

3.1.2 Draft Regulations on the Export Control of Dual-Use Items

Since ECL came into effect as from 1 December 2020, companies have encountered various export control compliance problems in practice. The existing decentralized administrative regulations and rules, regulating different categories of dual-use items, are no longer consistent with the export control supervision and law enforcement requirements under ECL. On 22 April 2022, MOFCOM announced the *Draft Regulations on the Export Controls of Dual-use Items* (the "Dual-use Draft Regulations"), which aims at unifying and streamlining the export control supervision and enforcement measures.

The Dual-use Draft Regulations is consisted of five chapters, respectively general provisions (Chap. 1), control policies, controls lists and control measures (Chap. 2), supervision and administration (Chap. 3), legal liabilities (Chap. 4), and supplementary provisions (Chap. 5), with 60 Articles in total. The major issues are summarized as follows:

---

[49] Order No. 760 of the State Council, 27 April 2023.

[50] Articles 31 of the *Regulations on the Administration of Commercial Cryptography.*

[51] State Cryptography Administration. (2020, April 2). Frequently Asked Questions (FAQs) No. 78 of the Policy of Cryptography. Retrieved September 14, 2023, from https://sca.gov.cn/sca/xxgk/2020-04/02/content_1060694.shtml.

[52] Articles 33 of the *Regulations on the Administration of Commercial Cryptography.*

[53] Ibid., Article 58.

A. **Scope of Controlled Items**

Article 2 of the Dual-use Draft Regulations reiterates that the Regulations shall apply to export control of any dual-use items. Besides, Article 59 of the Regulations supplements that "*This regulation applies to the export control of other goods, technologies or services related to safeguarding national security and interests, and fulfillment of nonproliferation and other international obligations. These items shall be regulated by reference to the regulations for dual-use items and included in the export control list of dual-use items*".

Under ECL, the export of technologies controlled relating to national security and interests, though not enlisted in the "Catalogue of Dual-use Items and Technologies Subject to Export License" but enlisted on the "Catalogue of Technologies Prohibited and Restricted from Export" for instance, are subject to ECL. However, the Regulations say that only items enlisted on the dual-use catalogue are regulated under the Regulations. The Author is curious why the Regulations are deviating from ECL on the scope of controlled items. At least it seems to me that ECL applies to export controls based on national security considerations and the penalty provisions of ECL also apply in the same manner, though the licensing mechanism can be different from those regarding the military, nuclear, and dual-use items.

Given the Dual-use Draft Regulations, the *Regulations on the Export Control of Nuclear Dual-use Items and Technologies, Regulations on the Export Control of Missiles and Missile-related Items and Technologies, Regulations on the Export Control of Dual-use Biological Items and Related Equipment and Technologies & Measures on the Export Control of Certain Chemicals and Related Equipment and Technologies* will be abolished in the future, as set forth in Article 60 of the Regulations.

B. **Removal of EBO Registration**

Pursuant to Article 11 of ECL, EBOs engaged in export of controlled items shall abide by this law and relevant laws and administrative regulations, and where any business qualification is legally required for export of any relevant controlled item, they shall obtain such qualification. This provision is in line with the *Administration Measures on the Business Registration for Exports of Sensitive Items and Technologies* last updated in 2015,[54] which requires that EBOs conducting export of sensitive items like nuclear dual-use items, missiles and missile-related items shall apply for registration to competent authorities in advance.[55]

The Dual-use Draft Regulations keep silent on this issue. Nevertheless, in its explanations, MOFCOM clearly states that the export business registration requirement for dual-use items is canceled, except for controlled chemicals. It is logically inferred that in the future, registration is no longer required for EBOs to conduct exports of dual-use items, which also means that the *Administration Measures* mentioned above may be annulled.

[54] Order No. 2 of 2015 of the MOFCOM, 28 October 2015.

[55] Article 3 of the *Administration Measures on the Business Registration for Exports of Sensitive Items and Technologies.*

C. **Export Control Supervision Code**

Article 13 of the Dual-use Draft Regulations provides that the list-based dual-use item controls adopt export control supervision code ("ECSC") to be assigned to each of the listed dual-use items. We understand that such ECSC functions in a manner similar to the export control classification number ("ECCN") under EAR of the U.S. As an implication, (i) the EBO and the foreign re-exporter are to classify accurately the ECSC for the list-controlled items to be exported; (ii) the EBO must declare such ECSC besides the tariff code of the list-controlled commodity to the Chinese Customs for export purposes, which would enable the Chinese Customs to supervise the export shipments of dual-use items more effectively; and (iii) the foreign re-exporter is to determine and declare through its agent in China the ECSC of the list-controlled item to MOFCOM before re-export of the same item in the importing country.

D. **Temporary Controls and Catch-all Controls**

(a) Temporary controls. Article 14 of the Dual-use Draft Regulations specifies the procedures of continuous control, if any, after the two-year temporary control elapses. The temporary control can either be canceled within such two years, or incorporated into the consolidated control catalogue, or announced again as subject to further temporary controls.
(b) Catch-all controls. Under Article 27 of the Dual-use Draft Regulations, if within three years after the export an EBO finds out that the exported goods, technologies, or services have a risk of falling into the catch-all control scope, it must report it to the competent commerce authority under the State Council in a timely manner. It is unclear whether such reporting obligation is also attached to foreign importers, re-exporters, and end-users.

E. **Dual-use Export Licenses**

(a) License categories. According to Article 16 of the Draft Regulations, China will maintain two types of the Dual-use Export License, respectively (i) Individual License and (ii) General/Multiple-Use License, which is in line with the existing *Administrative Measures for Import and Export License for Dual-use Items and Technologies*[56] and *Administrative Measures for General License of Export of Dual-use Items and Technologies.*[57] Specifically, an individual license allows an EBO to export one shipment of a given dual-use item within the validity period (generally one year). A general license allows an EBO to export multiple shipments of a range of dual-**use** items to multiple end-users for multiple times within the scope and validity period (generally two years) of the license.[58]

[56] Order No. 29 of 2005 of the MOFCOM and the GAC, 31 December 2005.

[57] Order No. 8 of 2009 of the MOFCOM, 13 May 2009.

[58] Currently, the validity for such general license is no longer than three years as set forth in Article 6 of the *Administrative Measures for General License of Export of Dual-use Items and Technologies.*

(b) Conditions for the issuance of multiple-use license. In Article 23 of the Dual-use Draft Regulations, four requirements shall be satisfied for applying for the multiple-use license, which include (i) a well-operated ICP, (ii) a record of dual-use export activities for two or more years, and licenses have been granted many times, (iii) regular sales channels and end-users, and (iv) other conditions as may be set forth by competent authorities. Under Article 24 of the Dual-use Draft Regulations, the EBO who has obtained such a multiple-use license is required to report the actual use of such license to MOFCOM periodically and accept its verification.

(c) License application procedures. EBOs are required to provide the following application and supporting documents: (i) a copy of the dual-use export contract or agreement; (ii) technical specifications or test report of the dual-use item to be exported; (iii) an end-user and end-use certification; (iv) statement of importers and end-users; (v) identification of legal representative, the main business manager and the person in charge of the EBO; and (vi) other documents as may be required by competent authorities. Please note that on 28 June 2021, the Bureau of Security and Control of MOFCOM issued an announcement on the paperless application of Dual-use Export/ Import License.[59] According to this announcement, EBOs can apply for export licenses electronically by visiting the following website (https:// ecomp.mofcom.gov.cn), or alternatively continue to submit paper-based materials in accordance with the original regulations.[60]

(d) License exceptions to export controls. For the first time, the Dual-use Draft Regulation by virtue of Article 25 introduces a "license exemption" scheme. Such license exemptions are limited to (i) the re-export after temporary import for inbound maintenance, repair, or testing, (ii) export for exhibition purposes, (iii) export of civil aircraft parts for maintenance purposes, and (iv) other circumstances as set forth by competent authorities. The license exemptions are applied in quite limited situations than those available under EAR of the U.S.,[61] and have not yet covered such scenarios as redelivery by export of technologies or items that were originally imported from overseas,

[59] Letter No. 209 of 2021 of the Bureau of Security and Control of the MOFCOM, 28 June 2021.

[60] It is worth noting that EBOs applying for the Dual-use Export License of nuclear, nuclear dual-use, biological, chemical, missiles and other sensitive items and technologies, and dredgers, as well as the Dual-use Export/Import License of commercial cryptographic products, are still required to send the original end-use/end-user certification and license application form (paper version) to the provincial departments of commerce.

[61] Under Part 740 of the EAR, a total of 18 kinds of license exemptions are enumerated including:

Shipments of limited value (LVS), Shipments to Country Group B countries (GBS), Technology and software under restriction (TSR), Computers (APP), Temporary imports, exports, reexports, and transfers (in-country) (TMP), License Exception Servicing and replacement of parts and equipment (RPL), Governments, international organizations, international inspections under the Chemical Weapons Convention, and the International Space Station (GOV), Gift parcels and humanitarian donations (GFT), Technology and software - unrestricted (TSU), Baggage (BAG), Aircraft, vessels and spacecraft (AVS), Additional permissive reexports (APR), Encryption commodities, software, and technology (ENC), Agricultural commodities (AGR), Consumer Communications Devices

or export of the new technologies derived in China from joint research and development efforts using overseas licensed technologies.

F. **End-user and End-use Controls**

(a) Procedures for the subsequent change of end-user or end-use. Under Article 30 of the Draft Regulations, MOFCOM's approval is required for the change of end-user or end-use as filed with MOFCOM of a dual-use item that has been exported. The importer and/or end-user may entrust the original Chinese EBO to file applications for such change.
(b) List of Controlled Parties. "List of Controlled Parties" is a term derived from Article 18 of ECL, which is a blacklist for those foreign entities and individuals who are found to be violating ECL. Under Articles 31, 32, and 33 of the Dual-use Draft Regulations, (i) an investigation is required before a designation onto this list of a given foreign importer or end-user; (ii) such Controlled Parties are prohibited from any access to export from China; (iii) the foreign importers and/or end-users need to undertake or have taken measures to prove that circumstances for being listed in this List no longer existed in order to seek removal from the List. Such removal can be triggered by the Controlled Parties' applications or ex officio.

G. **Obligation of Third-party Service Provides**

Under Article 20 of ECL, a service provider shall not provide service for illegal exports. Article 36 of the Dual-use Draft Regulations further requires that such service provider must immediately stop services and report to MOFCOM when it discovers the EBO's violation of export control regulations. Such a reporting scheme is compliance pressure on the EBOs who conduct controlled activities subject to ECL.

H. **Liabilities for Violations**

Liability provisions are further specified in the Draft Regulations. Article 52 lists the circumstances where "reduction or mitigation of penalties" may be applied to a given EBO or service provider, namely: (i) the party has taken proactive actions to eliminate or mitigate the harmful consequences; or (ii) the party was coerced or induced by others for such violations; or (iii) the party has voluntarily disclosed a violation which has not yet been detected; or (iv) the party has cooperated with and remarkably helped the investigation.

Furthermore, if an ICP is in place and operates well to prevent the further harmful consequences of the violation, MOFCOM may, at its discretion, impose a lighter penalty. However, it seems to us that the occurrence of the violation itself seemingly contradicts the allegation that the ICP runs well. Therefore, this provision needs to be adjusted.

(CCD), License Exception Strategic Trade Authorization (STA), Support for the Cuban People (SCP), and Authorized Cybersecurity Exports (ACE).

Table 3.1 Structure of the consolidated catalogue (2023)

No	Sub-catalogues of dual-use items	Items in total
1	Nuclear export control list	159
2	Nuclear dual-use items and related technologies export control list	204
3	Biological dual-use items and related equipment and technologies export control list	144
4	Controlled chemicals list	74
5	Certain chemicals and related equipment and technologies export control list	38
6	Missile and missile-related items and technologies export control list	186
7	Precursor chemical (I)	54
8	Precursor chemical (II)	17
9	Certain dual-use items and technologies	6
10	Special civil items and technologies	11
11	Commercial cryptography export control list	11

3.2 Consolidated Catalogue of Dual-Use Items and Technologies

Currently, all catalogues of the dual-use items and related technologies are consolidated into a comprehensive catalogue—"Catalogue of Dual-use Items and Technologies Subject to Export License" ("Consolidated Catalogue"), the latest version of which for the year 2023 was released by MOFCOM and the GAC on 30 December 2022.[62] This Consolidated Catalogue is regularly updated annually at the end of each calendar year. The 2023 version of the Catalogues includes 11 sub-catalogues or lists. Sub-catalogues 1–8 are mainly based on multilateral export control regimes, and sub-catalogues 9–11 in nature are unilateral export controls of China (Table 3.1).

3.2.1 Items Based on Multilateral Export Control Regimes

3.2.1.1 Nuclear Export Control List

This sub-catalogue of 2023 version is mainly based on the nuclear export control "Trigger List" developed by the Zangger Committee of which China is a member.

This sub-catalogue lists one hundred and fifty-nine items (including technologies) that are divided into eight categories: (i) nuclear materials (No. 1–5), (ii) nuclear reactors and especially designed or prepared equipment and components therefor (No. 6–17), (iii) non-nuclear materials for reactors (No. 18–20), (iv) plants

[62] Announcement No. 42 of 2022 of the MOFCOM and the GAC, 30 December 2022.

for the reprocessing of irradiated fuel elements, and equipment especially designed or prepared therefor (No. 21–25), (v) plants for the fabrication of nuclear reactor fuel elements, and equipment especially designed or prepared therefor (No. 26–35), (vi) plants for the separation of isotopes of natural uranium, depleted uranium or special fissionable material and equipment, other than analytical instruments, especially designed or prepared therefor (No. 36–137), (vii) plants for the production or concentration of heavy water, deuterium and deuterium compounds and equipment especially designed or prepared therefor (No. 138–148), and (viii) plants for the conversion of uranium and plutonium for use in the fabrication of fuel elements and the separation of uranium isotopes as defined in sections v and vi, respectively, and equipment especially designed or prepared therefor (No. 149–159).

Compared with the 2022 version, this list makes certain adjustments to the commodity name and description of nuclear grade graphite (No. 20), irradiated fuel element decladding equipment and chopping machines (No. 21), and dissolvers (No. 22), all of which are also included in the "Trigger List". The adjustment aims to pursue an illustration of these three items consistent with those in the "Trigger List". Detailed changes of these three items are summarized below (Table 3.2).

3.2.1.2 Nuclear Dual-Use Items and Related Technologies Export Control List

This sub-catalogue is mainly based on the "List of Nuclear Dual-use Equipment, Materials, Software, and Related Technology" developed by the NSG, of which China is a member.

A total of two hundred and four items (including technologies) are enlisted. This list is further divided into seven categories, respectively: (i) industrial equipment (No. 1–43), (ii) materials (No. 44–93), (iii) uranium isotope separation equipment and components other than items in the List of Nuclear Export Control (No. 94–132), (iv) heavy water production plant related equipment other than items in the List of Nuclear Export Control (No. 133–138), (v) test and measurement equipment for the development of nuclear explosive devices (No. 139–165), (vi) components for nuclear explosive devices (No. 166–195), and (vii) items subject to temporary control (No. 196–204).

Apart from Category (vii)-items subject to temporary control, each category is further divided into (1) equipment, assembles and components, (2) test and production equipment, (3) materials, (4) software, and (5) technology. Items subject to temporary control enlisted in Category (vii) mainly include tributyl phosphate[63] and graphite-related products.[64]

---

[63] Announcement No. 5 of 2003 on the Temporary Export Control on Tributyl Phosphate of MOFCOM and the GAC, 15 April 2003.

[64] Announcement No. 50 of 2006 on the Temporary Export Control on Graphite-Related Products of MOFCOM, State Administration of Science, Technology, and Industry for National Defense, and the GAC, 27 July 2006.

Table 3.2 Amendment of nuclear export control list

2022 Version	2023 Version
No. 20 Nuclear grade graphite Description: Explanatory Note– For the purpose of export control, the Government will determine whether or not the exports of graphite meeting the above specifications are for nuclear reactor use	**No. 20** Nuclear grade graphite Description: Explanatory Note– For the purpose of export control, the Government will determine whether or not the exports of graphite meeting the above specifications are for nuclear reactor use. Graphite having a purity level better than 5 ppm (parts per million) boron equivalent and with a density greater than 1.50 g/cm^3 not for use in a nuclear reactor is not covered by this control
No. 21 Irradiated fuel element chopping machines Description: Remotely operated equipment especially designed or prepared for use in a reprocessing plant and intended to cut or shear fuel assemblies, bundles or rods Explanatory Note– This equipment cuts the cladding of the fuel to expose the irradiated nuclear material for dissolution. Especially designed cutting shears are most commonly employed, although advanced equipment, such as lasers, may be used	**No. 21** Irradiated fuel element decladding equipment and chopping machines Description: Remotely operated equipment especially designed or prepared for use in a reprocessing plant and intended to breach the cladding of fuel assemblies, bundles or rods to expose the irradiated nuclear material Explanatory Note– This equipment cuts, shears or otherwise breaches the cladding of the fuel to expose the irradiated nuclear material for processing. Especially designed cutting shears are most commonly employed, although advanced equipment, such as lasers, peeling machines, may be used. Decladding involves removing the cladding of the irradiated nuclear fuel prior to its dissolution

(continued)

Table 3.2 (continued)

2022 Version	2023 Version
No. 22 Dissolvers Description: Criticality safety vessels (such as small diameter, annular, or slab tanks) especially designed or prepared for use in a reprocessing plant, intended for dissolution of irradiated nuclear fuel and which are capable of withstanding hot, highly corrosive liquid, and which can be remotely loaded and maintained. Dissolvers normally receive shredded, irradiated nuclear fuel. In such criticality safety vessels, the irradiated nuclear fuel is dissolved in nitric acid, and any undissolved cladding is removed	**No. 22** Dissolvers Description: Dissolver vessels or dissolvers employing mechanical devices especially designed or prepared for use in a reprocessing plant, intended for dissolution of irradiated nuclear fuel and which are capable of withstanding hot, highly corrosive liquid, and which can be remotely loaded, operated, and maintained Explanatory Note– Dissolvers normally receive the solid, irradiated nuclear fuel. Nuclear fuels with cladding made of material including zirconium, stainless steel, or alloys of such materials must be decladded and/or sheared or chopped prior to being charged to the dissolver to allow the acid to reach the fuel matrix. The irradiated nuclear fuel is typically dissolved in strong mineral acids, such as nitric acid, and any undissolved cladding is removed. While certain design features, such as small diameter, annular, or slab tanks, may be used to ensure criticality safety, they are not a necessity. Administrative controls, such as small batch size or low fissile material content, may be used instead. Dissolver vessels and dissolvers employing mechanical devices are normally fabricated of materials such as low-carbon stainless steel, titanium or zirconium, or other high-quality materials. Dissolvers may include systems for the removal of cladding or cladding waste and systems for the control and treatment of radioactive off-gases. These dissolvers may have features for remote placement since they are normally loaded, operated and maintained behind thick shielding

Compared with the 2022 version, this cab-catalogue mainly adjusts the tariff code of Zirconium (No. 83) and adds the tariff code for ten special materials (No. 184–193).

Regarding Zirconium, as a rare metal, it is widely used in aerospace, military, nuclear reaction, and atomic energy fields because of its excellent corrosion resistance, extremely high melting point, and ultra-high hardness and strength. Zirconium was assigned six tariff codes in the 2022 Catalogue and reduced to three in the 2023 Catalogue as 8109210090, 8109310000 and 8109910090. Those three deleted tariff codes actually correspond to zirconium with a hafnium content of no less than 1 part hafnium to 500 parts zirconium by weight, which does not meet the parameter threshold of zirconium subject to export control under this sub-catalogue.

Items No. 184–193 are materials for nuclear explosive devices falling into the scope of high-energy explosives subject to relatively high requirements in commercial transport practice. The 2023 Catalogue adds tariff codes for the materials based on the newly updated Tariff Schedule of the PRC for Imports and Exports (2023).

Details of the tariff code adjustments to these items are summarized below (Table 3.3).

3.2.1.3 Biological Dual-Use Items and Related Equipment and Technologies Export Control List

This sub-catalogue is formulated partly based on the "List Dual-use Biological Equipment and Related Technology and Software", the "List of Human and Animal Pathogens and Toxins", and the "List of Plant Pathogens" under the Australia Group.

A total of one hundred and forty-four items (including technologies) are enlisted. This list is further divided into seven categories, respectively: (i) human and zoonotic pathogens (No. 1–55), (ii) plant pathogens (No. 56–72), (iii) animal pathogens (73–90), (iv) toxins and subunits thereof (No. 91–109), (v) genetic material and genetically modified organisms (No. 110–115), (vi) dual-use biological equipment (No. 116–142) and (vii) related technology (No. 143–144).

3.2.1.4 Controlled Chemicals List

This sub-catalogue is formulated in parallel with the "Schedules of Chemicals" under CWC.

A total of seventy-four items (including technology), respectively, (i) controlled chemicals (No. 1–72), (ii) related technology (No. 73) and (iii) related production equipment (No. 74) is enlisted on this List. Specifically, the technology subject to control (No. 73) refers to all technologies to produce chemicals of Categories I, II, and III. The equipment subject to control (No. 74) refers to all special equipment for product synthesis, separation, purification, heat conduction and automatic control instruments required in the production of chemicals of Categories I, II, and III.

Table 3.3 Amendment of nuclear dual-use items and related technologies export control list

2022 version	2023 version
No.83 Zirconium Tariff Code: 8109210090 ~~8109290090~~ 8109310000 ~~8109390000~~ 8109910090 ~~8109990090~~	**No.83** Zirconium * Tariff Code: 8109210090 8109310000 8109910090
No. 184 Aminodinitrobenzo-furoxan or 7-amino-4,6 nitrobenzofurazane-1-oxide (ADNBF) (CAS 97096–78-1) Tariff Code: /	**No.184** Aminodinitrobenzo-furoxan or 7-amino-4,6 nitrobenzofurazane-1-oxide (ADNBF) (CAS 97096–78-1)* Tariff Code: 2934999081
No.185 1,1-diamino-2,2-dinitroethylene (DADE or FOX7) (CAS 145250–81-3)* Tariff Code: /	**No.185** 1,1-diamino-2,2-dinitroethylene (DADE or FOX7) (CAS 145250–81-3)* Tariff Code: 2921290020
No.186 2,4-dinitroimidazole (DNI) (CAS 5213–49-0) Tariff Code: /	**No.186** 2,4-dinitroimidazole (DNI) (CAS 5213–49-0)* Tariff Code: 2933290020
No.187 Diaminoazoxyfurazan (DAAOF or DAAF) (CAS 78644–89-0) Tariff Code: /	**No.187** Diaminoazoxyfurazan (DAAOF or DAAF) (CAS 78644–89-0)* Tariff Code: 2934999082
No.188 Diaminotrinitrobenzene (DATB) (CAS 1630–08-6) Tariff Code: /	**No.188** Diaminotrinitrobenzene (DATB) (CAS 1630–08-6)* Tariff Code: 2921519030
No.189 Dinitroglycoluril (DNGU or DINGU) (CAS 55510–04-8) Tariff Code: /	**No.189** Dinitroglycoluril (DNGU or DINGU) (CAS 55510–04-8) * Tariff Code: 2933990058
No.190 2,6-Bis (picrylamino)-3,5-dinitropyridine (PYX) (CAS 38082–89-2) Tariff Code: /	**No.190** 2,6-Bis (picrylamino)-3,5-dinitropyridine (PYX) (CAS 38082–89-2) * Tariff Code: 2933399071

(continued)

Table 3.3 (continued)

2022 version	2023 version
No.191 3,3′-diamino-2,2′,4,4′,6,6′-hexanitrobiphenyl or dipicramide (DIPAM) (CAS 17215–44-0) Tariff Code: /	**No.191** 3,3'-diamino-2,2′,4,4′,6,6′-hexanitrobiphenyl or dipicramide (DIPAM) (CAS 17215–44-0) * Tariff Code: 2921590034
No.192 Diaminoazofurazan (DAAzF) (CAS 78644–90-3) Tariff Code: /	**No.192** Diaminoazofurazan (DAAzF) (CAS 78644–90-3) * Tariff Code: 2934999083
No.193 1,4,5,8-tetranitro-pyridazino[4,5-d] pyridazine (TNP) (CAS 229176–04-9) Tariff Code: /	**No.193** 1,4,5,8-tetranitro-pyridazino[4,5-d] pyridazine (TNP) (CAS 229176–04-9) * Tariff Code: 2933990059

As mentioned before, China promulgated the *Regulations on the Administration of Controlled Chemicals* in 1995. The appendix of this Regulation, entitled "Catalogue of Controlled Chemicals", contained four categories (Category I, II, III, and IV) of chemicals subject to administration. However, only those chemicals falling into the scope of Categories I, II, or III are subject to export control and are transplanted into this Consolidated Catalogue.

Regarding seventy-two listed chemicals (No. 1–72), forty-seven of them are enlisted on the Schedules of Chemicals of the CWC and are consistently included in the List of Controlled Chemicals of China. The other twenty-five controlled chemicals can also be found in the Handbook on Chemicals, maintained by the Technical Secretariat of the OPCW as an important tool which aims at assisting States Parties in the identification of individual chemicals covered by the Schedules of Chemicals of the CWC.[65]

Compared with the 2022 version, this sub-catalogue mainly adjusts the tariff code of Saxitoxin (No. 23) and a special chemical (No. 41).

Saxitoxin (No. 23) is one of the most toxic marine biotoxins as known. It is reported that all countries have listed this chemical as a mandatory item for the safety inspection of aquatic products. The 2023 Catalogue only adjusts the tariff code of Saxitoxin from 3002491000 to 2939801000, which is consistent with the adjustment of Tariff Schedule of the PRC for Imports and Exports (2023).

As the most complex commodity in this sub-catalogue, chemical No. 41 is defined as "Chemicals, except for those listed in Category I, containing a phosphorus atom to which is bonded one methyl, ethyl or propyl (normal or iso) group but not further

[65] A total of 2134 chemicals are included in the latest version (2022) of the Handbook on Chemicals, Retrieved September 8, 2023, from https://www.opcw.org/sites/default/files/documents/2022/07/Handbook%20on%20Chemicals%202022.pdf.

carbon atoms. Exceptions: Fonofos: O-Ethyl S-phenyl ethylphosphonothiolothionate". In addition to a general description, fifteen types of chemicals controlled under this serial number are specified. Among these fifteen chemicals, the 2023 Catalogue adds the tariff code for each of such chemicals [1]–[14]. The current complete definition of controlled chemical No. 41 is presented below (Table 3.4).

3.2.1.5 Certain Chemicals and Related Equipment and Technologies Export Control List

This sub-catalogue is formulated in parallel with the "List of Chemical Weapons Precursors" and the "List of Dual-use Chemical Manufacturing Facilities and Equipment and Related Technology and Software" under the Australia Group. A total of thirty-eight items (including technologies) are enlisted, including (i) certain chemicals (No. 1–11), (ii) related production equipment (No. 12–35), (iii) dedicated detecting equipment and toxic gas monitors (No. 36–37), and (iv) related technology (No. 38).

Regarding eleven certain chemicals subject to control (No. 1–11) enumerated as follows, the 2023 Catalogues adds item potassium perchlorate (No. 11) to this sub-catalogue in accordance with the *Announcement on the export control of potassium perchlorate*, which came into effect on April 1, 2022.[66] In practice, potassium perchlorate can be used as a fuming agent, fire starter, oxidizer and chemical analysis reagent, and it is listed in the "List of Explosive Hazardous Chemicals" and controlled in accordance with the *Measures for the Security Management of Explosive Hazardous Chemicals* (Table 3.5).

As for certain dedicated detecting equipment and toxic gas monitors, they are further categorized into (1) valves (No. 12–14), (2) pumps (No. 15–22), (3) storage tanks, containers or receivers (No. 23–25), (4) multiwalled piping (No. 26), (5) distillation or absorption columns (No. 27–28), (6) heat exchangers or condensers (No. 29–30), (7) reaction vessels, reactors (No. 31–33), (8) incinerators (No. 34) and (9) filling equipment (No. 35).

Regarding dedicated detecting equipment and toxic gas monitors (No. 36–37), they are designed for continuous operation and usable for the detection of chemicals or organic compounds subject to export control containing phosphorus, sulfur, fluorine or chlorine at concentrations of less than 0.3 mg/m^3; or designed for the detection of cholinesterase-inhibiting activity.

Finally, regarding the related technology subject to control (No. 38), please note that controls on technology do not apply to information "in the public domain" or to "basic scientific research". Meanwhile, the approval for the export of any dual-use equipment mentioned above also authorizes the export to the same end-user of the minimum technology required for the installation, operation, maintenance, or repair of that item.

[66] Announcement No. 46 of 2021 of the MOFCOM and the GAC, 29 December 2021.

Table 3.4 Item No. 41 of the controlled chemicals list

Controlled chemicals (No. 41)
(2023 version)

No.	Commodity name	Description	Tariff code	Unit
41	Chemicals, except for those listed in Category I, containing a phosphorus atom to which is bonded one methyl, ethyl or propyl (normal or iso) group but not further carbon atoms. Exceptions: Fonofos: O-Ethyl S-phenyl ethylphosphonothiolothionate	Category II: chemicals which can be used as precursors of chemical weapons	2930909027	Kg
	1. Methylphosphonyl dichloride		2931510000	
	2. Dimethyl methylphosphonate		2931410000	
	3. Propylphosphonic acid		2931499020	
	4. Methylphosphonic acid		2931440000	
	5. Diethyl ethylphosphonate		2931430000	
	6. Cyclic phosphonate A Chemical name: (5-Ethyl-2-methyl-2-oxido-1,3,2-dioxaphosphinan-5-yl)methyl methyl methylphosphonate CAS: 41203–81-0		2931470000	
	7. Cyclic phosphonate B Chemical name: Bis[(5-Ethyl-2-methyl-2-oxido-1,3,2-dioxaphosphinan-5-yl)methyl] methylphosphonate CAS: 42595–45-9 8. Phosphonic acid, methyl-, polyglycol ester CAS: 294675-51-7		2931499020	
	9. Diethyl methylphosphonate		2931499020	

(continued)

Table 3.4 (continued)

Controlled chemicals (No. 41)
(2023 version)

No.	Commodity name	Description	Tariff code	Unit
	10. Methyl dichlorophosphine		2931590060	
	11. Trichloronate		2931590070	
	12. Monobutyl methylphosphite		2931499020	
	13. Amidinourea salt of methylphosphonic acid		2931450000	
	14. Diphenyl methylphosphonate		2931499020	
	15. Cyclic phosphonate CU Chemical name: Mixture of Cyclic phosphonate A and Cyclic phosphonate B CAS: 170836-68-7		3824999950	

Table 3.5 Items No. 1–11 of certain chemicals and related equipment and technologies export control List

No	Name of the commodity	Description	Tariff code	Unit
1	Electronic grade hydrofluoric acids		2811111000	Kg
	Other hydrofluoric acids		2811119000	
2	Sodium fluoride		2826192010	
3	Sodium sulfide		2830101000	
4	Sodium hydrogen difluoride		2826192020	
5	Ammonium hydrogen fluoride		2826191010	
6	Potassium fluoride		2826199010	
7	Potassium hydrogen fluoride		2826199020	
8	Diisopropylamine		2921199020	
9	2-Diethylaminoethanol (a.k.a. N,N-Diethylethanolamine)		2922192210	
10	2-Chloroethanol		2905590020	
11	Potassium perchlorate		2829900020	

3.2.1.6 Missile and Missile-Related Items and Technologies Export Control List

This sub-catalogue is mainly based on the "Annex of Equipment, Software and Technology under Missile Technology Control Regime", of which China has not yet become a member.

A total of one hundred and eighty-six items (including technologies) are enlisted in this sub-catalogue. Items on this sub-catalogue are grouped into fourteen categories, respectively: (i) completed delivery systems (No. 1–5), (ii) power system (No. 6–17), (iii) guidance (No. 18–23), (iv) materials (No. 24–47), (v) electronic equipment (No. 48–66), (vi) control system (No. 67–70), (vii) warhead (No. 171), (viii) ground equipment (No. 72–73), (ix) propulsion (No. 74–97), (x) software (No. 98–106), (xi) other components, assemblies (No. 107–119), (xii) design, testing, production facilities and equipment (No. 120–173), (xiii) related technology (No. 174–185), and (xiv) item subject to temporary control (No. 186).

For the item subject to temporary control (No. 186), it refers to unmanned aerial vehicle (UAV) system of specific parameters presented in the following table. Such special UAV system was added to this sub-catalogue in 2015 (Table 3.6).[67]

[67] Announcement No. 20 of 2015 of the MOFCOM, the GAC, State Administration of Science, Technology, and Industry for National Defense, and the General Equipment Department, 25 June 2015.

Table 3.6 Item No. 186 of the missile and missile-related items and technologies export control list

No	Name of commodity	Description	Tariff code	Unit
186	unmanned aerial vehicle system	1. A range of 300 km or more, 2. With any of the following characteristics, with autonomous flight control and navigation capability: i. Contains an aerosol dispensing system/device with a capacity of 20 L or more; or ii. Designed or modified to be equipped with an aerosol dispensing system/device with a capacity of 20 L or more 3. With any of the following characteristics, with the operator's ability to control the flight from beyond visual range: i. Contains an aerosol dispensing system/device with a capacity of 20 L or more; or ii. Designed or modified to be equipped with an aerosol dispensing system/device with a capacity of 20 L or more Note: Model aircraft designed for recreational or competition purposes is not subject to control	8806239010 8806249010 8806299010 8806939010 8806949010 8806990010	Set/ Kg

3.2.1.7 Precursor Chemical (I)

This sub-catalogue is formulated based on the *Single Convention on Narcotic Drugs* (1961), the *Convention on Psychotropic Substances* (1971), and the *United Nations Convention Against Illicit Traffic in Narcotic Drugs and Psychotropic Substances* (1988) in combination of the "List of Precursors and Chemicals Frequently Used in the Illicit Manufacture of Narcotic Drugs and Psychotropic Substances" maintained by the United Nations International Control Board.

A total of fifty-four categories of precursor chemicals are enumerated in the sub-catalogue which are illustrated below (Table 3.7).

At the end of 2021, chemicals No. 49–54 were added to this sub-catalogue according to the Letter from the General Office of the State Council.[68] Pursuant to this Letter, items No. 49–52 are classified into Category II of precursor chemicals,

[68] Letter No. 58 of 2021 of the General Office of the State Council, 7 June 2021.

Table 3.7 List of precursor chemical (I)

No	Name of commodity	Description	Tariff code	Unit
1	Ephedrine (ephedrine, ephedrine hydrochloride)	Can be used to make drugs	2939410010	Kg
2	Ephedrine sulfate		2939410020	
3	Racephedrine hydrochloride		2939410030	
4	Ephedrine oxalate		2939410040	
5	Pseudoephedrine (pseudoephedrine, pseudoephedrine hydrochloride)		2939420010	
6	Pseudoephedrine sulfate		2939420020	
7	Methylephedrine hydrochloride		2939490010	
8	DL-methylephedrine hydrochloride		2939490020	
9	Norephedrine and its salts		2939440000	
10	Ephedra extract and extract powder for pesticide		1302140011	
11	Ephedra extract and extract powder for medical		1302140012	
12	Other ephedra extract and extract powder		1302140019	
13	Saps and extracts of Ephedra		1302140020	
14	Ephedra powder for pharmacy		1211500011	
15	Ephedra powder for perfumery		1211500021	
16	Ephedra powder for other use		1211500091	
17	Single preparations of ephedrine salts [refers to (pseudo)ephedrine hydrochloride tablets, ephedrine hydrochloride injections, ephedrine sulfate tablets]		3004410010 3004420010	
18	Piperonal (piperonal, 3,4-methylenedioxybenzaldehyde, heliotropin)		2932930000	
19	Safrole (4-allyl-1,2-methylenedioxybenzene)		2932940000	
20	Isosafrole (4-propenyl-1,2-methylenedioxybenzene)		2932910000	
21	Ergometrine		2939610010	
22	Ergotamine		2939620010	
23	Lysergic acid		2939630010	
24	1-phenyl-2-acetone (propiophenone)		2914310000	
25	N-acetylanthranilicacid (N-acetylanthranilic acid, 2-acetylaminobenzoic acid)		2924230010	
26	3,4-Methylenedioxyphenyl-2-acetone		2932920000	
27	Potassium permanganate		2841610000	
28	Acetic anhydride		2915240000	

(continued)

Table 3.7 (continued)

No	Name of commodity	Description	Tariff code	Unit
29	Sassafras oil		3301299910	
30	Phenylacetic acid		2916340010	
31	Hydrochloric acid (hydrogen chloride)		2806100000	
32	sulfuric acid		2807000010	
33	Toluene		2902300000	
34	Diethyl ether		2909110000	
35	Acetone		2914110000	
36	Methyl ethyl ketone (butanone)		2914120000	
37	Anthranilic acid		2922431000	
38	Piperidine (hexahydropyridine)		2933321000	
39	Trichloromethane (chloroform)		2903130000	
40	Hydroximine and its salts		2925290020	
41	O-Chlorophenyl Cyclopentyl Ketone		2914399014	
42	1-Phenyl-2-bromo-1-propanone (a.k.a. bromopropiophenone, 2-bromopropiophenone, α-bromopropiophenone, etc.)		2914790016	
43	3-oxo-2-phenylbutyronitrile (a.k.a. α-cyanopropiophenone, α-phenylacetylacetonitrile, 2-phenylacetylacetonitrile, etc.)		2926909070	
44	N-phenethyl-4-piperidone		2933399092	
45	4-Anilino-N-phenethylpiperidine			
46	Bromine		2801302000	
47	1-phenyl-1-acetone		2914399015	
48	Ephedrine chloride		2939719014	
49	3-Oxy-2-phenylbutyrate methyl ester (a.k.a. α- Acetylphenylacetate methyl ester α- Methyl phenylacetate)		2918300021	
50	3-Oxy-2-phenylbutylamine (a.k.a. α- Acetyl phenylacetamide α- Acetanilide)		2924299061	
51	2-Mcthyl-3 - [3,4 - (mcthylenedioxy) phenyl] glycidyl acid (a.k.a. 3,4-methylenedioxyphenyl-2-acetone glycyrrhizin Oleic acid)		2932999093	
52	2-Methyl-3 - [3,4 - (methylenedioxy) phenyl] glycidyl acid methyl ester (a.k.a. 3,4-methylenedioxyphenyl-2-acetone glycidyl ester)		2932999093	
53	Benzeneacetonitrile		2926909081	
54	γ- Butyrolactone		2932209031	

which may potentially be used for making methamphetamine or ecstasies, while items No. 53–54 are classified into Category III of precursor chemicals.

3.2.1.8 Precursor Chemical (II)

Similar to Precursor Chemical (I), this sub-catalogue is also formulated on the same basis. Seventeen categories of precursor chemicals are thus enumerated as illustrated below (Table 3.8).

Table 3.8 List of precursor chemical (II)

No	Name of the commodity	Description	Tariff code	Unit
1	Ammonium chloride	Can be used to make drugs	2827101000 2827109000	Kg
2	Barium sulfate		2833270000	Kg
3	Palladium chloride		2843900010	Kg
4	Sodium acetate		2915291000	Kg
5	Ethanol		220710000022072000102207200090	Ltr/Kg
6	Sodium hydroxide		2815110000 2815120000	Kg
7	Sodium carbonate (soda ash)		2836200000	Kg
8	Sodium bicarbonate (baking soda)		2836300000	Kg
9	Activated carbon		38021010003802109000	Kg
10	Acetic acid		2915211100 2915211900 2915219010 2915219020 2915219090	Kg
11	Ethyl acetate		2915310000	Kg
12	Isopropanol		2905122000	Kg
13	Iodine		2801200000	Kg
14	Hydroiodic acid		2811199010	Kg
15	Red phosphorus		2804709010	Kg
16	Chloral		2913000010	Kg
17	Dihydrosafrol		2932999080	Kg

Please note that Dual-use Export License for the export of above seventeen categories of precursor chemicals is only required when they are exported to specific countries (regions) such as Myanmar, Laos, and Afghanistan.

3.2.2 *Items of Unilateral Controls*

3.2.2.1 Certain Dual-Use Items and Technologies

Sub-catalogue 9, titled "certain dual-use items and technologies", includes six categories of items and technologies as follows (Table 3.9).

China has always maintained strict controls on the export of unmanned aerial vehicles (UAVs). Since 2002, China has gradually implemented export controls on high-performance UAVs, and the control scope and technical standards are consistent with international standards.[69] However, in recent years, the rapid development of unmanned aerial vehicle technology has increased the risk of diversion of some high-specification, high-performance civilian UAVs to military use.[70] In this context, China started to maintain certain temporary export controls on consumer-grade UAVs above since 2015.[71]

Regarding the export control on advanced computing products (No. 4–6), China in recent years has made significant progress. For instance, Tianhe-2 of China (a.k.a. Milkyway-2), a supercomputer capable of operating as fast as 33.86 petaflops per second (Pflop/s), was the world's most powerful system in 2015 according to a biannual Top500 list of supercomputers released twice a year since June 1993.[72] However, some experts noted that the technical parameters for these controlled advanced computing items is not high enough which results in a wide control coverage, closer to coverage of like products under Wassenaar Arrangement.[73]

---

[69] The spokesman of the MOFCOM answered reporters' questions on certain media's groundless accusations of the export of China of unmanned aerial vehicles to the conflict zones in Ukraine. Retrieved September 8, 2023, from.
http://www.mofcom.gov.cn/article/xwfb/xwfyrth/202304/20230403405186.shtml.

[70] MOFCOM. (July 31, 2023). The spokesman of the MOFCOM answered reporters' questions on the export control policy of China of unmanned aerial vehicles. Retrieved September 8, 2023, from http://www.mofcom.gov.cn/article/xwfb/xwfyrth/202307/20230703424756.shtml.

[71] Announcement No. 31 of 2015 on Strengthening Export Controls on Certain Dual-use Items of MOFCOM and the GAC, 31 July 2015. In this sense, please note that on 31 July 2023, MOFCOM, the GAC, State Administration of Science, Technology, and Industry for National Defense, and the General Equipment Department has jointly published Announcements No. 27 & 28 to further implement export control on certain UAVs and UAVs-related items.

[72] China Daily. (November 19, 2013). Tianhe-2 retains title as world's fastest supercomputer. Retrieved September 8, 2023, from.
http://www.chinadaily.com.cn/china/2013-11/19/content_17114508.htm.

[73] Technology Daily. (August 7, 2015). Export control on supercomputers: comments from industry experts. Retrieved September 8, 2023, from.
http://m.haiwainet.cn/middle/348217/2015/0807/content_29031303_1.html.

Table 3.9 List of certain dual-use items and technologies

No	Name of the commodity	Description	Tariff code	Unit
1	Unmanned aerial vehicles or unmanned airships	Capable of controlled flight beyond the natural visual distance of the operator, and having any of the following: 1. Maximum endurance greater than or equal to 30 min less than 1 h, as well as the ability to take off and stable controlled flight in gusts greater than or equal to 46.3 km/h (25 knots) 2. Maximum endurance greater than or equal to 1 h Technical Note: "Operator" means a person who controls the flight of an unmanned aerial vehicle or unmanned airship, "Endurance" means the duration of flight converted to international standard atmospheric conditions (ISO 2533:1975) in zero wind at sea level, "Natural visual distance" means the visual distance of a person without any aids, with or without vision correction Note: Not applicable to model aircraft or model airships	8801009010 8806229010 8806239010 8806249010 8806299010 8806929010 8806939010 8806949010 8806990010	Set/ Kg
2	Equipment and components specially designed to convert manned aerial vehicles and manned airships into unmanned aerial vehicles and unmanned airships listed in item 1 above	Note: Not applicable to model aircraft or model airships		
3	Designed or modified for unmanned aerial vehicles and unmanned airships to fly above 15,420 m (50,000 feet) with aspirating piston or rotary internal combustion piston engines	Note: Not applicable to model aircraft or model airships	8407102010	Set/ Kg
4	Digital computers having an "Adjusted Peak Performance (APP)" exceeding 8.0 Weighted TeraFLOPS		8471411010 8471491010 8471501010	Set/ Kg

(continued)

Table 3.9 (continued)

No	Name of the commodity	Description	Tariff code	Unit
5	Electronic components specifically designed or modified to enable "Adjusted Peak Performance (APP)" exceeding 8.0 Weighted TeraFLOPS using processor aggregation			
6	External interconnection equipment specially designed to aggregate the performance of digital computers	Single link unidirectional communication rates in excess of 2.0Gbyte/s, but not for internal interconnect devices (e.g., backplane, bus), passive interconnect devices, network access controllers or communication channel controllers	8517623710 8517623910	Set/ Kg

3.2.2.2 Special Civil Items and Technologies

Sub-catalogue 10, titled "special civil and technologies", includes five kinds of dredgers and six kinds of high-pressure water cannons-related products (Table 3.10).

Regarding dredgers (No. 1–5), China maintains export controls on these dredgers since 2017.[74] As a major water and shipping nation, China has a long history of dredging from ancient times.[75] However, for a long time, the equipment of heavy dredger was monopolized by a few European countries such as Netherlands and Belgium, and a strict technology blockade was imposed on China. The items even if imported into China were encumbered with a high cost of purchase price.[76]

Recent years have witnessed advancement of China in the design, development and manufacturing of this machinery. The self-propelled cutter suction dredger, named Tianjing (a.k.a. Sky Whale), is one of the examples.[77] According to some Chinese military experts, China has developed advanced dredging technology

[74] Announcement No. 28 of 2017 of the MOFCOM and the GAC, 25 May 2017.

[75] There is a famous fairy tale named "King Yu combating the flood" in China, which describes the dredging of the Yellow River by ancient Chinese people.

[76] For example, China (CCCC Tianhang Bureau) bought an old drag suction dredger from the Netherlands at a cost of nearly 1.7 million pounds in 1966. It was named "Jinhangjun 102" after renovation and refurbishment. In 1985, China also purchased a cutter suction dredger from Japan.

[77] Tianjing has been hailed as a mighty tool for island building because of its strong excavation and hydraulic reclamation ability. According to a crew member, Tianjing can excavate 4,500 cubic meters of mixture from the seabed each hour - the equivalence of a 0.5-m-deep pit and a standard soccer field size. Retrieved September 8, 2023, from.

http://en.people.cn/n3/2017/0731/c90000-9249126.html.

Table 3.10 List of special civil items and technologies

No	Name of the commodity	Description	Tariff code	Unit
1	Drag suction dredger	1. Compartment capacity greater than or equal to 1500 m^3 2. Dredging depth greater than or equal to 15 m 3. With bow-blowing function and device	8905100010	Ship/ Kg
2	Cutter suction dredger	1. Reamer power greater than or equal to 500 kW 2. Digging depth greater than or equal to 15 m 3. Total installed power greater than or equal to 2000 kW		Ship/ Kg
3	Bucket dredger	1. Bucket capacity greater than or equal to 4 m^3 2. Digging depth greater than or equal to 15 m		Ship/ Kg
4	Sand suction dredger	1. Compartment capacity greater than or equal to 500 m^3 2. Total installed power greater than or equal to 1000 kW		Ship/ Kg
5	Self-propelled dump barge	1. Compartment capacity greater than or equal to 1000 m^3 2. With bow-blowing function and device	8901904110	Ship/ Kg
6	High-pressure water cannons	Meet all of the following characteristics 1. Maximum range greater than or equal to 100 m 2. Rated flow rate greater than or equal to 540 m^3 per hour 3. Rated pressure greater than or equal to 1.2 MPa Technical Note: High-pressure water cannon is a kind of equipment that uses a high-pressure water pump to do work on a liquid medium to form high-speed fluid that can be ejected in air at a long distance	8424899920	Set/ Kg
7	High-pressure water cannons (main body)	Major components and ancillary equipment specially designed for No. 6	8424909010	Kg
8	Electric vane pumps for high-pressure water cannons		8413603120	Set/ Kg
9	Other vane pumps for high-pressure water cannons		8413603902	Set/ Kg

(continued)

Table 3.10 (continued)

No	Name of the commodity	Description	Tariff code	Unit
10	High-pressure water cannon control system (for lines with voltages not exceeding 1000 V)		8537109040	Pcs/Kg
11	High-pressure water cannon control system		9032899092	Set/Kg

through its island-building projects.[78] The export control of this dredgers is based on national security considerations.

Regarding high-pressure water cannon-related products[79] (No. 6–11), they are reportedly the main weaponry in naval warfare during peacetime, capable of expelling foreign vessels from territorial waters and avoiding heavy casualties otherwise caused by shells or guns.[80] This control again is based on national security considerations.

3.2.2.3 Commercial Cryptography Export Control List

A total of eleven categories of commercial cryptography products are included in this List as follows (Table 3.11).

3.3 Conclusions

As manifested by the consolidated catalogue of export controls, China has vigorously implemented non-proliferation control lists of multilateral control regimes, and showed a sense of moderation in unilateral controls, even based on national security considerations. This means that manufacturing in China and exporting from China is convenient for items controlled under Wassenaar Arrangement, which are largely not controlled items in China.

[78] Hong Kong media said China restricts the export of dredgers for building islands: for national security reasons. Retrieved September 8, 2023, from https://baijiahao.baidu.com/s?id=1568793141441649&wfr=spider&for=pc.

[79] Announcement No. 31 of 2022 of the MOFCOM, the GAC, and the State Administration of Science, Technology, and Industry for National Defense, 1 November 2022.

[80] Why MOFCOM maintains export controls on high-pressure water cannons in addition to dredgers. Retrieved September 8, 2023, from https://www.sohu.com/a/602457201_121118977.

Table 3.11 Export control list of commercial cryptography

No	Name of the commodity	Description	Tariff code	Unit
I. Systems, equipment, and components				
1	Security chips	An integrated circuit chip achieving all or part of such functions as cryptographic operation, key management and random number generation, and having any of the following: 1. Containing a symmetric cryptographic algorithm with a key length of 64 bits or more, an integer factorization-based asymmetric cryptographic algorithm with a key length of 768 bits or more or an elliptic curve-based asymmetric cryptographic algorithm with a key length of 128 bits or more specifically for such fields as power, taxation, public security and finance; or 2. Containing a symmetric cryptographic algorithm with a key length of 64 bits or more, an integer factorization-based asymmetric cryptographic algorithm with a key length of 768 bits or more or an elliptic curve-based asymmetric cryptographic algorithm with a key length of 128 bits or more, and its symmetric cryptographic algorithm achieves an encryption-decryption rate of 10 Gbps or above or its asymmetric cryptographic algorithm achieves a signature rate of 50,000 times / second or above	8542311910 8542319010	Pcs/ Kg

(continued)

Table 3.11 (continued)

No	Name of the commodity	Description	Tariff code	Unit
2	Cryptographic machine (Cryptographic card)	Any device (including cryptographic card) with implementation of cryptographic operation as its main function, and having both of the following: 1. Containing a symmetric cryptographic algorithm with a key length of 64 bits or more, an integer factorization-based asymmetric cryptographic algorithm with a key length of 768 bits or more or an elliptic curve-based asymmetric cryptographic algorithm with a key length of 128 bits or more; and 2. Symmetric cryptographic algorithm encryption and decryption rate of 10Gbps or more or asymmetric cryptographic algorithm signature rate of 50,000 times/second or more	8543709950	Set/ Kg
3	Encrypted VPN device	Any device with IPSec / SSL VPN as its main function, and having both of the following: 1. Containing a symmetric cryptographic algorithm with a key length of 64 bits or more, an integer factorization-based asymmetric cryptographic algorithm with a key length of 768 bits or more or an elliptic curve-based asymmetric cryptographic algorithm with a key length of 128 bits or more; and 2. With a communication rate of 10 Gbps or above	8517622920 8517623920	Set/ Kg

(continued)

Table 3.11 (continued)

No	Name of the commodity	Description	Tariff code	Unit
4	Key management product	Any server device used to manage the generation, distribution and storage, etc., of symmetric or asymmetric keys as its function, and having both of the following: 1. Containing a symmetric cryptographic algorithm with a key length of 64 bits or more, an integer factorization-based asymmetric cryptographic algorithm with a key length of 768 bits or more or an elliptic curve-based asymmetric cryptographic algorithm with a key length of 128 bits or more; and 2. Supporting the management of more than 10,000 objects	8543709950	Set/ Kg
5	Dedicated cryptographic equipment	Any device containing a symmetric cryptographic algorithm with a key length of 64 bits or more, an integer factorization-based asymmetric cryptographic algorithm with a key length of 768 bits or more or an elliptic curve-based asymmetric cryptographic algorithm with a key length of 128 bits or more specifically for such fields as power, taxation, public security and finance		
6	Quantum cryptographic device	Any device using quantum technology to achieve the cryptographic function based on quantum mechanics and cryptography		
7	Cryptanalysis equipment	Any equipment used to crack, weaken, or bypass cryptographic technologies, products, or systems		
II. Test, inspection and production equipment				
8	Cryptography development and production device	Any device specifically designed for the development and production of the items specified in 1 to 7		

(continued)

Table 3.11 (continued)

No	Name of the commodity	Description	Tariff code	Unit
9	Cryptography test verification device	Any device specifically designed for measuring, testing, assessing or verifying the items specified in 1 to 7		
III. Software				
10	Any software specifically designed or improved for the development, production or use of the items specified in 1 to 9			
IV. Technology				
11	Any technology specifically designed or improved for the development, production or use of the items specified in 1 to 10			

Chapter 4
Export Control of Military Items

This chapter explores export controls of military items under Chinese law. Section 4.1 outlines the legal framework of export control of military items. Section 4.2 presents a brief introduction on the Military Item Export List of China. On this basis, Sect. 4.3 then makes certain commentaries on this List. Furthermore, Sect. 4.4 introduces the license application procedures. Finally, Sect. 4.5 provides the format of the Military Export License for reference.

4.1 Chinese Legal Framework

Export control of military items is common in many jurisdictions[1] since the export of military items is directly and closely related to national security, interests or foreign policies. Under ECL "military items" refers to equipage, special production equipment and other related goods, technologies and services that are used for military purposes.[2]

In this section, we would like to introduce the main legal instruments regulating the export of military items in China, i.e., ECL and the *Administration Regulations on the Export of Military Items.*

---

[1] For example, the U.S. has formulated *Arms Export Control Act* and *International Traffic in Arms Regulations* and maintained a corresponding Munitions List; the EU has established *Council Common Position 2008/944/CFSP* defining common rules governing the control of exports of military technology and equipment, and maintained a non-binding Common Military List, up to each Member to implement its own military export controls; Similarly, the Wassenaar Arrangement has also formulated its own Munitions List. Meanwhile, the UN has formulated the Arms Trade Treaty, which applies to all conventional arms within the following categories: (a) battle tanks, (b) armored combat vehicles, (c) large-caliber artillery systems, (d) combat aircraft, (e) attack helicopters, (f) warships, (g) missiles and missile launchers, and (h) small arms and light weapons.

[2] Article 2(5) of the ECL.

D. Zhao, *Contemporary Export Control Law of China*, Modern China and International Economic Law, https://doi.org/10.1007/978-981-99-9825-8_4

4.1.1 Export Control Law

Articles 23–27 of ECL provide for the export control mechanism for military items, which is summarized as follows:

(a) Export monopoly privilege. China maintains a monopoly scheme over the export of military items. EBOs that engage in the export of military items must be qualified to conduct such monopoly business which is approved and certified by the competent authorities and confine its export business within the authorized business scope.[3] The competent authorities refer to the State Administration of Science, Technology and Industry for National Defense ("SASTIND"), and the Equipment Development Department of the CMC.[4]
(b) Project approval. EBOs with qualified monopoly business scope of military products must also apply to the competent authorities for the review and approval of the export project proposal, and the export project or an export contract respectively, based on control policies and product attributes. If any key military product is involved, a joint review together with relevant departments is necessary, with a report to the State Council and the CMC for approval.[5]
(c) Military Export license. After obtaining one of the two approvals above, as the case may be, EBOs are further required to apply for the Military Export License, which is subject to the examination of the customs in export clearance of the goods.[6]
(d) Shipment. Please note that only certain shipping companies are eligible to conduct the export shipping of military products and other related activities.[7] However, the information on eligible shipping companies is not publicly available.[8]
(e) Overseas exhibition. EBOs or research institutes or manufacturers of military products who participate in any international exhibition of military products must also go through the above procedure.[9]
(f) Military activities overseas. However, the above procedure does not apply to the export of military products used for purposes of the use of armed forces overseas, external military-to-military contacts or military assistance, which are governed by separate laws and regulations instead of ECL.[10]

Please note that other provisions of ECL, except those specifically for the export control of dual-use items, also apply to the export of military items.

---

[3] Ibid., Article 23.

[4] White Paper, Part II, Section 2.

[5] Article 24 of the ECL.

[6] Ibid., Article 25.

[7] Ibid., Article 26.

[8] We are not sure whether the competent authorities maintained an unofficial regulation on the shipment issue.

[9] Article 27 of the ECL.

[10] Ibid., Article 47.

4.1.2 Administrative Regulations on Export of Military Items

Before the enactment of ECL, China has promulgated a separate administrative regulation on export control of military items, titled the "*Administrative Regulations on the Export of Military Items*" ("MER"), which was first published in 1997[11] and was subsequently revised in 2002[12], and remains unchanged since then.

The 1997 MER represented a major advance to a centralized and planned control.[13] However, the 1997 MER was not equipped with a control list of military items.[14]

To further strengthen the uniform and centralized controls,[15] the current MER introduces list-based controls with a Military Item List, which will be further explored in Sect. 4.2. The current MER consists of six chapters, namely general provisions (Chap. 1), trading companies of military items (Chap. 2), export administration of military items (Chap. 3), export order of military items (This chapter), legal liability (Chap. 5), and supplementary provisions (Chap. 6), with 30 Articles in total.

Chapter 1 mainly outlines the control policies. MER applies to the export trade of equipage, special production equipment, and other goods, technology, and related services, for military purposes or military uses.[16] The export of military items in China is subject to the supervision and administration by such authorities as SASTIND and the Equipment Development Department, under the leadership of the State Council and the CMC respectively.[17] Meanwhile, the export of above military items shall be subject to the following three principles, (i) the export shall be conducive to the capability for legitimate self-defense of the recipient country; (ii) the export shall cause no injury to the peace, security and stability of the region concerned and the world; and (iii) the export shall have no interference in the internal affairs of the recipient country.[18]

Chapter 2 introduces the concept of "trading companies of military items", e.g., EBOs of military items. In China, only those legal entities which have obtained the business monopoly privileges for military export are entitled to conduct such

---

[11] Order No. 234 of the Central Military Commission, 22 October 1997.

[12] Order No. 366 of the State Council and the Central Military Commission, 15 October 2002.

[13] Medeiros, E. S., & Gill, B. (2000). *Chinese Arms Exports: Policy, Players, and Process* (p.x). Strategic Studies Institute

[14] It is not clear at the time of the 1997 MER whether China maintained an unofficial Military Item List or simply referred to the international controlling list.

[15] Please note that the Chinese government underwent a huge structure reorganization in March 1998. For example, the Commission of Science, Technology and Industry for National Defense, originally established in 1982, was granted certain additional competence in the defense sector.

[16] Article 2 of the MER (2002).

[17] Ibid., Article 3.

[18] Ibid., Article 5.

exporting business within the approved business scope.[19] Currently in China, only ten enterprises are privileged to conduct trade of military items.[20]

Chapter 3 touches on the administration of the exports by way of Military Export License.[21] Specifically, the military items can be exported from China after all the following requirements are satisfied: (i) the export project has been examined and approved;[22] (ii) the export contract has been examined and approved;[23] and (iii) the Military Export License is granted with the approved export contract.[24] The specific examination measures for the military item export project and export contract and the issuance of the Military Export License are otherwise regulated,[25] which will be explained in Sect. 4.3.

This chapter regulates the export business order of military items. Firstly, it is reiterated that only eligible EBOs of military items are entitled to engage in the export of military items.[26] Secondly, EBOs of military items are prohibited from unfair competition, and from obtaining the Military Export License licenses through fraud, bribery or other improper means.[27] Finally, the competent authorities may, when deemed necessary or at the request of EBOs of military items, tackle any act obstructing the regularity of military exports.[28]

Chapter 5 specifies legal liabilities for violations. The EBOs not privileged in military exports shall be banned from illegal activities or otherwise shall be subject to criminal liabilities (e.g., the crime of illegal business operation) under *Criminal Law*, as the case may be. In case no criminal liabilities can be established, the competent authorities may give a warning, confiscate the illegal gains, and concurrently impose a fine of between one and five times of the illegal gains. If there are no illegal gains or the illegal gains are less than CNY 100,000, a fine of not less than CNY 100,000 but not more than CNY 500,000 shall be imposed.[29]

Chapter 6 contains supplement provisions. As provided in this chapter, the MER also applies to the export of police equipment.[30]

---

[19] Ibid., Article 7.

[20] They are China Precision Machinery Import & Export Corporation ("CPMIEC"), China National Aero-Technology Import & Export Corporation ("CATIC"), China Shipbuilding Trading Corporation ("CSTC"), China North Industries Corporation ("NORINCO"), Poly Technologies Corporation, CETC International ("CETCI"), "CSOC", China Electronics Import & Export Corporation ("CEIEC"), Aerospace Long-march International Trade Corporation ("ALIT"), and China Jing An Import & Export Corporation.

[21] Article 13 of the MER (2002).

[22] Ibid., Article 14.

[23] Ibid., Article 15.

[24] Ibid., Article 17.

[25] Ibid., Article 18.

[26] Ibid., Articles 20-21.

[27] Ibid., Article 22.

[28] Ibid., Article 23.

[29] Ibid., Article 26.

[30] Ibid., Article 29.

4.1.3 *Military End-Use*

Both ECL and the MER define military items as items used for military purposes,[31] and the special design for military application is not the test in determining whether an item is a military item or not. However, the Military Item List as introduced in Sect. 4.2 contains a catch-call or miscellaneous expression to the effect that all other products not explicitly included in that List with practical military applications and are specifically designed or modified for military purposes are regarded as *de facto* military items.[32] It is contradicting for the co-existence of the test of "military purposes" and the test of "special design" for determining whether it is a military item in practice, and it is also puzzling to determine whether any supplies to military units as the end-users would be treated as military items under ECL or the MER.

4.2 The Military Item List of China

4.2.1 *Introduction*

To implement Article 2 of the MER, the Commission of Science, Technology and Industry for National Defense (no longer existing since 2008), and the General Equipment Department of the Liberation Army of the PRC promulgated and released the Military Item List of China for the first time in 2002,[33] which is still in force now.

This List is layered with (i) definition of military items, (ii) specific categories of military items, (iii) major systems or components of military items, and parts and components directly related to, and (iv) technology and service. Please note that nuclear weapons (including their key components, raw materials and technologies) are not included in this List, which are not supposed to be exported.

While the military items on this List are divided into fourteen categories according to the conventional classification of weapons and equipment, the technology and service are not separately controlled, but mainly supplemental to such military weapons and equipment.

Structure of the Military Item List of China

Category no.	Description
1	Light weapons
2	Artillery and other launchers
3	Ammunition, mines, torpedoes, bombs, anti-tank missiles, and other explosive devices

(continued)

[31] Article 2(5) of the ECL, Article 2 of the MER.

[32] Category 14 (No. 14.1) of the Military Item List.

[33] Ke Gong Fa Order No. 828 of 2002, 1 November 2002.

(continued)

Structure of the Military Item List of China	
Category no.	Description
4	Tanks, armored vehicles and other military vehicles
5	Military engineering equipment and facilities
6	Military warships and special equipment and devices
7	Military aviation vehicles and special equipment and devices
8	Rockets, missiles, military satellites, and auxiliary equipment
9	Military electronics and fire control, ranging, optics, guidance, and control devices
10	Explosives, propellants, incendiaries, and related compounds
11	Military training equipment
12	Protective equipment and devices for nuclear, biological, and chemical weapons
13	Logistic equipment, materiel, and other auxiliary military equipment
14	Other products

Category One: Light weapons

1.1 Light weapons: weapons carried and used by individual soldiers or squads, including:

   1.1.1 Guns: firearms that primarily use energy such as gunpowder gas to fire a cartridge through a barrel with a caliber of less than 20 mm (0.78 inches), including pistols, submachine guns, rifles, machine guns, and other special-purpose firearms.
   1.1.2 Grenade weapons.
   1.1.3 Special equipment: weapons for demolition, mine-laying, mine detection, mine clearance, arson, smoke generation, illuminating, signaling, riot control, and other various special tasks.
   1.1.4 Lightweight laser jamming device.
   1.1.5 Cold weapons.

1.2 Optical sights, night sights, silencers, suppressors, and flash suppressors for all products listed in Sect. 1.1.
1.3 Parts, components, auxiliary accessories, attachments, fittings, spare parts, semi-finished products, and samples for all products listed in Sects. 1.1 to 1.2.
1.4 Technology, technique, equipment, technical data (including software), services directly related to the development, production, testing, trial, inspection, use, maintenance, and upgrading for all products listed in Sects. 1.1 to 1.3, and special raw materials and auxiliary materials for the production for all products listed in Sects. 1.1 to 1.3.

Category Two: Artillery and other launchers

2.1 Artillery: body-barreled firing weapons that use energy sources such as gunpowder gas pressure to throw projectiles with a caliber equal to and greater than 20 mm (0.78 inches).
2.2 New energy artillery.
2.3 Optical sights, night sights, rangefinders, launchers, and bases for all products listed in Sects. 2.1 to 2.2.
2.4 Military flamethrowers and associated components and devices.
2.5 Parts, components, auxiliary accessories, attachments, fittings, spare parts, semi-finished products, and samples for all products listed in Sects. 2.1 to 2.4.
2.6 Technology, technique, equipment, technical data (including software), services directly related to the development, production, testing, trial, inspection, use, maintenance, and upgrading for all products listed in Sections 2.1 to 2.5, and special raw materials and auxiliary materials for the production for all products listed in Sections 2.1 to 2.5.

Category Three: Ammunition, mines, torpedoes, bombs, anti-tank missiles and other explosive devices

3.1 Ammunition, including:

3.1.1 Bullets, artillery shells, rocket shells and grenades of various calibers, and other kinds of ammunition for all products listed in Categories 1 and 2.
3.1.2 Projectile, firing charge, bullet core, booster, detonation device, primer, safety and arming device, and one-time operation of high output power.
3.1.3 Ammunition belt and ammunition belt feeder.

3.2 Ammunition manufacturing machinery and loading machinery.
3.3 Mines, including:

3.3.1 Anti-tank mines, anti-infantry mines, and special mines.
3.3.2 Mine body and fuse.

3.4 Torpedoes, including:

3.4.1 River and water mines, beach water (ground) mines, and special mines.
3.4.2 Shell, fuse, charge, detonation device, auxiliary instrumentation, mine accessories, depth charges, and related components of torpedoes.

3.5 Bombs: ammunition and ammunition dispensers dropped by planes or other aircraft.
3.6 Anti-tank missiles.
3.7 Firing device, blasting device, detonation device, fire transmission device, detonator and aiming, night vision device and various equipment for all products listed in Sects. 3.1 to 3.6.

3.8 Handling, control, startup, monitoring, detection and dismantling device, software, and equipment for all products listed in Sects. 3.1 to 3.7.
3.9 Destruction and clearance equipment for military explosives.
3.10 Ablation-resistant materials processed or semi-processed from advanced composite materials (e.g., silicon, graphite, carbon/boron fiber filaments) specially designed or modified for all products listed in Category 3.
3.11 Parts, components, auxiliary accessories, attachments, fittings, spare parts, semi-finished products, and samples for all products listed in Sect. 3.1 to 3.9.
3.12 Technology, technique, equipment, technical data (including software), services directly related to the development, production, testing, trial, inspection, use, maintenance, and upgrading for all products listed in Sects. 3.1 to 3.11, and special raw materials and auxiliary materials for the production for all products listed in Sects. 3.1 to 3.11.

Category Four: Tanks, armored vehicles and other military vehicles

4.1 Tanks, including main battle tanks, amphibious tanks, reconnaissance tanks, and airborne tanks.
4.2 Armored vehicles: various tracked or wheeled military vehicles with armor protection.
4.3 Other military vehicles: all tracked or wheeled vehicles for military uses (except for military engineering vehicles and logistical support vehicles).
4.4 Chassis, power, and transmission device specially designed or modified for all products listed in Sects. 4.1 to 4.3.
4.5 Active armor, reactive armor device configured for all products listed in Sects. 4.1 to 4.2.
4.6 Parts, components, auxiliary accessories, attachments, fittings, spare parts, semi-finished products, and samples for all products listed in Sects. 4.1 to 4.5.
4.7 Technology, technique, equipment, technical data (including software), services directly related to the development, production, testing, trial, inspection, use, maintenance, and upgrading for all products listed in Sects. 4.1 to 4.6, and special raw materials and auxiliary materials for the production for all products listed in Sects. 4.1 to 4.6.

Category Five: Military engineering equipment and facilities

5.1 Equipment and facilities for military operations such as construction, bridging, float-crossing, fording, mine-laying, mine detection, mine clearance, mine removal, rescue, repair, blasting and clearance, and camouflage, including:

5.1.1 Military engineering construction vehicles and equipment.
5.1.2 Engineering, rescue, and repair vehicles.
5.1.3 Equipment, devices, and vehicles for mine-laying, mine detection, mine clearance, and mine removal.
5.1.4 Barrier-breaking equipment and facilities.

5.1.5 Engineering blasting equipment.
5.1.6 Testing and inspection equipment.
5.1.7 Camouflage and spoofing devices.

5.2 Parts, components, auxiliary accessories, attachments, fittings, spare parts, semi-finished products, and samples for all products listed in Sect. 5.1.
5.3 Technology, technique, equipment, technical data (including software), services directly related to the development, production, testing, trial, inspection, use, maintenance, and upgrading for all products listed in Sects. 5.1–5.2, and special raw materials and auxiliary materials for the production for all products listed in Sects. 5.1–5.2.

Category Six: Military warships and special equipment and devices

6.1 Military warships: ships designed, built, improved, modified and equipped for military purposes, capable of navigating on the surface, in the ground-effect wing area or underwater, including:

6.1.1 Combat ships (including nuclear-powered types).
6.1.2 Military auxiliary ships.

6.2 Shipboard weapon system: weapon system and its equipment specially designed and modified for the formation of naval combat capabilities from target detection to launch control, and taking military ships or naval vehicles as a platform.
6.3 Ship-specific equipment: special systems and equipment specially designed or modified for combat ships, including:

6.3.1 Ship power, propulsion, and control equipment.
6.3.2 Ship navigation systems and equipment.
6.3.3 Other special equipment and devices for ships.

6.4 Shipboard electronics and optical equipment.
6.5 Parts, components, auxiliary accessories, attachments, fittings, spare parts, semi-finished products, and samples for all products listed in Sects. 6.1 to 6.4.
6.6 Technology, technique, equipment, technical data (including software), services directly related to the development, production, testing, trial, inspection, use, maintenance, and upgrading for all products listed in Sects. 6.1 to 6.5, and special raw materials and auxiliary materials for the production for all products listed in Category 6.

Category Seven: Military aviation vehicles and special equipment and devices

7.1 Military aviation vehicles: aviation vehicles specially designed, modified, or equipped for military purposes.
7.2 Military aircraft engines: engines specially designed or modified for vehicles listed in Sect. 7.1.

7.3 Airborne equipment: equipment specially designed or modified for vehicles listed in Sect. 7.1.
7.4 Airborne weapon system.
7.5 Flight security equipment and facilities.
7.6 Parts, components, auxiliary accessories, attachments, fittings, spare parts, semi-finished products, and samples for all products listed in Sects. 7.1 to 7.5.
7.7 Technology, technique, equipment, technical data (including software), services directly related to the development, production, testing, trial, inspection, use, maintenance, measurement and calibration, upgrading for all products listed in Sects. 7.1 to 7.6, and special raw materials and auxiliary materials for the production for all products listed in Category 7.

Category Eight: Rockets, missiles, military satellites and their auxiliary equipment

8.1 Rockets: vehicles propelled by the reaction force generated by the rocket motor's ejected mass, including:

  8.1.1 Carrier rockets.
  8.1.2 Tactical Rockets.

8.2 Missile weapon systems: weapon systems consisting of a missile system and accompanying technical equipment and facilities, capable of performing combat missions independently.

  8.2.1 Missile systems: a general term for missiles and supporting technical equipment for testing and launching.
  8.2.2 Missiles: unmanned aerial weapons equipped with power devices, capable of controlling the flight trajectory, and carrying a payload.
  8.2.3 Direct combat equipment.
  8.2.4 Technical support equipment.
  8.2.5 Major system equipment of missiles.
  8.2.6 Components, equipment, programs, and software for missile weapon systems, including:
    8.2.6.1 All stages and sub-stages of missile systems, all stages and sub-stages of rockets, interstage mechanism of carrier vehicles, missile re-entry vehicles, etc.
    8.2.6.2 Liquid rocket engines, solid rocket engines, turbojet engines, turbofan engines, etc.
    8.2.6.3 Warhead, fuse, safety device, arming device, safety detonating device, etc.
    8.2.6.4 Guidance and control devices.
    8.2.6.5 Missile command control systems.
  8.2.7 Missile production testing equipment.
  8.2.8 Special software related to the above products and equipment.

8.3 Military satellites: satellites for military uses, including:

  8.3.1 Military communication satellites, military reconnaissance satellites, military navigation and positioning satellites, military meteorological satellites, military remote sensing satellites, military mapping satellites, and military test satellites.
  8.3.2 Satellite components.
  8.3.3 Satellite ground equipment, including data receiving equipment, data processing equipment, etc.

8.4 Special parts, components, auxiliary accessories, attachments, fittings, spare parts, semi-finished products, and samples for all products listed in Sect. 8.1 to 8.3.
8.5 Technology, technique, equipment, technical data (including software), services directly related to the development, production, testing, trial, inspection, use, maintenance, measurement and calibration, upgrading for all products listed in Sects. 8.1 to 8.4, and special raw materials and auxiliary materials for the production for all products listed in Category 8.

Category Nine: Military electronics and fire control, ranging, optics, guidance and control devices

9.1 Electronic equipment for military purposes or specially designed, modified, or configured for military use, including:

  9.1.1 Command automation system and equipment.
  9.1.2 Radar systems and their sensors.
  9.1.3 Electronic warfare equipment.
  9.1.4 Intelligence reconnaissance equipment.
  9.1.5 Communication and navigation equipment.
  9.1.6 Identification and location systems and equipment.
  9.1.7 Security and confidentiality systems.

9.2 Fire control systems, rangefinders and devices, optical systems (including military telescopes, and periscopes), optoelectronic systems, and optoelectronic systems of weapons in this List.
9.3 Guidance and control devices.
9.4 Parts, components, auxiliary accessories, attachments, fittings, spare parts, semi-finished products, and samples for all products listed in Sects. 9.1 to 9.3.
9.5 Technology, technique, equipment, technical data (including software), services directly related to the development, production, testing, trial, inspection, use, maintenance, measurement and calibration, upgrading for all products listed in Sects. 9.1 to 9.4, and special raw materials and auxiliary materials for the production for all products listed in Category 9.

Category Ten: Explosives, propellants, incendiaries and related compounds

10.1 Military gunpowder, military explosives, propellants, military incendiaries, military fuel thickeners, and military pyrotechnics for weapons in this List, including:

  10.1.1 Gun propellants and components: gunpowder used to launch gun projectiles.
  10.1.2 Propellants and components.
  10.1.3 Military explosives and components: explosives for various munitions and military demolition projects.
  10.1.4 Military combustibles and components.
  10.1.5 Military fuel thickeners and components thereof.
  10.1.6 Military pyrotechnics and components thereof.

10.2 Compounds specifically configured for products listed in Category 10.

10.3 Technology, technique, equipment, technical data (including software), services directly related to the development, production, testing, trial, inspection, use, and measurement for all products listed in Sects. 10.1 to 10.2, and special raw materials and auxiliary materials for the production for all products listed in Category 10.

Category Eleven: Military training equipment

11.1 Military training and teaching equipment and devices, including:

  11.1.1 Training, simulation, teaching equipment, and devices for army weapon equipment.
  11.1.2 Training, simulation, teaching equipment, and devices for naval ships and special weapons and equipment.
  11.1.3 Training, simulation, teaching equipment, and devices for military aviation vehicles and special weapons and equipment.
  11.1.4 Training, simulation, teaching equipment, and devices for special weapons and equipment.

11.2 Parts, components, auxiliary accessories, attachments, fittings, spare parts, semi-finished products, and samples for all products listed in Sect. 11.1.

11.3 Technology, technique, equipment, technical data (including software), services directly related to the development, production, testing, trial, inspection, use, maintenance, measurement and calibration, upgrading for all products listed in Sects. 11.1 to 11.2, and special raw materials and auxiliary materials for the production for all products listed in Category 11.

Category Twelve: Protective equipment and devices for nuclear, biological and chemical weapons

12.1 Equipment and devices for protecting against nuclear, chemical and biological weapons attacks, including:

  12.1.1 Detection equipment and devices.

12.1.2 Protective equipment and devices.
12.1.3 Decontamination equipment and devices.
12.1.4 First aid equipment and devices.

12.2 Parts, components, auxiliary accessories, attachments, fittings, spare parts, semi-finished products, and samples for all products listed in Sect. 12.1.

12.3 Technology, technique, equipment, technical data (including software), services directly related to the development, production, testing, trial, inspection, use, maintenance, measurement and calibration, upgrading for all products listed in Sects. 12.1 to 12.2, and special raw materials and auxiliary materials for the production for all products listed in Category 12.

Category Thirteen: Logistic equipment, materiel and other auxiliary military equipment

13.1 Logistic equipment.

13.1.1 Quartermaster equipment and materiel, including:
13.1.1.1 Military quits and clothing.
A. Military uniform.
B. Military caps, military ties, military logos, and military buttons.
C. Military shoes and boots.
D. Military fabrics.
E. Others, military gloves for example.
13.1.1.2 Military fittings.
A. General fittings.
B. Protective equipment, including steel helmets, and bulletproof vests.
C. Others.
13.1.1.3 Cooking equipment.
13.1.1.4 Other quartermaster materiel.
13.1.2 Health equipment and supplies, including:
13.1.2.1 Health equipment for motorized carriers.
13.1.2.2 Additional devices for the wounded transport equipment.
13.1.2.3 Battlefield first aid equipment.
13.1.2.4 Field medical technical support equipment.
13.1.2.5 Field blood station equipment.
13.1.2.6 Field epidemic prevention and protective equipment.
13.1.2.7 Military specially required medicines.
13.1.3 Military transportation equipment, including:
13.1.3.1 Special transport equipment.
13.1.3.2 Military loading, unloading and reinforcement equipment.
13.1.3.3 Specialized repair protection equipment.
13.1.3.4 Military vehicles transport service equipment.

13.1.4 Oil equipment, including:
- 13.1.4.1 Field oil equipment.
- 13.1.4.2 Military oil.

13.1.5 Camping equipment, including:
- 13.1.5.1 All types of military tents and camping heating and cooling equipment.
- 13.1.5.2 Field water extraction, purification, storage, sub-package, and desalination equipment.
- 13.1.5.3 Field generator sets and power supply networks.

13.1.6 Warehouse equipment, including:
- 13.1.6.1 Field material loading and unloading machinery.
- 13.1.6.2 Automated equipment for field warehouse material management.

13.1.7 Automated equipment for logistics command and management, including:
- 13.1.7.1 Field logistics command and operation equipment.
- 13.1.7.2 Military logistics information, graphics, sound and image, data transmission, management (handling) equipment, software and technology.

13.1.8 Navy special logistics equipment, including:
- 13.1.8.1 Naval ship replenishment equipment and devices.
- 13.1.8.2 Shipboard helicopter replenishment equipment and devices.
- 13.1.8.3 Maritime casualty search and rescue equipment and devices.
- 13.1.8.4 Coastal motorized security equipment and devices.
- 13.1.8.5 Naval special oil detection equipment.

13.1.9 Air force special logistics equipment, including:
- 13.1.9.1 Aviation fuel storage, transportation, refueling, testing equipment and facility, field airfield fuel supply systems.
- 13.1.9.2 Airport rapid opening, bomb disposal, repair, maintenance equipment and devices, airport road sweeping devices, airport positions and logistics facilities camouflage protection equipment and materials.
- 13.1.9.3 Training clothes, work clothes and food specially for aircrew, ground crew, and paratroopers.
- 13.1.9.4 Runway rapid repair equipment and devices, field airport laydown equipment and devices.
- 13.1.9.5 Air transport, airdrop, bundled equipment for fuel and supplies.
- 13.1.9.6 Special equipment and devices for military aviation medicine.

13.1.10 Missile forces special logistics equipment and devices, including:
13.1.10.1 Logistics support equipment for fixed positions and mobile launch positions of missile tunnels.
13.1.10.2 Other missile forces special logistics equipment.

13.2 Auxiliary military equipment, including:

13.2.1 Military photography, stereo mapping, and measurement equipment.
13.2.2 Military self-contained diving equipment and underwater breathing equipment.
13.2.3 Military energy conversion devices.

13.3 Parts, components, auxiliary accessories, attachments, fittings, spare parts, semi-finished products, and samples for all products listed in Sects. 13.1 to 13.2.
13.4 Technology, technique, equipment, technical data (including software), services directly related to the development, production, testing, trial, inspection, use, maintenance, measurement and calibration, upgrading for all products listed in Sects. 13.1 to 13.3, and special raw materials and auxiliary materials for the production for all products listed in Category 13.

Category Fourteen: Other products

14.1 All other products not explicitly included in this List with practical military applications and specifically designed or modified for military purposes. Whether any of these products should be included in Category 14 shall be determined by competent authorities.
14.2 Parts, components, auxiliary accessories, attachments, fittings, spare parts, semi-finished products, and samples for all products listed in Category 14.
14.3 Technology, technique, equipment, technical data (including software), services directly related to the development, production, testing, trial, inspection, use, maintenance, measurement and calibration, upgrading for all products listed in Category 14, and special raw materials and auxiliary materials for the production for all products listed in Category 14.

4.3 Commentary on the Military Item List of China

The Military Item List of China is a bit hysteretic since it has not been updated for over 20 years since its formulation. The Technical notes or parameters of this List are not sufficient enough in some cases for EBOs to determine whether an item falls within the scope of military items. Meanwhile, compared with Dual-use Consolidated Catalogue, items under Military Item List are not equipped with tariff codes for reference.

Furthermore, Category 13 ***Logistic equipment, materiel, and other auxiliary military equipment*** enumerates logistic equipment, materiel, and other auxiliary equipment, some of which are relatively common in the commercial world but identified as military items according to this List. For instance, bulletproof helmets with higher safety performance may just look like ordinary safety helmets. However, they are clearly defined as "protective equipment" under Category 13.1.1.2 (B) of the List, according to an administrative punishment decision made by Tianjin Xingang Customs.[34] In addition, camouflage clothing is another type of products that is common in daily life but is likely to be identified as military products.[35]

4.4 License Application Procedures

4.4.1 Military Export Business Privilege and Business Scope

Only State-owned military enterprises or enterprises designated by competent authorities without records of export violations or tainted reputation during the last three years are entitled to submit documents titled "*Request on granting the military export business operation right to the company [XXX]*" to the SASTIND, and the Equipment Development Department.

The application documents shall normally contain a detailed description of the overall enterprise situation, the necessity of applying for military export business operation right, the supply channels of weapons and equipment, future development plans, international marketing system construction, and after-sales service guarantee system construction and so forth.

SASTIND and the Equipment Development Department are required to decide within 20 working days and deliver the decision within 10 working days.[36]

4.4.2 Approval of the Military Export Proposal

Military-industrial groups, provincial offices (including autonomous regions and municipalities directly under the Central Government) for national defense science and technology, or other departments designated by competent authorities are requested to submit documents titled "*Request of company [XXX] on the export proposal of products [XXX]*".

---

[34] Jin Xin Gang Guan Ji Cha/Wei Zi [2022]0175, 津新港关缉查/违字〔2022〕0175号, 21 December 2022.

[35] Peng Guan Ji Kuai Wei Zi [2023]1, 鹏关缉快违字〔2023〕1号, 25 April 2023.

[36] SASTIND. (18 July 2022). Military Export License—Right to Operate and Scope of Operation. Retrieved 1 September 2023 from http://www.sastind.gov.cn/n6195634/n6195706/n6195716/n6427863/n6428033/c6429000/content.html.

The application documents shall contain a brief description of the proposed project product, the background and capability of the research and development unit, system compositions, main functions and uses, main features and advantages, and market prospects. Appendixes submitted together include (i) a comprehensive illustration report, (ii) an overall technical plan, and (iii) expert opinions.

SASTIND and the Equipment Development Department are required to decide within 45 working days. The period may extend to 60 working days for significant and sensitive military items. For projects that have an important impact on national diplomatic and military security, an extra opinion of the Ministry of Foreign Affairs and the relevant departments of the Joint Staff Department of the Military Commission is required. The final decision shall be delivered to the applicant within 5 working days.[37]

4.4.3 Approval of a Specific Military Export Project

For a specific military export project (which means the export project proposal has been approved already), EBOs of military products are required to submit documents titled "*Request on exporting military products [XXX] to country [XXX]*" to SASTIND for a comprehensive examination.

Generally, the application documents shall include the name, model, and quantity of the military products to be exported, the destination country or region, and the expected amount of the transaction, accompanied by the approval documents of the export project proposal (or provide the export project proposal approval number).

SASTIND is required to make a decision within 15 working days and deliver the decision within 5 working days.[38]

4.4.4 Approval of the Military Export Contract

EBOs of military products are also required to submit documents titled "*Request on the approval of CONTRACT on exporting military products [XXX] to country [XXX]*" to the SASTIND for review.

---

[37] SASTIND. (18 July 2022). Military Export License—Project Proposal Approval. Retrieved 1 September 2023 from
http://www.sastind.gov.cn/n6195634/n6195706/n6195716/n6427863/n6428038/c6429028/content.html.

[38] SASTIND. (18 July 2022). Military Export License—Project Approval. Retrieved 1 September 2023 from
http://www.sastind.gov.cn/n6195634/n6195706/n6195716/n6427863/n6428043/c6429055/content.html.

The contract is supposed to include contract signing time, parties to the contract, contract number, the name, model, unit price, and quantity of the military products to be exported, the destination country or region, the expected amount of the transaction, domestic supplier of the products, time of delivery, port of delivery, mode of transport, and mode of payment. Other documents include an extra copy of the contract, end-use or end-user certification, the approval documents of the export project initiation.

SASTIND is required to decide within 20 working days after receiving the contract and deliver the decision within 5 working days.[39]

4.5 Format of Military Export License

The format of Military Export License is provided as follows for your reference.

Military Export License of the People's Republic of China

No̲ ()

[39] SASTIND. (18 July 2022). Military Export License—Contract Approval. Retrieved 1 September 2023 from

http://www.sastind.gov.cn/n6195634/n6195706/n6195716/n6427863/n6428048/c6429085/content.html.

1. Exporter		3. License no.		
2. Consignor		4. License expiry date		
5. Contract no.		8. Country/region of import		
6. Port of delivery		9. Mode of shipment		
7. Port of clearance		10. Value of the goods		
11. No.	12. Description & mode of the goods	13. Unit	14. Quantity	15. Supplementary details
(1)				
(2)				
16. Total				
17. Supplementary details		18. Issuing authority's stamp and signature 19. License date		

Chapter 5
Certain Unilateral Export Controls: Non-dual Use Goods and Technologies

This chapter discusses unilateral export controls of China on non-dual use goods and technologies. Section 5.1 explores the policy considerations behind such export controls. Sections 5.2 and 5.3 outline the specific export control measures upon such goods and technologies, including the legal framework and control mechanism, controlled items, license application procedures, and special issues under ECL.

5.1 Policy Considerations

5.1.1 Overview

We have analyzed export controls over dual-use, nuclear, and military items. However, the items subject to export control are not limited to such typical items. Under ECL, export controls can also be extended to those goods, technologies, and services if relevant to the maintenance of national security and interests.[1] Apart from the catalogues we have discussed, China does maintain separate restrictive or prohibitive export control lists over certain goods and technologies, which may be based on national security considerations. If there is a violation of such restrictive or prohibitive lists, there may be consequences under ECL. Under this book, we term such restrictive or prohibitive export controls as "Certain Unilateral Controls" or "CUC", which is distinct from the unilateral export controls over dual-use, nuclear, or military items.

[1] Article 2 of the ECL.

D. Zhao, *Contemporary Export Control Law of China*, Modern China and International Economic Law, https://doi.org/10.1007/978-981-99-9825-8_5

Legislatively, the Certain Unilateral Controls are empowered by Chapter 3 of the Foreign Trade Law. For one of the following reasons, China may restrict or prohibit the export of goods or technologies[2]:

(i) national security, public interest, or public ethics;
(ii) protecting the health or safety of the people, life or health of animals and plants, and the ecological environment;
(iii) implementing the measures on the import and export of gold or silver;
(iv) shortage of supplies or as important natural resources that are in danger of depletion within China;
(v) the limited market in the importing countries or regions;
(vi) severe disruption in the export order;
(vii) reasons in accordance with domestic laws and administrative rules; and
(viii) restriction or ban of import and export by international treaties or agreements.

With introduction of ECL, Certain Unilateral Controls can also be governed by ECL if the controls are based on national security reasons.

China may specify the policy considerations for a given control under CUC. Some goods prohibitive of export are given a reason for commitments under certain international conventions concerning environmental protection and human health.[3] Under such circumstances, such CUC may be still relevant to ECL as it is based on considerations covered by the grand concept of national security and interest. In some other instances, technologies restrictive of export have been controlled based on considerations of maintaining national economic security.[4] In such a case, it is obviously an issue of control under ECL as national economic security is a part of the concept of national security.

If a given CUC does not specify the control reasons, a legal analysis or enquiry to the competent authority may be desirable to understand whether it is governed by ECL.

---

[2] Article 15 of the Foreign Trade Law.

[3] For example, the 3rd round of Catalogues of Goods Prohibited from Export was promulgated in 2005 to fulfill the international obligations under the Rotterdam Convention on the Prior Informed Consent Procedure for Certain Hazardous Chemicals and Pesticides in International Trade and the Stockholm Convention on Persistent Organic Pollutants. The 6th round of Catalogues of Goods Prohibited from Export was promulgated in 2020 to fulfill the international obligations under the Stockholm Convention on Persistent Organic Pollutants and the Minamata Convention on Mercury.

[4] MOFCOM. (2020, August 31). *The Official of the Department of Trade in Services Answers Reporters' Questions on the Release of the Updated Catalogue of Technologies Prohibited or Restricted from Export by China.* China Trade Remedies Information. Retrieved 20 October 2023, from http://cacs.mofcom.gov.cn/article/gnwjmdt/gn/202008/165955.html.

5.1.2 Concept of National Security and Interest

Understandably, a definition of "national security and interests" under Chinese law is far-reaching and ambiguous, leaving a discretionary power upon the Chinese government to determine whether there is an issue of national security and interest or whether an endangerment of such national security or interest may occur or has occurred under given circumstances.

Under Chinese law, "national security" refers to a *state of condition* in which the State power, sovereignty, unity and territorial integrity, people's well-being, sustainable economic or social development, or other significant national interests are *relatively free* from danger and internal and external threats, as well as *the State's ability to safeguard the continuous security.*[5] Honestly, the ordinary person or entity is not capable of such an affirmation that the State is "relatively free from danger and internal and external threats", or whether such "State's ability to safeguard the continuous security" may exist in practice. Such a person with such capability cannot be anyone but the government of a certain level.

The author suggests that the concept of national security or interest is to be clarified so that the business community can easily see the boundaries in which they behave themselves. Otherwise, they do have no idea as to how they can behave, with an anxiety of violations deemed by the government. Upon pondering over such clarification, one must first ask himself/herself a few questions: why a conception of national security is imposed in this context? What specific national security risks may ensue even when all the other laws and regulations are observed by the given individual or entity? If there is indeed a specific security issue, the author suggests the concept of national security as far as export control and other relevant laws are concerned is confined to such specific issue only, leaving other violations to be conditional upon prior notice of risks from the relevant authority of the Chinese government.

For the business community, it is worth noting that violation of CUC may simultaneously incur liabilities and consequences under ECL. Apart from this, the goods and technologies as controlled under CUC may be subject to control lists and licensing and control procedures separate from those of ECL or regulations under ECL, which is further elaborated in the following sections.

[5] Article 2 of the National Security Law.

5.2 Certain Unilateral Controls on Goods

5.2.1 Legal Framework and Control Mechanism

Apart from the Foreign Trade Law, CUC on goods are governed by the Administrative Regulations of the People's Republic of China on the Import and Export of Goods ("RIEG") and the Administrative Measures for Export Licenses for Goods ("MELG"). RIEG came into force on 1 January 2002, which regulates the control mechanism for CUC on goods. MELG prescribes the licensing procedures and requirements, which are different from the licensing procedures for dual-use, nuclear, and military items under ECL.

5.2.1.1 CUC Controls of Goods

RIEG classifies goods into three categories for regulatory purposes: goods that are free to export, restricted from export or prohibited from export.[6] The Foreign Trade Law and other laws or regulations[7] are the legal basis for restricting or prohibiting certain goods from export. Goods are restricted from export in two ways: where there are quantitative limits set by the State on goods restricted from export, the goods shall be subject to quota control, and other goods restricted from export shall be subject to license control.[8]

5.2.1.2 Control Lists and Other Control Measures

The goods restrictive or prohibitive of export under a CUC measure are specified on special lists. For goods that are restricted from export, China releases the Catalogue of Goods Subject to Export Licensing every year as a general practice, specifying the goods subject to quota control or license control.[9] For goods that are prohibited from export, China publishes the Catalogue of Goods Prohibited from Export. As of March 2023, China has released different goods for seven times which are prohibitive

[6] Article 4 of the Administrative Regulations of the People's Republic of China on the Import and Export of Goods.

[7] Article 33 and 35 of the Administrative Regulations of the People's Republic of China on the Import and Export of Goods. Regarding laws and regulations other than the Foreign Trade Law that regulates the export control of goods, for example, the Administrative Regulation on the Ozone Depleting Substances stipulates that China may restrict or prohibit the export of ozone depleting substances.

[8] Article 36 of the Administrative Regulations of the People's Republic of China on the Import and Export of Goods.

[9] For example, on 30 December 2022, the MOFCOM and the General Customs of the PRC published the Catalogue of Goods subject to Export Licensing (2023), which came into force on 1 January 2023, and has replaced the Catalogue of Goods subject to Export Licensing (2022).

of export, which means that no export of the enlisted goods is permissible in any case.

Goods not listed in such catalogues may be controlled under special circumstances. After approved by the State Council, the department in charge of foreign trade may provisionally restrict or prohibit the export of specific goods that are not listed in the aforementioned catalogues.[10]

RIEG also regulates the export business of the exporters. According to Chapter 4 of RIEG, China may require that the export of certain goods to be subject to State monopoly or monopolistic privilege. The foreign trade department formulates and publishes the list of such goods as well as the list of enterprises qualified to conduct such privileged business.[11]

5.2.1.3 Export Licenses for Goods

To export the goods on the restrictive lists (as elaborated below), whether the goods are subject to a quota or license, the exporter shall apply for an export license which is not a Dual-use Export License.[12]

Export licenses have different categories in practice, which are respectively classified as *one license for one given customs, for one particular batch of goods* or *for multiple batches* of the same goods. All export licenses are permissible to be used within their terms of validity. If a license is issued (a) for one given customs, the export license can only be used once with the given customs; or (b) for one particular batch of goods, the export license can only be used once for the particular shipment of goods with any customs; or (c) as "non-one-batch license", it can be used for multiple times but no more than 12 times.[13] Such license requirements are specified on the Catalogue of Goods subject to Export Licensing which may be revised from time to time.[14]

An export license will be valid for 6 months and in any case the expiration date shall not be later than December 31 of the year of issuance. MOFCOM may revise the terms of validity of export licenses for some goods under some special circumstances. Export licenses are supposed to be used within their terms of validity. Where a

[10] Article 18 of the Foreign Trade Law and Article 57–58 of the Administrative Regulations of the People's Republic of China on the Import and Export of Goods.

[11] Chapter 4 of the Administrative Regulations of the People's Republic of China on the Import and Export of Goods.

[12] Article 6 of the Administrative Measures for Export Licenses for Goods.

[13] Article 22 of the Administrative Measures for Export Licenses for Goods.

[14] In the Catalogue of Goods subject to Export Licensing (2023), the following goods are subject to "non-one-batch license": wheat, corn, rice, wheat flour, corn flour, rice flour, live cattle, live pigs, live chickens, beef, pork, chicken, crude oil, refined oil, coal, motorbikes (including all-terrain vehicles) and their engines and frames, automobiles (including complete sets of spare parts) and their chassis (new vehicles only), export goods under processing trade, export goods under compensatory trade. For one particular batch of the following goods, the export license can only be used once for the particular shipment of goods: ozone depleting substances and automobiles (second-hand).

license is used beyond expiration, the customs will not approve the release of the goods for export.[15] For goods subject to quota control, the export quota is valid before December 31 of the year of issuance unless otherwise indicated. The exporter shall additionally apply before the year-end for the export license within the term of validity of the quota.[16]

5.2.1.4 Customs Clearance

The exporters shall present the export license to the customs offices for export declaration and clearance with the customs.[17] As required by the Customs Law, in the absence of an export license, goods whose export is restricted by the State shall not be released.[18] If such goods are fraudulently exported without a license, there will likely be a criminal consequence of smuggling of goods "prohibitive of export". A good if restrictive of export would become prohibitive of export if no export license was obtained.

5.2.1.5 Legal Liabilities

According to the Criminal Law of China, RIEG, the Customs Law, and the Implementing Regulations of the Customs of China on Administrative Penalties, exporting goods restricted or prohibited from export may incur criminal liabilities or administrative liabilities which are summarized in the following table.

Violations	Criminal Liability	Administrative Liability[19]
Exporting goods that are prohibited from export[20]	Criminal liability imposed according to the provisions on the crime of smuggling under the PRC Criminal Law	• Order to transport the goods back to China and impose a fine of no more than RMB 1 million[21]

(continued)

[15] Article 30 of the Administrative Measures for Export Licenses for Goods.

[16] Article 28 of the Administrative Measures for Export Licenses for Goods.

[17] Article 41 and 43 of the Administrative Regulations of the People's Republic of China on the Import and Export of Goods.

[18] Article 24(1) of the Customs Law.

[19] The penalties stipulated in the Administrative Regulations of the People's Republic of China on the Import and Export of Goods also include suspending and even revoking the foreign trade business license. However, the registration requirement for foreign trade operators has been abolished. The 38th session of the Standing Committee of the Thirteenth National People's Congress of China on 30 December 2022 decided to delete Article 9 of the Foreign Trade Law of the PRC, and the foreign trade operators engaging in import and export of goods or technologies no longer need to make the registration.

[20] Article 64 of the Administrative Regulations of the People's Republic of China on the Import and Export of Goods.

[21] Articles 13 of the Implementing Regulations of the Customs of the PRC on Administrative Penalties.

(continued)

Violations	Criminal Liability	Administrative Liability
		• If the violations constitute smuggling,[22] confiscate any smuggled goods and illegal income, and a fine of no more than RMB 1 million can be imposed[23]
Exporting goods that are restricted from export without an approval[24]		• Not release the goods and impose a fine of no more than 30% of the goods' value[25] • If the violations constitute smuggling, confiscate any smuggled goods and illegal income, and a fine of no more than the goods' value can be imposed[26]

(continued)

[22] According to Article 82 of the Customs Law, exporting goods that are prohibited or restricted from export may constitute smuggling. In China, the smuggling with severe circumstances (for example, evading a relatively large amount of tax payable) constitutes a crime while others do not. The Customs Law and the Implementing Regulations of the Customs of the PRC on Administrative Penalties stipulate administrative liabilities for smugglings that do not constitute a crime.

Article 82 of the Customs Law: Any of the following acts of evasion of Customs control, Customs duties, and State import and export prohibited or restricted control in violation of this Law and other related laws and administrative regulations shall constitute an act of smuggling:

1. transporting, carrying, or sending by post into or out of the territory goods and Articles which are prohibited or restricted by the State from being imported or exported, or which are dutiable;
2. the sale in the territory of China of any bonded goods imported by special permission or listed for special duty reduction or exemption, as well as other goods, Articles, or overseas means of transport entering the territory without approval of the Customs, payment of Customs duties, or presentation of the requisite certificates;
3. any other act of evasion of Customs control which constitutes smuggling.

For any act listed in the above clauses which does not constitute a crime, the Customs shall confiscate any smuggled goods and Articles and illegal income and impose a fine. Goods, Articles, and means of transport involved in smuggling on multiple occasions shall also be confiscated. Specially made equipment used to conceal smuggled goods shall be destroyed or confiscated.

Any act in the above clauses which constitutes a crime shall be punishable with criminal charges.

[23] Articles 9 of the Implementing Regulations of the Customs of the PRC on Administrative Penalties.

[24] Article 64 of the Administrative Regulations of the People's Republic of China on the Import and Export of Goods.

26

[25] Articles 14 of the Implementing Regulations of the Customs of the PRC on Administrative Penalties.

[26] Articles 9 of the Implementing Regulations of the Customs of the PRC on Administrative Penalties.

(continued)

Violations	Criminal Liability	Administrative Liability
Exporting goods that are restricted from export beyond the scopes approved or permitted[27]	Criminal liability imposed according to the provisions on the crime of smuggling or the crime of illegal operation under the PRC Criminal Law	
Counterfeiting, altering, buying, or selling certificates of export quota, approval documents or licenses[28]	Criminal liability imposed according to the provisions on the crime of illegal business operation or the crime of counterfeiting, altering, buying, or selling official documents, certificates, seals of State organs under the PRC Criminal Law	• The certificates of export quota, approval documents or licenses acquired by deception or other unfair means shall be taken back[29] • Any illegal income shall be confiscated and a fine shall be imposed[30]

5.2.2 Lists of Goods Prohibitive or Restrictive of Export

5.2.2.1 The Catalogue of Goods Prohibited from Export

As of March 2023, China has released for seven rounds of prohibitive controls in terms of the Catalogue of Goods Prohibited from Export. The Catalogue includes the tariff code and commodity name of the goods prohibited from export. For some of the goods, there are also annotations functioning as clarification of the controlled

[27] Article 65 of the Administrative Regulations of the People's Republic of China on the Import and Export of Goods.

[28] Article 66 of the Administrative Regulations of the People's Republic of China on the Import and Export of Goods.

[29] Article 67 of the Administrative Regulations of the People's Republic of China on the Import and Export of Goods.

[30] Article 84 of the Customs Law. The Customs Law does not specify the exact amount of the fine.

goods with illustrations[31] or parameters.[32] The Catalogue of Goods Prohibited from Export[33] is summarized in the following table.

Rounds	Effective date	Legal basis	Prohibitive goods	Note
1st	December 20, 2001	Foreign Trade Law RIEG	Certain tiger bones, certain rhinoceros horns, certain logs, certain platinum, and so forth	The export of certain platinum by way of processing trade is not prohibited
2nd	October 1, 2004		Charcoal made from wood other than bamboo	
3rd	January 1, 2006	International conventions[34] Foreign Trade Law RIEG	Crocidolite, dioxin and other hazardous chemicals, pesticides, and pollutants	The catalogue was issued to protect human health, maintain environmental safety, and eliminate outdated products

(continued)

[31] For example, in the Catalogue of Goods Prohibited from Export (5th round), "forest litter that is not chemically treated" with the HS code of 3101001910 is prohibited from export, and there is a comment box enumerating that the "forest litter that is not chemically treated" includes decaying leaves, decaying roots, barks, leaves, roots, and other forest litter.

[32] For example, in the Catalogue of Goods Prohibited from Export (6th round), "fuel cells containing mercury" with the HS code of 8506800091 are prohibited from export, and there is a comment box with specific parameters qualifying the goods subject to control: the mercury content $\geq$0.0001% of the weight of the cell and the mercury content of the button cell $\geq$0.0005% of the weight of the cell.

[33] For detailed descriptions of the goods, please refer to the Catalogue on the following websites. Retrieved October 24, 2023, from: (1) 1st round of control: http://www.mofcom.gov.cn/zfxxgk/article/gkml/202104/20210403055952.shtml; (2) 2nd round of control: http://www.mofcom.gov.cn/article/b/e/200409/20040900279399.shtml; (3) 3rd round of control: http://www.mofcom.gov.cn/article/b/g/200602/20060201575919.shtml; (4) 4th round of control: http://www.mofcom.gov.cn/article/b/c/200604/20060401872048.shtml; (5) 5th round of control: http://www.mofcom.gov.cn/article/b/c/200812/20081205948343.shtml; (6) 6th round of control: http://www.mofcom.gov.cn/article/b/c/202012/20201203027805.shtml; and (7) 7th round of control: http://www.mofcom.gov.cn/article/zwgk/gkzcfb/202306/20230603414825.shtml.

[34] The Rotterdam Convention on the Prior Informed Consent Procedure for Certain Hazardous Chemicals and Pesticides in International Trade and the Stockholm Convention on Persistent Organic Pollutants.

(continued)

Rounds	Effective date	Legal basis	Prohibitive goods	Note
4th	May 1, 2006	Foreign Trade Law RIEG	Silica sand, quartz sand, and other natural sand	
5th	January 1, 2009		Forest litter that is or is not chemically treated; peat (grass peat)	
6th	January 1, 2021	International conventions[35] Foreign Trade Law RIEG	Certain insecticides and other chemicals; certain batteries, switches, cosmetics and other products containing mercury, certain fluorescent lamps, and so forth	
7th	June 6, 2023	International convention[36] Foreign Trade Law Drug Administration Law RIEG	Hexachlorobutadiene; pentachlorophenol and its salts and esters; dicofol; perfluorohexane sulfonic acid, its salts and its related compounds; certain polychlorinated naphthalenes; hexabromocyclododecane	The catalogue was issued to protect human health and safety and protect the environment

The policy considerations behind the Catalogue are mainly protecting the environment and human health as well as conserving crucial natural resources of China, which is in conformity with Chapter 3 of the Foreign Trade Law, and difficult to be insulated from the conception of national security. Some goods are prohibited from export due to international conventions related to environmental protection. Most goods in the catalogues are animal and plant products, hazardous chemicals, and mineral resources.

5.2.2.2 Non-list-Based Prohibitive Export Controls

Please note that some goods may be prohibited from export under other laws and regulations of China, but such goods are not so listed in any catalogue. What follows are some examples of such non-list-based prohibitive export controls as of March 2023.

[35] The Stockholm Convention on Persistent Organic Pollutants and the Minamata Convention on Mercury.

[36] The Stockholm Convention on Persistent Organic Pollutants.

Non-list-based prohibitive export controls	Legal basis
State-owned and valuable non-state-owned cultural relics	PRC Cultural Relics Protection Law
Any endangered wild animals and plants as well as the product thereof, whose export is prohibited by the Convention on International Trade in Endangered Species of Wild Fauna and Flora (the "CITES") for any purpose of commercial trade	1. Regulation on the Administration of the Import and Export of Endangered Wild Animals and Plants 2. CITES
Raw plasma	Regulations on the Administration of Blood Products
Printed matter, audio, and video products containing messages including but not limited to State secrets, opposing the fundamental constitution principles, defaming the Chinese government, disturbing social order	Measures of the Customs for the Supervision and Administration of printed matter, audio, and video products entering and leaving the territory of China
Goods infringing intellectual property rights	Regulations on Customs Protection of Intellectual Property Rights

The goods as described above are prohibited from export for purposes of safeguarding national security and interests, fulfilling international obligations, and so forth. The exporters in China must consult the most updated laws and regulations of China to see if the goods in question not listed are prohibitive of export.

5.2.2.3 Catalogue of Goods Subject to Export License

If goods are subject to license for export from China, such goods fall into the scope of goods restrictive of export. The Catalogue of Goods Subject to Export License is normally updated annually[37] and released in December for implementation in the next year. The latest catalogue, the Catalogue of Goods Subject to Export License (2023) ("ELC") was published on 30 December 2022 and is effective since 1 January 2023. This Catalogue includes the tariff code, commodity type, and commodity name of the goods that are subject to export license. Each commodity type includes several specific commodities.

ELC is summarized as follows.[38]

[37] Article 3 of the Administrative Measures for Export Licenses for Goods.

[38] For all the goods or their detailed descriptions, please refer to the website. Retrieved 24 October 2023 from http://images.mofcom.gov.cn/wms/202212/20221230211147281.pdf.

Summary of Catalogue of Goods Subject to Export License (2023)		
No	Description	Note
1	Live cattle	For exports to Hong Kong and Macao, the certificates of export quota shall be provided when applying for the export license
2	Live pig	
3	Live chicken	For exports to Hong Kong, the certificates of export quota shall be provided when applying for the export license
4	Beef	
5	Pork	
6	Chicken	
7	Wheat	The certificates of export quota shall be provided when applying for the export license
8	Corn	
9	Rice	
10	Flour	
11	Corn flour	
12	Rice flour	
13	Ephedra used as medicinal materials (artificial cultivation)	
14	Licorice and licorice products	
15	Mat rush and mat rush products	
16	Natural sand	
17	Alumina	
18	Phosphate ore	
19	Magnesia	
20	Talc blocks (powder)	
21	Fluorite (fluorspar)	
22	Rare earths	
23	Tin and tin products	
24	Tungsten and tungsten products	
25	Molybdenum and molybdenum products	
26	Antimony and antimony products	
27	Coal	The certificates of export quota shall be provided when applying for the export license
28	Coke	
29	Crude oil	The certificates of export quota shall be provided when applying for the export license

(continued)

(continued)

Summary of Catalogue of Goods Subject to Export License (2023)

No	Description	Note
30	Refined oil	The certificates of export quota shall be provided when applying for the export license (excluding lubricating oil, grease, and lubricating base oil)
31	Paraffin wax	
32	Certain metals and metal products	
33	Disodium sulfate	
34	Silicon carbide	
35	Ozone depleting substances	
36	Citric acid	
37	Sawn timber	The certificates of export quota shall be provided when applying for the export license
38	Cotton	
39	Silver	
40	Platinum	
41	Indium and indium products	
42	Motorcycles (including all-terrain vehicles) and their engines and frames	
43	Automobiles (including complete knock-down kits) and their chassis	

In the annotations to ELC, the tariff codes are stated for reference only, and the license control is based on the type and name of the goods.

5.2.3 *Licensing Procedures*

5.2.3.1 Application and Approval of Export Quota for Goods

As is illustrated above, some goods restricted from export are subject to quota control, and the certificates of export quota shall be provided when applying for the export license. Currently, 17 types of goods are subject to quota control as is specified in the table in Sect. 5.2.2.3. The certificates of export quota of wheat, corn, rice, coal, and cotton are issued by the National Development and Reform Commission ("NDRC") while MOFCOM issues export quota certificates for other goods.[39]

To apply for the certificate of export quota, the exporter applicant shall submit an export quota application and its business license. Besides, the applicant must

[39] Approval of the Quotas of Goods Restricted from Export. Retrieved 24 October 2023 from http://egov.mofcom.gov.cn/xzxksx/18014/.

ascertain that all other export requirements are satisfied when applying for the quota. If a manufacturer would like to apply for the export quota of wheat flour, it shall meet the following requirements, including but not limited to obtaining the Export Food Hygiene License and other licenses or approval, maintaining advanced production processes, reaching the minimum export amount and production amount of the wheat flour.[40]

The annual overall national export quota for the next year is announced no later than October 31 of each year. The applicant shall apply for the quota of the next year between November 1 and 15 of each year. After receiving applications for export quota, NDRC or MOFCOM is required to decide whether to grant the export quota within 30 days and no later than December 15 of the current year.[41]

5.2.3.2 Application and Approval of Export License for Goods

MOFCOM is the authority to administer the application and approval of export licenses for goods. However, MOFCOM only accepts and reviews applications for export licenses for some types of goods, currently including wheat, corn, coal, crude oil, refined oil (excluding lubricating oil, grease, and lubricating base oil), cotton, and so forth.[42] Such goods may change when the catalogue is updated, or the official approval guideline of export licenses issued by MOFCOM is revised. The application of export licenses for other commodities restricted from export is handled by the provincial department in charge of commerce.

To apply for an export license for goods, the exporter applicant shall submit the application, its business license, export contract, and other documents if required, which depend on the specific requirements according to different types of goods. For example, to apply for the export license for automobiles, the exporter must submit the overall construction of the overseas after-sale service network; to apply for the export license for wheat and other goods subject to quota control, the exporter must submit the approved certificates of export quota.

[40] MOFCOM. (2008, January 19). 2008 Grain-based Flour Export Quota Application Requirements and Declaration Procedures. Retrieved 24 October 2023 from http://www.mofcom.gov.cn/aarticle/b/e/200801/20080105345729.html.

[41] Article 38 of the Administrative Regulations of the People's Republic of China on the Import and Export of Goods.

[42] License Approval for Goods Restricted from Export. Retrieved October 24, 2023, from http://egov.mofcom.gov.cn/xzxksx/18008/.

The authority shall issue the export license within 3 working days as of the receipt of the applications that meet the requirements, according to the Administrative Measures for Export Licenses for Goods.[43] However, in practice, as stated in the latest official approval guideline of export licenses issued by MOFCOM,[44] after accepting the application, MOFCOM will complete its review process and decide on whether to grant the export license within 30 working days from the date of acceptance; in addition, the time required to consult relevant departments or industries will not count in running the time limit. Practically it may take more than 30 working days to issue an export license.

The export license can be either a paper certificate or an electronic certificate, both of which have the same legal effect.[45]

The format of export license for goods restricted from export is illustrated below.

Export License of the People's Republic of China

No. ()

[43] Article 19 of the Administrative Measures for Export Licenses for Goods.

[44] The official approval guideline, named "License Approval for Goods Restricted from Export", was last revised in 2022, which may be further revised in 2023 according to the Catalogue of Goods subject to Export Licensing (2023).

[45] Article 3 of the Work Specifications for the Application, Issuance and Use of Export Licenses.

<table>
<tr><td colspan="3">1. Exporter</td><td colspan="3">3. Export license No.</td></tr>
<tr><td colspan="3">2. Consignor</td><td colspan="3">4. Export license expiry date</td></tr>
<tr><td colspan="3">5. Terms of trade</td><td colspan="3">8. Country/Region of purchase</td></tr>
<tr><td colspan="3">6. Contract No.</td><td colspan="3">9. Payment</td></tr>
<tr><td colspan="3">7. Place of clearance</td><td colspan="3">10. Mode of transport</td></tr>
<tr><td colspan="3">11. Description of goods</td><td colspan="3">Code of goods</td></tr>
<tr><td>12. Specification</td><td>13. Unit</td><td>14. Quantity</td><td>15. Unit Price</td><td>16. Amount</td><td>17. Amount in USD</td></tr>
<tr><td>1</td><td></td><td></td><td></td><td></td><td></td></tr>
<tr><td>2</td><td></td><td></td><td></td><td></td><td></td></tr>
<tr><td></td><td></td><td></td><td></td><td></td><td></td></tr>
<tr><td></td><td></td><td></td><td></td><td></td><td></td></tr>
<tr><td></td><td></td><td></td><td></td><td></td><td></td></tr>
<tr><td></td><td></td><td></td><td></td><td></td><td></td></tr>
<tr><td></td><td></td><td></td><td></td><td></td><td></td></tr>
<tr><td></td><td></td><td></td><td></td><td></td><td></td></tr>
<tr><td>18. Total</td><td></td><td></td><td></td><td></td><td></td></tr>
<tr><td colspan="2">19. Supplementary details</td><td></td><td colspan="3">20. Issuing authority's stamp & signature

21. License date</td></tr>
</table>

5.2.4 *Issues Under China Export Control Law*

On the ELC there are some dual-use goods. In such case, a dual-use Export License would suffice.

For the goods that are restricted from export and are only listed in the ELC, the export of such goods may also trigger severe penalties under ECL if such goods endanger national security, or may be used for WMD-related or terrorist purposes.

5.3 Certain Unilateral Controls on Technologies

5.3.1 Legal Framework and Control Mechanism

Certain Unilateral Controls on technologies are based on the Administrative Regulations of China on Technology Import and Export ("TIER") and the Measures for Administration of Technologies Prohibited or Restricted to be Exported ("TPREM").

TIER was first introduced in 2001, with subsequent revisions in 2011, 2019, and 2020, which has been the framework of technology export and import control. TPREM focuses on licensing issues and procedures relevant to the Technology Export License.

5.3.1.1 Meaning of Technology Export

TIER defines "technology export" as transferring technology from any location inside China to outside of China by way of trade, investment, or economic and technical cooperation, including assignment of patent or patent application, patent licensing, assignment of technical know-how, technical service, and other means of technology transfer.[46] The definition is broad enough to cover any outbound transfer of technology, whether by trade or other means, which are all subject to CUC on technologies.

However, it seems from the definition of "technology export" that the re-export and retransfer of technologies originating in China is not subject to the CUC scheme, nor the concept of "deemed export" under ECL can be triggered in CUC scheme on technologies, which deemed export refers to the provision of technologies to foreign entities within or outside the territory of China.

Please note that the export of certain technologies may involve cross-border data transfer if the related data are exported as well. The export of such technologies may be subject to the administration of cross-border data regulations under Chinese law.

5.3.1.2 Categories of Technologies

TIER classifies technologies into three categories subject to different export controls, which are free, restrictive, and prohibitive.[47]

(a) Free technologies: technology export contracts shall be filed with the commerce authority after execution of the same. Otherwise, the same technology is free from control.

---

[46] Article 2 of the Administrative Regulations of China on Technology Import and Export.

[47] Article 5, 29 and 30 of the Administrative Regulations of China on Technology Import and Export.

(b) Restrictive technologies: such technologies may not be exported from China without an export license issued by the commerce authority.
(c) Prohibitive technologies: such technologies may not be exported from China.

5.3.1.3 Filing Technology Export Contracts

The export contracts of free technologies need to be registered online, and an application, copy of the contract (with translation in Chinese), and documents showing the legal standing of the contracting parties shall be submitted as well. MOFCOM will then verify these documents and issue a registration certificate within 3 working days upon the receipt of complete documents.[48] Such export contract of free technologies can take effect from the time when the contract is entered into and the registration is not a condition for effectiveness of the contract.[49]

For restrictive technologies, the exporter is required to file an application for technology export to the competent commerce authority and obtain a letter of comfort to permit the technology export from such authority before any substantial negotiations can commence between the parties to the export transaction. After concluding such technology export contract, the exporter must still submit the contract to the commerce authority for its review and decision on whether to issue a Technology Export License. Such technology export contract cannot take any effect until the issuance of the Technology Export License.[50]

5.3.1.4 Export and Other Formalities

To handle formalities of foreign exchange, banking, tax, and customs, the exporter shall provide the Technology Export License or the registration certificate of the technology export contract, as the case may be.[51] If the technology export involves customs formalities (e.g., in the case of exporting technologies through a tangible medium), the exporter shall provide the Technology Export License when clearing such medium with the customs. The customs will check the Technology Export License before releasing the medium containing such technologies.[52]

[48] Article 8 of the Measures for the Administration of Registration of the Contracts for Import or export of Technologies.

[49] Article 36 of the Administrative Regulations of China on Technology Import and Export.

[50] Articles 11 and 14 of the Measures for Administration of Technologies Prohibited or Restricted to Be Exported.

[51] Article 39 of the Administrative Regulations of China on Technology Import and Export.

[52] Article 18 of the Measures for Administration of Technologies Prohibited or Restricted to Be Exported.

5.3.1.5 Legal Liabilities

Under TIER, penalties for violating the regulatory requirements for technologies prohibited or restricted from export are as follows[53]:

<table>
<tr><th>Violations</th><th>Criminal liability</th><th>Administrative liability[54]</th></tr>
<tr><td>Exporting technologies prohibited from export</td><td rowspan="2">Criminal liability imposed according to the provisions on the crimes of smuggling, illegal business operation, divulging State secrets, or others under the PRC Criminal Law</td><td rowspan="2">• Penalties imposed according to the Customs Law; or
• Penalties from the foreign trade authorities including issuing a warning, confiscating illegal income, and imposing a fine ranging from 1 to 5 times of the illegal income</td></tr>
<tr><td>Exporting technologies restricted from export without a license</td></tr>
<tr><td>Exporting technologies restricted from export beyond the scope of license</td><td>Criminal liability imposed according to the provisions on the crime of illegal business operation or other crimes under the PRC Criminal Law</td><td>• Penalties imposed according to the Customs Law; or
• Penalties from the foreign trade authorities including issuing a warning, confiscating illegal income, and imposing a fine ranging from 1 to 3 times of the illegal income</td></tr>
</table>

The Customs Law does not specify penalties for illegal export through intangible means (by way of emails and other instant communication platforms) of technologies prohibited or restricted from export. However, illegally exporting technologies through tangible media may incur legal liabilities under Customs Laws and regulations as well.

5.3.2 Catalogue of Technologies Prohibitive or Restrictive of Export

5.3.2.1 Overview

The Catalogue of Technologies Prohibitive or Restrictive of Export ("CUC Catalogue on Technologies") was first published in 2001, and it has been substantially revised in 2008 and 2020.

---

[53] Articles 43 and 44 of the Administrative Regulations of China on Technology Import and Export.

[54] The penalties stipulated in the Administrative Regulations of China on Technology Import and Export also include "suspending and even revoking the foreign trade business license". However, the registration requirement for foreign trade operators has been abolished. The 38th session of the Standing Committee of the Thirteenth National People's Congress of China on 30 December 2022 decided to delete Article 9 of the Foreign Trade Law of the PRC, and the foreign trade operators engaging in import and export of goods or technologies no longer need to make the registration.

Under the Catalogue, each technology, its name, and control points are specified. The control points generally include some examples and parameters to identify the controlled technology. Technology entries on the Catalogue are arranged according to industrial sectors. The industrial sectors comprise traditional industries and high-tech industries, including but not limited to agriculture, food manufacturing industry, chemical product manufacturing industry, metal products manufacturing and processing industry, equipment manufacturing industry, telecommunication industry, computer industry, and software industry.

5.3.2.2 Revision to CUC Catalogue on Technology in 2020

The CUC Catalogue on Technology was last revised in 2020 in response to the trade tensions between China and the US. During the Q&A session on the 2020 revision, an official of the Division of Trade in Services of MOFCOM pointed out that one of the main purposes of revising the Catalogue was to maintain national economic security.[55] Technology trade may have a profound impact on the security of politics, economy, national defense, culture, society, ecology, resources, and other fields, and China accordingly needs to adhere to a holistic view of national security to ensure stability and sustainability of the opening up of the technology sector.[56] More technologies appear on the Catalogue as restricted from export, including unmanned aerial vehicle technology, password security technology, artificial intelligence interactive interface technology, and personalized information push service technology based on data analysis of the information processing technology, and so forth. Among them, the control points of artificial intelligence interactive interface technology and personalized information push service technology based on data analysis were of big concern in a cross-border acquisition project involving the export of such technologies from a Chinese high-tech company.

The table that follows is a summary of the 2020 revision.

Entries deleted	4 entries of prohibited technologies	(1) Microbial fertilizer technology (2) Caffeine production technology (3) Riboflavin production process, and (4) Vitamin fermentation technology

(continued)

[55] MOFCOM. (2020, August 31). The Official of the Department of Trade in Services Answers Reporters' Questions on the Release of the Updated Catalogue of Technologies Prohibited or Restricted from Export by China. Retrieved October 26, 2023, from http://cacs.mofcom.gov.cn/article/gnwjmdt/gn/202008/165955.html.

[56] Han, J., & Chen, W. (2020, August 29). Expanding Technology Exchanges with Foreign Countries on the Basis of Maintaining National Security—Experts Explain the Release of the Updated Catalogue of Technologies Prohibited or Restricted from Export by China. Retrieved 26 October 2023 from http://www.gov.cn/zhengce/2020-08/29/content_5538422.htm.

(continued)

	5 entries of restricted technologies	(1) Newcastle disease vaccine technology (2) Natural medicine production technology (3) Functional polymer material preparation and processing technology (4) Chemical synthesis and semi-synthetic medicine production technology, and (5) Information security firewall software technology
Entries added	23 entries of restricted technologies	(1) Artificial breeding technology of agricultural wild plants (2) Genetic engineering (genes and vectors) (3) Cashmere goat breeding technology (4) Cashmere goat breed nurturing technology (5) 3D printing technology (6) Application technology of construction machinery (7) Basic common technology of machine tool industry (8) Large-scale high-speed wind tunnel design and construction technology (9) Large-scale vibration platform design and construction technology
		(10) Petroleum equipment core component design and manufacturing technology (11) Large-scale petrochemical equipment basic process technology (12) Heavy machinery industry strategic new product design technology (13) Offshore island reef utilization and safety assurance equipment technology (14) Aerospace bearing technology (15) Unmanned aerial vehicle technology (16) Laser technology (17) Large-scale power equipment design technology (18) Password security technology (19) Efficient detection technology (20) Information defense technology (21) Information countermeasure technology (22) Basic software security enhancement technology, and (23) Space remote sensing image acquisition technology
Entries amended	5 entries of prohibitive technologies	(1) Silkworm species, breeding and cocoon collection, and processing technology (2) Spacecraft measurement and control technology (3) Mapping technology (4) Space data transmission technology, and (5) Satellite application technology

(continued)

(continued)

	16 entries of restrictive technologies	(1) Crop (including pasture) germplasm resources and their breeding technology (2) Aquatic germplasm breeding technology (3) Veterinary drug production technology (4) Chemical raw material production technology (5) Biological pesticide production technology (6) Biotechnology drug production technology (7) Tissue engineering medical device product preparation and processing technology (8) Artificial crystal growth and processing technology (9) Criminal technology (10) Medical diagnostic equipment and equipment manufacturing technology (11) Space instrument and equipment manufacturing technology (12) Mapping technology (13) Space data transmission technology (14) Satellite application technology (15) Information processing technology, and (16) Vacuum technology

5.3.2.3 Proposed Revisions to CUC Catalogue on Technologies

On 30 December 2022, the Department of Trade and Commercial Services of MOFCOM issued the *Circular Seeking Public Comments on the Revised Catalogue of Technologies Prohibited or Restricted from Export by China* (the "2022 Circular"), featuring substantial deletion of technology entries and refinement of the control points of many technology entries. According to the 2022 Circular, 32 entries may be deleted from the Catalogue, with 36 maybe amended and 7 added, and the Catalogue may control 139 entries in total, including 24 prohibited and 115 restricted ones for export purposes.

Most of the envisaged deleted entries are related to traditional industries such as agriculture, food, textile, chemical, and equipment manufacturing industries. Few entries proposed for deletion are from high-tech industries. Except for the "applied technology for engineering machinery", the proposed deleted entries are all entries added in 2008 and almost all entries created in the 2020 Catalogue are retained. The new entries as proposed this time fall into scope of crucial and emerging industries such as biological research, rare earth, photovoltaics, smart cars, and so forth, reflecting the considerations of protection of national security and social and economic public interests. The entries as maybe amended are across various industries. Except for the narrowing of a few control points, most amendments are made in terms of adding control points or refining control points by illustrations or adding descriptions or parameters.

According to the 2022 Circular, this revision aims to create positive conditions for strengthening international technical cooperation.[57] It can be seen from the content of the revision that the Catalogue may loosen the control of technologies in agriculture, food industry, textile industry, and other traditional industries.

Although the tone for this revision is set to promote international technical cooperation, the export control of high and new technologies has not been loosened and the trend is to focus on controls on high-tech and emerging technologies, which is in concert with the holistic view of national security of China. The proposed amendments to the CUC Catalogue on Technologies are summarized as follows:

A. **Entries Deleted**

Industry	Technology name
Technologies prohibitive from export	
Agriculture, forestry, animal husbandry and fishery service industries	Production technologies of growth regulators of green plants
Non-ferrous metal ore mining and separating industry	Mining engineering technologies
Agricultural and sideline food processing industry	Meat processing technologies
Beverage manufacturing industry	Beverage production technologies
Non-ferrous metal smelting and rolling processing industry	Non-ferrous metal metallurgical technologies
Manufacturing industry of special equipment	Manufacturing technologies of agricultural machinery
Technologies restrictive from export	
Agriculture, forestry, animal husbandry, and fishery service industries	Production technologies for livestock feed and animal growth regulators
	Processing technologies for livestock products
	Technologies for bee breeding and collection, processing, and utilization of bee products
	Forest pest and disease prevention and control technologies
Agricultural and sideline food processing industry	Cereal processing technologies
	Egg product processing technologies
Food manufacturing industry	Production technologies for food additives
Beverage manufacturing industry	Beverage production technologies

(continued)

[57] MOFCOM. (2022, December 30). The Circular of Public Comments Sought on the Revised Catalogue of Technologies Prohibited or Restricted from Export by China. Retrieved 26 October 2023 from http://fms.mofcom.gov.cn/article/tongjiziliao/202212/20221203376696.shtml.

(continued)

Industry	Technology name
Textile industry	Natural fiber textile products and their processing technologies
	Manufacturing technologies for soybean fibers
Papermaking and paper product industry	Papermaking technologies
Chemical raw material and chemical product manufacturing industry	Production technologies for chemical raw materials
	Production technologies for chemical pesticides
	Dye production technologies
	Production technologies for catalysts
	Production technologies for photosensitive materials
	Production technologies for synthetic resin and its products
	Industrial explosives and their production technologies
	Industrial detonator production technologies
Non-metal mineral product industry	Production technologies for domestic ceramics and their products
	Production technologies for fireproof materials
General equipment manufacturing industry	Combustion technologies for boiler manufacturing
	Application technologies for engineering machinery (Note: added in the 2020 revision, deleted in this revision)
Special equipment manufacturing industry	Firefighting technologies
	Criminal technologies
Electrical machinery and equipment manufacturing industry	Production technologies for electrical materials
Water transport industry	Liquid cargo transport technologies

B. **Entries Added**

Industry	Technology name	Control points
Technologies prohibitive from export		
Research and experimental development	Cell cloning and gene editing technologies for human use	1. Somatic cell cloning technologies, including nucleus extraction and removal technology, nucleus transfer technology, embryo transfer technology, and cell activation of key enzymes 2. Gene editing technologies for human use, including ZFN, TALEN, and CRISPR technology, specific nucleases, homologous recombination technology, point knockout technology, gene introduction and fragment deletion technology, and multilocus mutagenesis technology
Technologies restrictive from export		
Agriculture	Techniques for exploiting the advantages of hybridization in agricultural crops	1. Endangered, rare, and important species in China and the resources such as individuals, organs, tissues, cells, genes of such species which are usable for regeneration, or seeds and genetic information of these species that can be used for reproduction 2. Hybrid breeding technologies for endangered, rare, and important species in China
Non-ferrous metal ore mining and separating industry	Mining engineering technologies	Leaching technology of ionic rare earth in mine
Non-metal mineral product industry	Photovoltaic silicon wafer preparation technologies	Large-size silicon wafer technology, black silicon preparation technology, super-efficient ingot casting single crystal/ polycrystalline process, etc
General equipment manufacturing industry	Bulk material handling and conveying technologies	Design and manufacture technology for three-car and four-car tippers, large belt conveyors, and large ship loaders
Manufacturing industry for communication equipment, computer and other electronic equipment	Laser radar system	Vehicle mounted laser detection and ranging system technology
Research and experimental development	CRISPR gene editing technologies	1. Applications in ethically controversial areas, including gene editing of embryonic cells, egg cells, and sperm cells 2. Applications in research that could have significant harmful consequences

(continued)

(continued)

Industry	Technology name	Control points
	Synthetic biology technology	1. Major technologies such as efficient synthesis and assembly of DNA, directed evolution, and creation of cell factories 2. Synthesis technologies of major chemicals such as amino acids, proteins, starch, etc 3. Application technologies that may cause significant harmful consequences

C. **Entries Amended**

Industry	Technology name	Main changes	Note
Technologies prohibitive from export			
Medicine manufacturing industry	Extraction and processing technologies of medicinal components of precious and endangered plants in China	Amend the industry name (originally "Animal Husbandry") and the technology name (originally "technologies of species resources unique to China")	The control points remain unchanged as "paclitaxel and relevant technologies"
Medicine manufacturing industry	Traditional Chinese medicinal material resources and production technologies	Reduce control points	
Non-ferrous metal smelting and rolling processing industry	Refining, processing and utilization technologies of rare earth	Significantly amend the control points	Move some control points to the catalogue of technologies restrictive from export
Manufacturing industry of transportation equipment	Spacecraft measurement and control technologies	Add examples to the control points	
Telecom and other information transmission service industries	Computer network technologies	Add examples to the control points	
	Satellite application technologies	Slightly supplement the control points	

(continued)

(continued)

Industry	Technology name	Main changes	Note
Technologies restrictive from export			
Agriculture	Cultivation and breeding technologies for commercial crops	Significantly amend the control points	The control points in the revised Catalogue are technologies related to tobacco; technologies related to ramie in the original Catalogue are entirely deleted
Forestry	Tree germplasm resources and breeding technologies	Change the wording of the control points	
	Breeding technologies for landscape plants and ornamental plants	Change the wording of the control points	
	Artificial breeding and protection technologies for wild animals	Add control points	
Agriculture, forestry, animal husbandry, and fishery professional and auxiliary activities	Veterinary drug production technologies	Add and reduce control points	Amend the industry name (originally "agriculture, forestry, animal husbandry, and fishery service industries")
	Veterinary hygiene and quarantine technologies	Reduce control points	
	Traditional hand-made paper technologies	Amend the technology name (originally "processing technologies for forest chemical products"); reduce control points	
Chemical raw material and chemical product manufacturing industry	Biopesticide production technologies	Add and reduce control points	
	Production technologies for synthetic fibers	Reduce control points	
Medicine manufacturing industry	Traditional Chinese medicinal material resources and production technologies	Add and reduce control points	

(continued)

(continued)

Industry	Technology name	Main changes	Note
	Production technologies for biotech drugs	Reduce control points	This entry was added in the 2020 revision and further amended this time
Rubber and plastic product industry	Production technologies for rubber products	Add parameters to the control points	Amend the industry name (originally "rubber product industry")
Non-metal mineral product industry	Growth and processing technologies for artificial lenses	Add control points	
Non-ferrous metal smelting and rolling processing industry	Non-ferrous metal metallurgical technologies	Add control points	Add technologies related to rare earth
General equipment manufacturing industry	3D printing technologies	Add control points	This entry was added in the 2020 revision and further amended this time
	Basic common technologies for machine tool industry	Compact the control points	This entry was added in the 2020 revision and further amended this time
Special equipment manufacturing industry	Design and construction technologies for large high-speed wind tunnels	Add control points	This entry was added in the 2020 revision and further amended this time
Transportation equipment manufacturing industry	Hull form design and testing technologies	Add descriptions to illustrate the control points	
Communication equipment, computer and other electronic equipment manufacturing industry	Computer core hardware manufacturing technologies	Amend the technology name and the parameters to illustrate the control points	The original technology name is "computer hardware and external equipment manufacturing technology"
	UAV technology	Add control points	This entry was added in the 2020 revision and further amended this time

(continued)

(continued)

Industry	Technology name	Main changes	Note
Instrumentation manufacturing industry	Manufacturing technology for mechanical value measuring apparatus and instruments	Amend the parameters to illustrate the control points	Amend industry name (originally "instrumentation, culture and office machinery manufacturing industry")
Electric power and heating power production and supply industry	Design technologies for large electric power equipment	Refine the descriptions of the control points	This entry was added in the 2020 revision and further amended this time
Water transport industry	Port equipment manufacturing technologies	Significantly amend the control points	
Telecommunications, radio, television and satellite transmission services	Computer network technology	Amend the parameters to illustrate the control points	Amend the industry name (originally "telecommunications and other information transmission services")
	Communication transmission technology	Reduce control points	
Computer service industry	Information processing technologies	Add and reduce control points; add descriptions to illustrate the control points	Enumerate types of "personalized information push service technology based on data analysis" (a control point added in the 2020 revision)
	Password security technologies	Change the wording of the control points	This entry was added in the 2020 revision and further amended this time
	High-performance detection technologies	Add control points; add parameters to the control points	This entry was added to the Catalogue in 2020 and amended this time
Software industry	General computer software programming technologies	Amend the parameters to illustrate the control points	
Professional and technical services industry	Acoustic engineering technologies	Refine the descriptions of the control points	

5.3.3 Licensing Procedures

MOFCOM has released the "Guideline on Import and Export Licensing of Technologies Restricted from Import or Export", which specifies the application procedures for the Technology Export License.[58] According to the guideline, the application for technology export shall be submitted to the provincial commerce departments.

After receiving the application documents, the provincial commerce department, together with the department in charge of science and technology, examines the application of technology export, and the departments decide to approve or disapprove the application within 30 working days from the reception of the application. If the application is approved, the commerce authority will issue a letter of comfort to permit the technology export (valid for 3 years). After obtaining the letter of comfort, the applicant may enter substantial negotiations on or concluding a technology export contract. The commerce authority will examine the authenticity of the contract and decide on whether to issue the Technology Export License within 15 workings from the receipt of the required documents.

To apply for the Technology Export License, the following documents shall be submitted: an application, a copy of the contract (with translation in Chinese), a list of technical materials to be exported, and documents showing the legal standing of the contracting parties.

The application of exporting technologies restricted from export will be reviewed from the perspective of trade and technology respectively. The review from the perspective of trade focuses on (i) whether the export is in conformity with foreign trade policies of China and helps promote exports of China; (ii) whether the export is in conformity with industrial export policies of China and helps promote the development of the national economy of China; and (iii) whether the export is in conformity with commitments of China to foreign countries.[59] The review from the perspective of technology focuses on (i) whether the export jeopardizes national security of China; (ii) whether the export is in conformity with technological development policies of China and helps facilitate the technological development of China; and (iii) whether the export is in conformity with industrial technology policies of China and helps drive the manufacturing of large and complete equipment as well as development of economic and technical cooperation.[60]

The format of the Technology Export License of China is illustrated below.

Technology Export License of the People's Republic of China

[58] Guideline on Import and Export Licensing of Technologies Restricted from Import or Export. Retrieved 26 October 2023 from http://egov.mofcom.gov.cn/new140923/table/D18002zhinan.pdf.

[59] Article 8 of the Measures for Administration of Technologies Prohibited or Restricted to Be Exported.

[60] Article 9 of the Measures for Administration of Technologies Prohibited or Restricted to Be Exported.

1. Exporter	2. No. of technology export license
3. Importer	4. Technology owner
5. Technology item Control point Code	
6. Technology item	7. Mode of technology export
8. License attachments Attachment title Pages	
9. Supplementary detail	10. Issuing authority stamp & signature 11. Issuing date

5.3.4 *Issues Under China Export Control Law*

It should be noted that CUC Catalogue on Technologies and its corresponding laws and regulations such as TIER and TPREM mainly regulate the export of technologies. ECL, on the other hand, focuses on the export of technologies related to dual-use items, military items and nuclear items.

According to Article 42 of TIER, exporting a nuclear technology, a technology of nuclear products for both military and civilian purposes, a technology for supervising or monitoring the manufacture of chemicals, a technology for military purposes, or any other technology under export control shall be conducted pursuant to the relevant administrative laws and regulations. According to Article 21 of TPREM, these measures are not applicable to the export of nuclear technologies and technologies in relation to dual-use nuclear products, dual-use chemical products, dual-use biological products, missiles, national defense, and military products.

Though the licensing system under TIER and CUC Catalogue on Technologies are different from the export control of dual-use items, military items and nuclear items, the boundary between the technology scopes under these two regulatory systems is not completely clear when there is an element of national security in the export controls as far as ECL is concerned. Therefore, the exporters must be aware that violation of TIER may also result in violation of ECL, if the reason for control of the technologies is national security considerations, or if such export endangers the national security of China, so that the severe penalties under ECL may be imposed on such exporters in violation.

For any foreign trade, investment or commercial transaction projects, if there is an element of cross-border transfer of technologies from China, the legal and trade compliance due diligence is a must before the negotiation and conclusion of the transactions.

Chapter 6
National Security and Extraterritorial Jurisdiction

This chapter discusses the issue of national security and rules and practices of extraterritorial jurisdiction under ECL. Section 6.1 explores the legal meaning of national security under Chinese law. Section 6.2 analyzes export control issues relevant to national security. Section 6.3 analyzes the extraterritorial jurisdiction of export controls of China, especially its impacts on foreign parties. Section 6.4 then gives a brief conclusion.

6.1 National Security Under Chinese Law

"National security" is a key term in the export-control-related legislations and practices in almost every jurisdiction,[1] and this term is particularly significant under ECL as the enlisted items under China Unilateral Controls are controlled largely on the basis of national security considerations, and those unlisted items if controlled are also mainly based on national security concerns. ECL exhibits itself with twelve provisions with reference to national security.[2] Under ECL, national security and

[1] Take the U.S. for instance, the *Export Control Reform Act of 2018* ("ECRA") of the U.S. comes straight that this Act is to authorize the President to control the export, re-export, and transfer of commodities, software, and technology to protect the national security, and to promote the foreign policy, of the United States, and for other purposes. The EAR also makes it clear that the export control provisions of the EAR are intended to serve the national security, foreign policy, non-proliferation of weapons of mass destruction, and other interests of the United States, which in many cases are reflected in international obligations or arrangements. The EU also emphasizes the security concern by stressing that EU dual-use regulation aims to ensure that in the area of dual-use items, the Union and its Member States fully take into account all relevant considerations including international obligations and commitments, obligations under relevant sanctions, considerations of national foreign and security policy.

[2] Please note that under the ECL, the complete expression always takes the form of "national security and interests".

D. Zhao, *Contemporary Export Control Law of China*, Modern China and International Economic Law, https://doi.org/10.1007/978-981-99-9825-8_6

interest were placed ahead of the non-proliferation and other international commitments, which is a signal different from the First Reading of the draft ECL (2019) where the purpose of "fulfill non-proliferation and other international obligations" was stressed in the first place, followed by the wording "maintain national security and interest".[3]

Understandably, national security is a legal term with a politically sensitive nature, which normally leaves the State with the discretion to decide whether a specific export activity may endanger its national security.[4] Although ECL does not define its inherent connotations, the term exists elsewhere under Chinese legal framework.[5]

Article 28 of the *Constitution Law of the PRC* regulates that "*the State shall maintain public* order, *suppress treason and other criminal activities that jeopardize national security, punish criminal activities, including those that endanger public security or harm the socialist economy, and punish and reform criminals.*"

The term of national security was not clarified in the first[6] and the second[7] versions of the *National Security Law of the PRC*. The updated National Security Law of the PRC[8] announced on 1 July 2015 defines "national security" as a status in which the regime, sovereignty, unity, territorial integrity, welfare of the people, sustainable economic and social development, and other major interests of the State are relatively not faced with any danger and not threatened internally or externally, and the capability to maintain a sustained security status.[9] Besides, sixteen specific elements of "national security" are specified in this law, including **(i)** political security, **(ii)** homeland security, **(iii)** military security, **(iv)** economic security, **(v)** cultural security, **(vi)** social security, **(vii)** technological security, **(viii)** cybersecurity, **(ix)** ecological security, **(x)** resource security, **(xi)** nuclear security, **(xii)** overseas interest security, **(xiii)** biosecurity, **(xiv)** space security, **(xv)** polar security, and **(xvi)** deep-sea security.

On 21 April 2022, China proposed the concept of "global security", reflecting China's emphasis on both internal security and international security. The core principles and priorities of cooperation were delivered by the Foreign Minister of China in the forum "The Global Security Initiative: Proposals of China for Solving Security

---

[3] Article 1 of the First Reading Draft of the ECL (2019) prescribes that "*the Law is hereby formulated for the purpose of fulfilling international obligations such as nonproliferation, maintaining the state security and benefits and strengthening export control*". Article 1 of the Second Reading Draft of the ECL (2020) and the Final ECL regulates that "*this Law is enacted to protect national security and interest, fulfill non-proliferation and other international obligations, and strengthen and regulate export control*".

[4] Ren, Q., & Zhao, D. (2020). Developments in Mainland China and Hong Kong. In Rachel Barnes and others (eds.), *The Guide to Sanctions* (1st ed., p. 243). Global Investigations Review.

[5] The term "national security" exists and is specially highlighted in the *National Intelligence Law of the PRC* (Article 2), *Cryptography Law of the PRC* (Article 3), *National Defense Law of the PRC* (Article 4), *Coast Guard Law of the PRC* (Article 4), *Biosecurity Law of the PRC* (Article 3), *Hainan Free Trade Port Law of the PRC* (Article 3), and *Data Security Law of the PRC* (Article 4).

[6] Order No. 68 of the President of the PRC, 22 February 1993.

[7] Order No.18 of the President of the PRC, 27 August 2009.

[8] Order No.29 of the President of the PRC, 1 July 2015.

[9] Article 2 of the *National Security Law of the PRC*.

Challenges" on 21 February 2023.[10] Thus, it is understandable that in its summary report released on 15 April 2023, Chinese national security authority states that the concept of "national security" enriches itself with more ingredients and coverage, and wider territorial effect of space and time."[11]

The term "national security" has also been referred to under other laws, regulations, and underlying rules or measures. Table 6.1 as exhibited an unexhausted summary of provisions referring to "national security" under Chinese law (not including regulations, rules, or measures).

6.2 National Security Issues in Export Controls

As illustrated in other sections of this book, "national security" means *a status of being relatively free from* danger and not threatened internally or externally, as well as the *State's ability to safeguard continuous security*. But how could a person or entity determine its own behavior or certain involving activities may affect such a status of the State relatively free from danger or the State's ability to safeguard its continuous security? Only the State government may have the ability or discretion to determine. For the business community, it is difficult to ascertain whether a given export activity may endanger national security of China and whether an export license is required.

"National security" appears under ECL in such manners as summarized in the table (See Table 6.2).

6.2.1 Policies of Controls Over Dual-Use Items and Military Items

These dual-use and military export control lists under ECL are controlled either by reason of national security and interests or non-proliferation considerations. If the list-based controls are unilateral controls, they are generally based on national security and interest reasons; if such list-based controls are multilateral controls, they can be also viewed as based on national security and interest reasons simply based on the legal concept of national security of China embodies the international security components. For the list-based controls, the EBOs simply comply with the list-based controls, end-user and end-user controls, and resolve the red flags of the transactions before proceeding with or implementing the export transaction. In this way, the EBOs can resolve national security concerns to a certain extent.

[10] The Global Security Initiative Concept Paper, 21 February 2023. In this Paper, China calls on all parties to carry out single or multiple cooperation in 20 aspects.

[11] Legal Daily. (2023, April 15). National Security Authorities Warn against Activities Endangering National Security of the PRC. Retrieved 20 September 2023 from http://www.chinapeace.gov.cn/chinapeace/c100007/2023-04/15/content_12649335.shtml.

Table 6.1 "National security" as appears under Chinese law

Effective date	Name of the laws	Articles
1 July 2015	*National Security Law*	Throughout the whole text
1 June 2017	*Cybersecurity Law*	Articles 1, 12, 28, 31, 35, 58
27 April 2018	*National Intelligence Law*	Articles 1, 2, 6, 11
26 October 2018	*Company Law*	Article 213
1 January 2020	*Foreign Investment Law*	Articles 6, 35
1 January 2020	*Cryptography Law*	Articles 1, 3, 12, 21, 26, 27, 28, 32
30 June 2020	*Law on Safeguarding National Security in the Hong Kong Special Administrative Region of the PRC*	Throughout the whole text
1 December 2020	*Export Control Law*	Articles 1, 2, 3, 9, 10, 12, 13, 18, 32, 43, 44, 48
1 January 2021	*National Defense Law*	Article 4, 31
1 February 2021	*Coast Guard Law*	Articles 4, 39, 43, 44
1 March 2021	*Criminal Law*	Articles 2, 56, 66, 102–113, 277
15 April 2021	*Biosecurity Law*	Articles 1, 2, 3, 20, 55
10 June 2021	*Anti-Foreign Sanctions Law*	Articles 1, 13, 15
10 June 2021	*Hainan Free Trade Port Law*	Articles 3, 18, 55
1 September 2021	*Data Security Law*	Articles 2, 4, 8, 21, 24, 25, 35
1 November 2021	*Personal Information Protection Law*	Articles 10, 42
1 August 2022	*Anti-Monopoly Law*	Article 38
1 July 2023	*Anti-Espionage Law*	Throughout the whole text

Table 6.2 National security provisions under ECL

Art. 1	This law is enacted to protect **national security** and interests, fulfill non-proliferation and other international obligations, and strengthen and regulate export control
Art. 2(1)	This law shall apply to the State's export control of dual-use items, military products, nuclear materials, and *other items such as goods, technologies, or service that are related to the protection of* ***national security*** *and interests* or the fulfillment of non-proliferation or other international obligations (hereinafter collectively referred to as the "controlled items")
Art. 3	Export control shall stay in line with a holistic approach to **national security** and be performed for maintaining international security, balancing security and development, and improving export control administration and services
Art. 9(2)	As needed for protecting **national security** and interests or for fulfilling non-proliferation or other international obligations, subject to the approval of the State Council or the approval of both the State Council and the Central Military Commission, the State export control authorities may, together with relevant departments, impose a temporary control on the export of any goods, technologies, or services outside the control lists, which shall be publicly announced
Art. 10	As needed for protecting **national security** and interests or fulfilling non-proliferation or other international obligations, subject to the approval of the State Council or the approval of both the State Council and the Central Military Commission, the State export control authorities may, together with relevant departments, prohibit the export of any relevant controlled item or prohibit the export of any relevant controlled item to any specified destination country or region or to any specified organization or individual
Art. 12(3)	If an exporter knows or ought to know or is notified by the State export control authorities that any relevant goods, technologies or services outside the control lists that are to be exported by it may pose any of the following risks, it shall apply to the State export control authorities for a license: 1. Endangerment to **national security**…
Art. 13(1)	The State export control authorities shall review the application for the export of any controlled item made by any exporter and make a decision to grant a license or not based on an overall consideration of the following factors: 1. **National security** and interests…
Art. 18(1)	The State export control authorities shall establish control lists regarding importers and end-users identified as falling into any of the following circumstances: 1. Breach of the regulatory requirements regarding end-users or end-uses; 2. Posing of a potential endangerment to **national security** and interests; or…
Art. 32(2)	The provision of any export control-related information by any organization or individual within the territory of the People's Republic of China to an overseas recipient shall be conducted under the law, and any such provision that may endanger **national security** and interests shall be prohibited
Art. 43(1)	Any violation of any regulatory requirement on export control in this law which endangers **national security** and interests shall be handled and subjected to penalties under this law as well as any relevant laws or administrative regulations

(continued)

Table 6.2 (continued)

Art. 44	Any violation of any regulatory requirement on export control in this law by any organization or individual outside the territory of the People's Republic of China which endangers the **national security** and interests of the People's Republic of China or obstructs the fulfillment of non-proliferation or other international obligations shall be handled and investigated for legal liability according to law
Art. 48	The People's Republic of China may, depending on the actual situation, take reciprocal measures against any country or region whose abuse of export control measures endangers the **national security** and interests of the People's Republic of China

6.2.2 CUC Policies

By virtue of Article 2(1) of ECL, any items such as goods, technologies, or services whose export is controlled by reason of national security protection, even if not covered by the Consolidated Catalogues and temporary controls, are also covered by ECL. China does have a separate list-based restrictive and prohibitive controls of goods and technologies. If these unilateral controls are based on national security reasons, the EBOs must consider incorporating such controlled items into their export control compliance program so that the national security concerns can be properly addressed. For details on such unilateral controls, please see Chap. 5.

6.2.3 Catch-All Control

For such non-list-based controls, given the ambiguity of the concept of national security and the difficulty in ascertaining the relativity status of the State as free from danger and threat and of its capability to maintain its continuous security, no person or entity other than the government in China is able to identity and determine such relativity status and capability. Therefore, it seems that EBOs can do nothing further than focus on due diligence on the legitimate destination, end-user and end-uses and red flags of the envisaged transactions, if any. If MOFCOM otherwise informs EBOs of the national security risk, EBOs must follow the instructions of MOFCOM immediately.

6.2.4 Provision of Export Control Information

The provision of export control information overseas may also trigger national security concerns. Pursuant to Article 32 of ECL, "*any provision of information related to export control by an organization or individual within the territory of the People's Republic of China to those outside the territory of China shall be conducted in accordance with the law; any such provision that may endanger national security and interests shall be prohibited*".

It is uncertain what is "the information of export control", the provision of which may endanger national security. It is said that the purpose of Article 32 is to forbid the provision by a person or entity in China of any information from China to overseas if such information is relevant to the export controls by a foreign country. However, such an interpretation is far from what can be understood from the literal meaning of Article 32. Again, it remains an issue of how national security may be endangered if the provision of the information has complied with all other laws and regulations.

6.3 Extraterritorial Jurisdiction Under ECL

6.3.1 Extraterritorial Jurisdiction: An Overview

Traditionally, the exercise of jurisdiction by a State was primarily limited to persons, property and acts within its territory and to exceptional situations in which its nationals traveled beyond its borders.[12] Nowadays, the exercise of extraterritorial jurisdiction by a State with respect to persons, property, or acts outside its territory has become a phenomenon, though the lawfulness of such extraterritorial jurisdiction remains quite unclear.

According to the landmark *Lotus* case, a State is entitled to exercise jurisdiction in its own territory in respect of any case which relates to acts that have taken place abroad, if not prohibited by international law.[13] On this basis, the International Law Commission has defined "extraterritorial jurisdiction" as the existence of sovereign power or authority by a State outside of its territory.[14] Naturally, such competence may be exercised by way of prescription, adjudication or enforcement.[15]

In the context of extraterritorial jurisdiction, there are certain similar terms such as "extraterritoriality", "extraterritorial jurisdiction" (the prerequisite), "extraterritorial

[12] United Nations, International Law Commission. (2006). *Report of the Commission to the General Assembly on the work of its fifty-eighth session.* Yearbook of the International Law Commission. /CN.4/SER.A/2006/Add.l (Part 2). Annex V, p. 229. Retrieved September 22, 2023, from https://legal.un.org/ilc/publications/yearbooks/english/ilc_2006_v2_p2.pdf.

[13] *Lotus* Case, PCIJ Series A, Judgement of 7 September 1927, pp. 18–19. Please note that this principle refers specifically to the exercise of enforcement jurisdiction and not to prescriptive or adjudicative jurisdiction.

[14] Supra note 12.

[15] Prescriptive jurisdiction refers to a State's authority to lay down legal norms. Adjudicative jurisdiction refers to a State's authority to decide competing claims. Enforcement jurisdiction refers to a State's authority to ensure compliance with its laws. See: Kamminga, M. T. (2012). "Exterritoriality". *Max Planck Encyclopedia of Public International Law.* Max Planck Institute for Comparative Public Law and International Law. Heidelberg and Oxford University Press.

application" (the process), and "extraterritorial effect" (the consequence).[16] Though the accurate legal connotation of these terms are not entirely identical, we will not strictly distinguish these expressions for the purpose of this book in this section.[17]

6.3.2 Extraterritorial Jurisdiction of ECL

In terms of U.S. export control, EAR is conspicuous for its control of items subject to EAR regardless of where the given items are located and no matter who is disposing of the export, deemed export, re-export, or in-country transfer. The extraterritorial jurisdiction is reflected in the control of dual-use items re-exported by a foreign company to a third country, for instance.

Facing the enforcement of export controls and economic sanctions intensified against Chinese companies, the Chinese government accelerated the construction of an export control legal system "which can bite". The extraterritorial jurisdiction provisions of ECL are one of tools that can enable such bites.

Article 44 of ECL handles and investigated legal liabilities "*any violation of any regulatory requirement on export control in this Law on the part of any organization or individual outside the territory of the People's Republic of China which endangers the national security and interests of the People's Republic of China or obstructs the fulfillment of non-proliferation or other international obligation*". This provision was afresh in the Second Reading of the Draft ECL (2020) and was retained in the final ECL, functioning as an overall and dominant provision of extraterritorial jurisdiction under ECL.

Unlike EAR, ECL does not technically cover and control the re-export of foreign-made items, which shows self-restraint to a certain degree on long-arm jurisdiction. EAR extends its jurisdiction over those activities in foreign countries the effect of which undermines the legislative objectives of ECL, namely considerations of protecting national security, securing non-proliferation and honoring international commitments.

---

[16] For example, the term "extraterritorial effect" refers to the process of applying domestic laws with extraterritorial effects to persons, objects and acts outside the jurisdiction of the State to endow domestic law with extraterritorial effect. See: Liao, S. (2019). Extraterritorial Application of Domestic Law and Its Response—The Extraterritorial Application of U.S. Law As an Example, *Global Law Review*, 41(03), 168.

[17] Another analogous concept which is more frequently used and easy to be confused is "long-arm jurisdiction", referring to jurisdiction over persons or entities domiciled or resident outside the territory of the sanctioning state, first established by the U.S. Supreme Court in the case of International Shoe *Co. v. State of Washington* (1945), see: The Ministry of Foreign Affairs. (2023, February 3). The U.S. Willful Practice of Long-arm Jurisdiction and its Perils. Retrieved 25 September 2023 from https://www.mfa.gov.cn/wjbxw_new/202302/t20230203_11019274.shtml.

A foreign party (entity or individual) will implicate itself in violations of ECL relevant to controls of China over (**i**) re-export by re-exporters; (**ii**) end-use or end-user including foreign importers and end-users; and (**iii**) foreign third-party provision of services.

6.3.2.1 Re-exporter in a Foreign Country or Region

As mentioned in Chap. 1, ECL applies to the re-export of controlled items.[18] Generally, the re-export refers to the export of original controlled items from a foreign country (region) to another, although the term "re-export" only appears once in ECL and has not been well explained.[19] Legislatively, the provision on re-export controls has experienced significant changes.

Draft ECL (2017)	Final ECL (2020)
[Article 64] **The export from overseas to another foreign country (region)** of controlled items or foreign-made items containing a certain proportion of controlled items of China shall be governed by the relevant provisions of this law The proportion of content as specified in the preceding paragraph and the administrative measures in this regard shall be stipulated by the State Council or the Central Military Commission separately	[Article 45] The transit, transshipment, through transportation or **re-export** of controlled items, or the export of controlled items from any bonded areas, export processing zones or other special customs supervision zones or export supervised warehouses, bonded logistics centers or other bonded supervision premises to overseas shall be governed by the relevant provisions of this law

The initial draft provision on re-export considered the U.S. *de minimis* rule on the U.S.-origin controlled contents. However, this consideration disappeared in the subsequent draft versions and the final ECL. It can be inferred that the re-export of foreign-made items with some Chinese-controlled origins is not subject to the controls of ECL. The policy reasons may be twofold: (**i**) such self-restraint on re-export control of foreign products helps the export sale from China of materials, components, and parts; and (**ii**) it is practically difficult for the authorities to set the appropriate threshold number for *de minimis* rule and monitor and enforce against

[18] Different jurisdictions may have distinct understandings of the concept of "re-export". Under U.S. law, re-export means (a) an actual shipment or transmission of an item subject to the EAR from one foreign country to another foreign country, including the sending or taking of an item to or from such countries in any manner; (b) releasing or otherwise transferring "technology" or source code subject to the EAR to a foreign person of a country other than the foreign country where the release or transfer takes place (a deemed re-export); or (c) transferring by a person outside the United States of registration, control, or ownership of certain spacecraft. While in the context of EU export control, re-export is referred to as that within the meaning of Article 270 of the Union Customs Code, i.e., taking non-Union goods out of the customs territory of the Union.

[19] The term "re-export" was defined as "the export from overseas to another foreign country (region)" in the initial draft version of the ECL but was deleted subsequently.

violations of the same control.[20] Please note that any entity or individual in a foreign country can be treated as the ex-exporter subject to ECL if it enters into and performs such re-export transactions.

In practice, an issue may arise as to whether the item imported from China may be treated as a foreign-made item when the item undergoes a certain process of adding value so that the re-export restriction no longer applies. The ECL is silent on this point. There may be two alternative approaches to address this issue:

(a) Simple process approach: if the value-added process is only a simple processing as defined by customs regulations, it may not be treated as foreign-made and retains its status as an item exported from China as a China-origin item and still is subject to controls for re-export or change of end-use or end-user.[21]
(b) Substantial transformation: if the value-added process has substantially transformed the item imported from China according to the country-of-origin rules of China, such processed item will be deemed as a foreign-made item and no longer subject to ECL.[22]

Another question is whether "deemed re-export" is subject to control under ECL. It seems that the deemed re-export is controlled as ECL defines deemed export as occurring in provision of controlled items from a Chinese party to a foreign citizen no matter whether such provision occurs within in China or not. In other words, a Chinese person or an entity incorporated in China may be exposed to deemed export risks if the same party provides China-controlled items in a foreign country to a foreign national or entity.

6.3.2.2 Foreign End-Use or End-User

Besides the export license, foreign end-use and end-user control is another crucial tool for ensuring the designated civil and peaceful use of the controlled item in a foreign country. Under EAR, a concept of "transfer (in-country)" is invoked to control such an activity, i.e., a change in end-use or end-user of an item within the same foreign country is not permissible unless the licensing requirements are satisfied.[23]

---

[20] Liu, Y., & Li, Q. (2021). Construction of Specific Extraterritorial Applicable Legal Rules of China's Export Control Law. *International Economic Review*. 2021(04), 56.

[21] For example, Article 51 of the *Measures of PRC Customs for Assessing and Determining the Duty-paid Value of Imported and Exported Goods* defines the term "minor processing" as the dilution, mixing, classification, simple assembling, repacking or other similar processing.

[22] For example, Article 3 of the *Provisions on the Standards for Substantial Changes in the Non-Preferential Rules of Origin* regulates that the standard for determining the substantial changes in imports and exports shall be on the basis of the change in tariff classification, and where the change in tariff classification cannot reflect substantial change, ad valorem percentage and manufacturing or processing procedure shall be supplementary referred to.

[23] § 734.16 of EAR—Transfer (in-country).

Though ECL does not contain the concept of in-country transfer, the in-country transfer is factually controlled under ECL through licensing requirements on the part of the end-use or end-user.

Before the enactment of ECL, those decentralized underlying regulations on dual-use items as illustrated in Chap. 3 commonly contain a provision that "*the recipient undertakes not transfer the items and technologies to third parties other than the stated end-user without the permission of the Chinese government*",[24] which can be regarded as preliminary export control rules with extraterritorial effects. Under the above regulations, the consequence of non-compliance on the part of the end-user is merely the suspension or revocation of the Dual-use Export License if issued, without any other direct effects on foreign importers.[25]

ECL which came into effect on December 2020 includes a provision that the State export control authorities shall establish a risk management system for end-users and end-uses of controlled items to assess and review the end-users and end-uses and tighten the control over them.[26] It further regulates that end-users shall undertake not to change the end-use of the controlled items or transfer the items to any third party without the approval of the competent authorities. Where foreign importers find that the end-user or end-use may be changed, they shall immediately report the case to the authorities in compliance with regulations.[27]

On this basis, the *Dual-use Draft Regulations* further strengthen and specify the end-use and user controls. It expressly requires that MOFCOM's approval is a must prerequisite for the change of end-user or end-use of a dual-use item that has been exported. As a matter of procedure, the end-user may entrust the original Chinese EBO to file applications for such change.[28]

Given the end-user is committed to its specified end-use by reason of law or end-use certificate it furnished to MOFCOM through the EBO in China, it is advisable for the end-user *per se* to act as the importer of the controlled items from China, if possible, in practice. Upon further substantial manufacturing activities, the imported Chinese-origin item may become a foreign-made item which is not subject to ECL any longer and can be sold free to a certain extent. However, please bear in mind if the further sale of foreign-made items is for military or other proliferation use, such end-user of Chinese items is advised to conduct a national security assessment before proceeding with such further sales.

---

[24] Article 6 of the *Regulations on the Export Control of Nuclear Dual-use Items and Technologies*; Article 6 of the *Regulations on the Export Control of Missiles and Missile-related Items and Technologies*; Article 7 of the *Regulations on the Export Control of Dual-use Biological Items and Related Equipment and Technologies*; and Article 5 of the *Regulations on the Export Control of Nuclear*; Article 6 of the *Measures on Export Control of Certain Chemicals and Related Equipment and Technologies.*

[25] Liao, S. (2019). Legal System of Extraterritorial Application of Chinese Laws: Status, Issues and Improvements. *Chinese Jurisprudence.* 2019(06), 25.

[26] Article 17 of the ECL.

[27] Ibid., Article 16.

[28] Article 30 of the *Dual-use Draft Regulations.*

If the items imported from China are for inventory use temporarily, the identity of the end-user is not fixed at the time of license application. Some importers if simply indicate themselves as end-users without disclosing the exact end-use are not in conformity with MOFCOM's supervision requirements. The problem may be solved by indicating inventory purposes, with regular and timely reports to MOFCOM regarding the actual end-users and end-use. However, such an approach may not be feasible if the given items are sensitive from MOFCOM's perspective.

6.3.2.3 Foreign Third-Party Service Providers

Under ECL, no organization or individual may provide any agency, freight, delivery, customs clearance, third-party e-commerce trading platform, financial or other services to any exporter engaged in any violations of export control provisions.[29] The above third-party service providers will be exposed to legal liabilities if they knowingly facilitate an illegal export activity.[30] Obviously, such third-party service can be provided by foreign parties, which triggers the extraterritorial application of ECL.

The provision on third-party service providers under ECL shares some similarities with *General Prohibition Ten* under EAR, which forbids providing services to certain transactions with the knowledge that a violation has occurred or is about to occur.[31] Please note that the term "knowingly" is likely to include the scenario where the service provider should have known the underlying trade was illegal under ECL (constructive knowledge) though no positive knowledge can be established.[32] If there is no ICP at all within the organization of the service provider, and the management turning a blinking eye in conducting the service business, it is likely that such service

---

[29] Article 20 of the ECL.

[30] Ibid., Article 36.

[31] § 736.2(b)(10) of EAR—*General Prohibition Ten—Proceeding with transactions with knowledge that a violation has occurred or is about to occur (Knowledge Violation to Occur).* You may not sell, transfer, export, re-export, finance, order, buy, remove, conceal, store, use, loan, dispose of, transport, forward, or otherwise service, in whole or in part, any item subject to the EAR and exported, re-exported, or transferred (in-country) or to be exported, re-exported, or transferred (in-country) with knowledge that a violation of the Export Administration Regulations, the Export Control Reform Act of 2018, or any order, license, license exception, or other authorization issued thereunder has occurred, is about to occur, or is intended to occur in connection with the item. Nor may you rely upon any license or license exception after notice to you of the suspension or revocation of that license or exception. There are no-license exceptions to this General Prohibition Ten in part 740 of the EAR.

[32] § 772 of EAR: [Definition of "Knowledge"] Knowledge of a circumstance (the term may be a variant, such as "know", "reason to know", or "reason to believe") includes not only positive knowledge that the circumstance exists or is substantially certain to occur, but also an awareness of a high probability of its existence or future occurrence. Such awareness is inferred from evidence of the conscious disregard of facts known to a person and is also inferred from a person's willful avoidance of facts.

provider may be held with a "constructive knowledge" of violation of the underlying transactions in need of the service.

In a recent case, a court of appeal in the U.S. held that FedEx, a global business that provides its customers with transportation, e-commerce, and business solutions was subject to strict liability for serving its Entity List customer's goods in violation of EAR, the liability of which does not seem to necessarily depend on the knowledge element on the part of FedEx.[33] China has not gone that far under ECL, which depends on the actual or constructive knowledge of the third-party service provider before liability can be established on them under ECL.

6.4 Conclusions

Though the meaning of national security is ambiguous and hard to grasp, the foreign importer, re-exporter, and end-user are supposed to avoid endangering national security of China in handling items controlled under ECL. If an ICP is strictly implemented in place for ECL, it may effectively avoid or reduce the national security risks as well as the extraterritorial exposures under ECL.

[33] *Federal Express Corporation v. U.S. Department of Commerce, et al.*, 39 F.4th 756 (DC Cir. 2022). https://law.justia.com/cases/federal/appellate-courts/cadc/20-5337/20-5337-2022-07-08.html.

Chapter 7
Export Control Enforcement

This chapter discusses the export control authorities, legal liabilities, and violation cases related to export control enforcement. Section 7.1 introduces two export control authorities in export control practice, MOFCOM, and the customs. Section 7.2 specifies consequences of violations under legal frameworks of China. Section 7.3 summarizes some administrative and criminal enforcement cases against EBOs who violate ECL and/or customs laws.

7.1 Export Control Authorities

The State export control authorities as mentioned in Article 5 of ECL[1] include MOFCOM and the customs.

7.1.1 MOFCOM

MOFCOM as the Ministry of Commerce is a department subordinate to the State Council of China.[2] Its predecessors can be traced back to the Ministry of Foreign Trade that was established in 1952 and the General Administration of Foreign

---

[1] Article 5 of the ECL prescribes that departments under the State Council and departments under the Central Military Commission that undertake the functions of export control (hereinafter collectively referred to as the "State export control authorities") shall be responsible for the export control within their respective jurisdictions. Other relevant departments under the State Council or the Central Military Commission shall be responsible for other work related to export control within their respective jurisdictions.

[2] The official website of the MOFCOM can be found at: http://www.mofcom.gov.cn/.

D. Zhao, *Contemporary Export Control Law of China*, Modern China and International Economic Law, https://doi.org/10.1007/978-981-99-9825-8_7

Economic Liaison established in 1961, both of which were merged with other departments to form the Ministry of Foreign Economic Relations and Trade in 1982, and was renamed as the Ministry of Foreign Trade and Economic Cooperation in 1993. In 2003, MOFCOM was established by merging the Ministry of Foreign Trade and Economic Cooperation with other departments.

The division within MOFCOM responsible for export control is the Bureau of Industry Security and Import & Export Control (BISIEC).[3] BISIEC undertakes the functions of implementing national export controls, end-user and end-use management, industry and technology risk assessment, constructing the national export control supervision system,[4] and investigating and enforcing laws and regulations against violations.[5]

MOFCOM's supervision and enforcement powers are summarized as follows:

(a) to supervise and inspect export of controlled items, especially the export of intangible technologies, data and services;
(b) to establish expert consultation mechanism to give advice on export controls;
(c) to release export control guidelines for industries;
(d) to verify application documents and issue export licenses;
(e) to investigate violations and impose penalties thereon.

Please note that such supervisions and enforcement power also apply to the exported commodities though the same is cleared with the customs.

7.1.2 The Customs

The General Administration of Customs[6] ("GAC") is a department subordinate to the State Council, responsible for supervision and control over the (tangible) commodities and personal belongings entering or exiting the customs territory of China.[7] The customs' system consists of a "three-tier" hierarchy, with GAC at the top level, with a total of 42 regional customs led by GAC on the next level and the affiliated local customs under the regional customs.

Given that the customs have jurisdiction over exported goods, the customs also have the power to supervise and control export declaration and clearance of dual-use goods, nuclear goods as well as military goods, which will request license or no-license certificate from MOFCOM or other authorities. GAC cooperates closely with MOFCOM and other related authorities to regulate the export of controlled items, engages in investigating and handling violations, carries out risk prevention

[3] The official website of the BISIEC can be found at: http://aqygzj.mofcom.gov.cn/.

[4] Introduction to the BISIEC, available at: http://aqygzj.mofcom.gov.cn/article/gywm/202009/20200903002890.shtml.

[5] White Paper, Part III, Section 2.

[6] The official website of the GAC can be found at: http://www.customs.gov.cn/.

[7] Article 2 of the *Customs Law*.

and control, and conducts enforcement of ECL against exported goods in violation. It is reported in recent years that the customs have increased inputs into export control supervision equipment to detect radioactive, biological, and chemical items, as well as illegal exports, more efficiently.[8]

Pursuant to ECL and the *Dual-use Draft Regulations*, the customs are empowered to enforce the following administrative measures:

(a) not to release the controlled goods without an export license (Dual-use Export License or Military Export License);
(b) not to release the controlled goods if they are not declared as controlled items. but the customs suspect that they are controlled items;
(c) to request export control authorities to organize identification or assessment of the nature of goods as controlled or not;
(d) to work with MOFCOM and other authorities to enforce ECL and other regulations and rules and conduct investigations;
(e) to impose administrative penalties if there is a violation.

An important organ within the customs' system is the Anti-Smuggling Bureau ("ASB") under GAC,[9] which is empowered to investigate both administrative and criminal violations of the *Customs Law*, and ECL as well if concerned with exported commodities. ASB with local organs within the regional and some local Customs is subjected to the dual leadership of the Ministry of Public Security and GAC.

7.2 Legal Liabilities

Violations of ECL may result in (**i**) administrative penalties and/or (**ii**) criminal penalties.

7.2.1 Administrative Penalties

Administrative penalties may be imposed by both MOFCOM or the customs depending on the nature of the controlled items, and such administrative penalties may include (**i**) an order to cease the illegal activity, (**ii**) confiscation of goods or illegal proceeds, (**iii**) monetary fines, (**iv**) an order to suspend business, and/or (**v**) revocation of exporting business qualification for the controlled items.

Prior to the enactment of ECL, MOFCOM was empowered to impose administrative penalties under the fragmental export control regulations and rules on different categories of export control items. For instance, under the *Regulations on the Export Control of Nuclear Dual-use Items and Technologies*, MOFCOM is entitled to impose

[8] White Paper, Part III, Section 2.

[9] The official website of the ASB of the GAC can be found at: http://jsj.customs.gov.cn/.

(**i**) a fine not less than CNY 50,000 but no more than CNY 250,000, if the illegal proceeds are less than CNY 50,000, (**ii**) a warning and a fine not less than the same amount of but no more than the 5 times of the amount of the illegal proceeds, and/ or (**iii**) confiscation of any illegal gains. With the enactment of ECL, MOFCOM has been authorized to impose penalties prescribed by the provisions of ECL which are more severe on the violating party. For instance, pursuant to Article 37 of ECL, any EBO that trades under an export transaction with an overseas importer or end-user designated onto the List of Controlled Parties in violation of ECL shall be given a warning, ordered to cease its illegal activity, faced with confiscation of illegal gains, and such EBO shall also be fined between ten and twenty times the illegal business value if the illegal business value exceeds CNY500,000 or be fined between CNY500,000 and CNY5 million if there are no illegal business value or the illegal business value is below CNY500,000; and in serious cases, an order may be imposed to suspend business for rectification and even up to the revocation of export business qualification for the relevant controlled items. For other forms of violations of ECL by the EBO, the main difference is the amount penalty, which ranges from five to ten times of the illegal business value, with a minimum penalty of CNY 500,000. For the service providers in violation of ECL, the penalties would range from three to five times the illegal business value, with a minimum penalty of CNY 100,000.

China Customs have been enforcing against export violations under the *Customs Law* and the *Regulations on the Implementation of Customs Administration Penalties* ("*Customs Implementation Regulations*"). Among other things, a failure to submit proper exporting licenses required to export dual-use items or military items may be subject to a fine of no more than 30% of the value of the goods.[10] However, commencing from 2023, the customs tend to impose such penalties against illegal export of controlled goods pursuant to ECL, which will be further elaborated in Sect. 7.3.

7.2.2 Criminal Penalties

Violation of export controls, if committed knowingly, or with constructive knowledge, may constitute a crime under the *Criminal Law*, generally including the crimes of (**i**) smuggling (Articles 151 & 152) without export licenses, (**ii**) illegal business operation without obtaining special authorization (Article 225), (**iii**) divulging state secrets intentionally or negligently through releasing controlled information, data or technology (Article 398) or (**iv**) forging, altering, trading, stealing, and dealing with documents, certificates, or seals of State organs in terms of fake license document (Article 280).[11]

---

[10] Article 14(1) of the *Customs Implementation Regulations*.

[11] Ren, Q., & Zhao, D.M. (2020). Developments in Mainland China and Hong Kong. In R. Barnes et al. (eds.), *The Guide to Sanctions, Global Investigations Review* (p. 239).

Under the *Criminal Law*, the intentional unauthorized export of controlled goods may amount to the crime of "smuggling goods and articles **prohibited** for import and export" (Article 151(3)[12]) or of "smuggling ordinary goods and articles" (Article 153[13]). Given the restrictive nature of the controlled goods under ECL, it is interesting to note that there is no crime named as "smuggling goods and articles **restricted** for import and export" under the *Criminal Law.* In this connection, a document entitled the *Interpretative Opinion of the Supreme People's Court and the Supreme People's Procuratorate on Certain Issues concerning the Application of Law to Handling of Criminal Cases Involving Smuggling*[14] (the "*Interpretative Opinion*") has been released to provide some guidance. According to Article 21 of the *Interpretative Opinion*, whoever, without licenses, imports or exports goods or articles restricted by the State, if constituting a criminal offense, shall be convicted of the crime such as "smuggling goods and articles prohibited for import and export" and punished in accordance with Articles 151 and 152 of the *Criminal Law*. Besides, whoever imports or exports goods or articles restricted by the State with licenses but the quantity of the imported or exported goods or articles exceeds the authorized quantity, if constituting a criminal offense, shall be convicted of the crime of smuggling ordinary goods or articles and punished in accordance with Article 153 of *Criminal Law* of China. Therefore, an intentional export without a license under ECL will be convicted of the crime of smuggling goods prohibitive of export, while intentional undue use of export licenses may be convicted of the crime of smuggling ordinary goods.

Another controversy centers around the criminal penalties related to the export of military items. Since Article 151(1) of the *Criminal Law* lays out another "crime of smuggling weapons and ammunition", the question is what if the smuggled military items though enlisted on the Military Item List do not qualify as such traditional weapons and ammunition under the *Criminal Law*. Combined with the *Interpretative Opinion*, it is very likely that the smuggling of military items if not as weapons and ammunition may be interpreted as covered by Article 151(3) of the *Criminal Law*, i.e., smuggling goods and articles prohibited for import and export.

---

[12] Article 151(3) of the *Criminal Law* prescribes that whoever smuggles rare plants or products thereof or any other goods or articles that are prohibited from being imported or exported shall be sentenced to fixed-term imprisonment not more than five years or criminal detention, and/or be fined; or if the circumstances are serious, shall be sentenced to fixed-term imprisonment not less than five years and be fined. Where an entity commits a crime as provided for in this Article, the entity shall be sentenced to a fine, and its directly responsible person and other directly liable persons shall be punished according to the provisions of this Article.

[13] Article 153 of the *Criminal Law* prescribes that whoever smuggles goods or articles other than those as regulated in Articles 151, 152, and 347 shall be punished in light of the graveness of the crime according to the following provisions.

[14] Fa Shi [2014] No. 10, 法释 [2014]10 号, 12 August 2014, effective as of 10 September 2014.

7.3 Enforcement Cases

Since ECL came into force on 1 December 2020, MOFCOM and the customs have intensified enforcement against violations of ECL. Such reported enforcement cases can be summarized in two categories: (**i**) administrative cases and (**ii**) criminal cases.

7.3.1 Administrative Cases

In theory, both MOFCOM and the customs are empowered to impose administrative penalties on EBOs who violate ECL concerning exported goods. However, as far as exported goods are concerned, the customs have been more proactive in enforcing ECL. Cases regarding the illegal export of (**i**) dual-use items and (**ii**) military items handled by the customs are summarized and analyzed as follows.[15]

7.3.1.1 Administrative Penalties on Export of Dual-Use Items

Case 1: On 12 December 2022, a company in Gansu Province declared an export shipment of 21 tons of carburant through Tianjin Xingang Customs, with a total FOB value of USD 23,100. After inspection and testing, the items were identified as artificial graphite under the China tariff code 3801 1000 90 subject to the Dual-use Export License. The company was held as exporting controlled items without an export license and was imposed a fine of CNY 24,000 pursuant to Article 34 of ECL and Article 32(5) of the *Administrative Punishment Law*.[16]

Case 2: During the period from 20 March 2020 to 9 December 2021, a company in Zhuhai of Guangdong Province has continuously declared to export 11 shipments of detergents and laundry gels containing 10% triethanolamine through Gongbei Customs. The customs decided that the contents of triethanolamine contained in the products were controlled chemicals subject to the Dual-use Export License. Accordingly, a fine of CNY 85,000 was imposed on the company pursuant to Article 14(1) of the *Customs Implementation Regulations*.[17]

[15] Currently, only two related administrative cases imposed by the MOFOM are online available as follows. In May 2004, a company in Jiangsu Province and a chemical company in Shandong Province were found illegally exporting items enlisted on the *Missile and Missile-related Items and Technologies Export Control List*. Both two companies were subject to monetary penalties and no more information was disclosed. In March 2008, a chemical equipment company in Shandong Province was found illegally exporting items enlisted on the *Certain Chemicals and Related Equipment and Technologies Export Control List*. The company was subject to a fine of CNY 450, 000.

[16] Jin Xin Gang Guan Ji Wei Zi [2023]0012, 津新港关缉违字 (2023) 0012号, 22 February 2023.

[17] Gong Dou Guan Ji Wei Zi [2023]0003, 拱斗关缉违字 (2023) 0003号, 14 February 2023.

Case 3: During the period from 26 February 2021 to 24 June 2021, a company in Shenzhen of Guangdong Province has separately declared to export "aircraft engines" through Meisha Customs. Meisha Customs determined that the shipments were "small and combustion-efficient lightweight turbofan engines" classified as falling into the scope of China tariff code 8411 1210 00, enlisted on the *Missile and Missile-related Items and Technologies Export Control List*, and subject to the Dual-use Export License. The company was found exporting controlled items without a license and was imposed a fine of CNY 40,000 pursuant to Articles 34(1) and 40 of ECL and Article 32(1) of the *Administrative Punishment Law*.[18]

Case 4: On 27 October 2022, a company in Suzhou of Jiangsu Province entrusted a customs broker to export a shipment including certain glass-lined reactors with a value of CNY 1,365,236.93 through a custom in Shanghai. After inspection, the commodities were identified as biological dual-use ferments under the tariff code 8479 8200 10 subject to the Dual-use Export License. Accordingly, a fine of CNY 120,000 was imposed on the company pursuant to Article 86(3) of the *Customs Law* and Article 15(3) of the *Customs Implementation Regulations*.[19]

Case 5: On 2 January 2023, a company in Tianjin declared to export 200 graphite crucibles as a matter of general trade through Tianjin Xingang Customs, with a total CIF price of USD 4,060. After inspection and testing, the commodities were identified as graphite or other carbon products for non-electrical purposes under tariff code 3801 9090 00 subject to the Dual-use Export License. Accordingly, the company was found exporting controlled items without a license and was imposed a fine of CNY 7,000 pursuant to Article 34 of ECL and Article 32 of the *Administrative Punishment Law*.[20]

7.3.1.2 Administrative Penalties on Export of Military Items

Case 1: On 18 August 2022, a company in Beijing declared to export a shipment of goods through Tianjin Customs, including safety helmets (No. 18), uniforms (No. 19), and protective equipment (No. 20). After inspection, Tianjin Customs determined that above items were bulletproof helmets (No. 18), bulletproof undershirts (No. 19), and bulletproof plugs (No. 5), all of which were enlisted under Category 13.1.1.2 of the Military Item List of China, subject to the Military Export License when exported. In accordance with Articles 82(1) and 82(2) of the *Customs Law* and Articles 7(2), 9(1), and 9(2) of the *Customs Implementation Regulations*, the items were confiscated. No fines were imposed against the violating company.[21]

Case 2: On 7 February 2023, a company in Ningbo of Zhejiang Province entrusted a customs broker to export a cargo of goods, including 60,552 big lip caps with a value of CNY 2,260,700 through Ningbo Customs. After inspection and testing, the

[18] Mei Sha Guan Ji Pu Wei Zi [2023]0005, 梅沙关缉普违字 (2023) 0005号, 11 May 2023.

[19] Hu Wai Gang Guan Ji Wei Zi [2023]5032, 沪外港关缉违字 (2023) 5032号, 12 May 2023.

[20] Jin Xin Gang Guan Ji Wei Zi [2023]0038, 津新港关缉违字 (2023) 0038号, 25 April 2023.

[21] Jin Xin Gang Guan Ji Cha/Wei Zi, 津新港关缉查/违字 (2022) 0175号, 21 December 2022.

commodities were identified as police caps subject to the Military Export License. Accordingly, the company was found exporting controlled items without a license in violation of Article 19(1) of ECL and was imposed a fine of CNY 319,200 pursuant to Articles 34 of ECL and Article 32(5) of the *Administrative Punishment Law*.[22]

Case 3: On 31 October 2022, a company in Wenzhou of Zhejiang Province entrusted a customs broker to export a shipment of goods in cross-border e-commerce mode through Ningbo Customs, including knitted fabric (No. 1), training vest (No. 2), and bags (No. 3). After inspection, the commodities were identified as camouflage fabric of 8471.9 m, tactical vests, and tactical triple magazine bags, all of which were subjected to the Military Export License when exported with a value of CNY 973,100. Accordingly, the company was found exporting controlled items without a license in violation of Article 19(1) of ECL and was imposed a fine of CNY 116,700 pursuant to Articles 34 of ECL and Article 32(5) of the *Administrative Punishment Law*.[23]

Case 4: On 6 September 2022, a company in Guangzhou of Guangdong Province entrusted a customs broker to export a shipment of goods through Ningbo Customs, declared as men's casual suits. After inspection, the commodities were determined as military uniforms subject to the Military Export License when exported, with a value of CNY 1,832,300. Accordingly, the company was found exporting controlled items without a license in violation of Article 19(1) of ECL and was imposed a fine of CNY 219,800 pursuant to Articles 34 of ECL and Article 32(5) of the *Administrative Punishment Law*.[24]

Case 5: On 2 February 2023, a company in Beijing declared to export a shipment of goods through Tianjin Customs, including tool kits (No. 1), blankets (No. 2), socks (No. 3), hats (No. 4), traveling bags (No. 5), and cotton clothes (No. 6). However, after inspection, the customs determined that certain above items were boxes of 90-IA aerial arrows explosive bombs (No. 1), military blankets and military green towel quilts (No. 2), tank hats (No. 4), and front transport bags (No. 5), all of which were enlisted under Category 13.1.1.4 of the Military Item List of China, subject to the Military Export License when exported. In accordance with Articles 82(1) and 82(2) of the *Customs Law* and Articles 7(2) and 9(1) of the *Customs Implementation Regulations*, the items were confiscated. No fines were imposed against the violation party.[25]

7.3.1.3 Analysis and Comments

The above administrative enforcement cases by the customs reflect some common problems faced by both EBOs and the customs in practice.

[22] Yong Bei Guan Ji Wei Zi [2023]255, 甬北关缉违字 (2023) 255号, 2 June 2023.
[23] Yong Bei Guan Ji Wei Zi [2023]225, 甬北关缉违字 (2023) 225号, 24 April 2023.
[24] Yong Mei Guan Ji Wei Zi [2023]0001, 甬梅关缉违字 (2023) 0001号, 1 March 2023.
[25] Jin Xin Gang Guan Ji Cha Zi [2023]1, 津新港关缉查字 (2023) 1号, 8 May 2023.

(a) **Identification of Controlled Items**

The definition of controlled items is a precondition for the export license requirement and the basis for EBOs' export control compliance and the enforcement by the Customs.

From EBOs' perspective, the administrative enforcement cases show that the major cause for their failure to accurately identify whether the items are subject to export control is the misclassification of the China tariff codes, or the failure to identify the attributes as controlled items even when they are correctly classified. In addition, it is erroneous to merely rely on the tariff codes to determine the export control items. Although admittedly most commodities under the Dual-use Export Catalogue of China are annotated with corresponding tariff codes, the Catalogue, however, especially remarks that the attributes as controlled or not controlled shall be determined according to the given names and descriptions, and the tariff codes are provided for reference only. Furthermore, the items under the Military Item List of China are presented simply with names and descriptions without any tariff code. In this sense, there exist high risks in the determination and identification of controlled items if EBOs solely rely upon the tariff code classification.

From the perspective of the customs, the customs are granted the power under ECL to "request the State export control authorities to organize an assessment and not to release the goods for export during the assessment or questioning period".[26] In some of the above-summarized cases, some local customs have actively exercised this power by applying for identification and inspection of the goods in doubt. For the goods not declared by EBOs as military items but with apparent military characteristics, many local customs chose to contact State export control authorities, including the Equipment Development Department of the CMC, to identify the nature of such goods.[27]

(b) **Third-Party Service Providers**

It is not unusual for EBOs in the summarized cases to entrust third-party customs brokers to declare their exports. However, in all cases, only EBOs themselves were penalized except for one decision made by the Lianyungang Customs.[28] In that case, a freight forwarder was found cooperating with an EBO to export sodium carbonate (soda ash) from Lianyungang of China to Yangon of Myanmar, by falsely declaring the port of destination as Singapore, with a knowledge that a Dual-use Export License is required for this export to Myanmar. The Lianyungang Customs emphasized that this freight forwarder "knowingly" provided services for an illegal export. Nevertheless, it is still unclear whether a third-party service provider will be penalized if it should have the knowledge that a violation has occurred or is about to occur.

[26] Article 19(2) of the ECL.

[27] Hang Ji Guan Ji Wei Zi [2023]0004, 杭机关缉违字[2023]0004号, 20 February 2023; Hu Yang Shan Guan Ji Wei Zi [2023]258, 沪洋山关缉违字〔2023〕258号, 7 June 2023; Peng Guan Ji Kuai Wei Zi [2023]1, 鹏关缉快违字 (2023) 1号, 25 April 2023.

[28] Lian Guan Ji Cha Zi [2023]0054, 连关缉查字[2023]0054号, 6 January 2023.

Combined with *Administrative Penalties Law* of China, it is generally acknowledged that "fault" is not a necessary element for imposing administrative penalties, while the latest amendment of this law adds a new provision that if a party concerned has sufficient evidence to prove that there is no fault, no administrative penalty shall be imposed.[29] Regarding this issue, under ECL, Article 20 prescribes that no organization or individual may provide any agency, freight, delivery, customs clearance, third-party e-commerce trading platform, financial or other services to any exporter engaged in any violations of export control provisions. This seems to be an expression of strict liability, without regard to whether the third party knows or should have known that the export activity is illegal at the time the service was provided. However, under Article 36 of ECL, the penalty is conditional upon the knowingly provision of services to an exporter engaged in violations of ECL. In fact, Article 36 is the only provision under ECL that contains the wording "knowingly".

(c) **Exported Goods Containing Chemicals**

A major concern in recent years is whether the export of goods containing special chemical contents, controlled chemicals, certain chemicals, precursor chemicals (I), and precursor chemicals (II), for instance, is subjected to Dual-use Export License management. Common examples of such goods include cleaner containing triethanolamine,[30] lubricants containing triethanolamine,[31] industrial compounds containing sodium carbonate,[32] and ink products containing ethyl acetate.[33]

Regarding this issue, it is reported that GAC has issued an instruction to the regional customs that for industrial products like detergents, and make-ups containing triethanolamine, if the triethanolamine is already neutralized and cannot be extracted in monomer, the export of such products is exempted from Dual-use Export License; otherwise, a license is still required even the content of controlled triethanolamine is extremely low.[34] It seems that this logic can be applied to other types of goods containing chemicals, as long as the chemical monomer can still be extracted, a Dual-use Export License will be required for the export of the goods containing such chemicals, unless otherwise regulated.

The second issue is under the circumstances of exporting goods containing chemicals, whether the illegal transaction value shall be determined on the basis of the value of the whole goods, or only the value of chemical component itself, which is not explained under ECL or other related rules and regulations. Regarding this question,

[29] Article 33(2) of the *Administrative Penalties Law*.

[30] Gong Dou Guan Ji Wei Zi [2023]0003, 拱斗关缉违字 (2023) 0003号, 14 February 2023.

[31] Gong Dou Guan Ji Wei Zi [2023]0002, 拱斗关缉违字 (2023) 0002号, 10 February 2023.

[32] Nan Guan Ji Wei Zi [2023]0009, 南关缉违字 (2023) 0009号, 12 January 2023; Da Gang Guan Ji Wei Zi [2023]17, 大港关缉违字 (2023) 17号, 29 June 2023; Da Gang Guan Ji Wei Zi [2023]16, 大港关缉违字 (2023) 16号, 29 June 2023.

[33] Yong Guan Cha/Wei Zi [2023]0002, 永关查/违字 (2023) 0002号, 2 March 2023.

[34] Letter of Department of General Operation of the General Administration of Customs on the Clarification of import/export license regulatory requirements of mixtures containing triethanolamine, 28 October 2022.

Article 7 of the *Administration Provisions on Import and Export of Precursor Chemicals* stipulates that mixtures containing precursor chemicals should be converted into pure products based on content to determine whether a license is required, except for compounded pharmaceutical preparations containing precursor chemicals. In line with this logic, a potential interpretation is that in determining the amount of the illegal transaction value for penalty purposes, the calculating base shall be the value of the chemical component contained, instead of the whole goods. However, it seems that many local customs authorities tend to directly take the value of the goods or mixtures as the base, which may be challenged for EBOs on a case-by-case basis.

(d) **Application of Article 40 of ECL**

Article 40 of ECL provides that violations of export control provisions of ECL shall be subjected to penalty by the State export control authorities; and for those violations that are subjected to penalty by the customs according to any laws or administrative regulations, the penalty imposed by the customs shall be governed by ECL.

Prior to entry into force of ECL, the customs imposed administrative penalties on the party in violation of export control regulations on the basis of the *Administrative Penalties Law*, the *Customs Law*, and/or the *Customs Implementation Regulations*. After the entry into force of ECL on 1 December 2020, the jurisdiction of the customs over exported controlled goods remains intact, save that the customs must impose penalties for such violations pursuant to ECL. Given this phenomenon of concurrent liabilities under different laws,[35] the customs face an abrupt psychological switch from the less stringent customs law penalties to the stringent penalties under ECL, which is normally five to ten times of the illegal transaction value, while Article 15(3) of the *Customs Implementation Regulations* provides a fine of not less than 5% and not more than 30% of the value of the goods for unauthorized exports without a license.

In practice, it seems that the customs have adopted a considerate approach to violations of ECL in the first two years after the entry into force of ECL. The customs tend to apply customs' laws and regulations as the basis and the *Administrative Penalties Law* as well to justify its less stringent penalties on ECL violations, in cases of violations of a minor nature, so ECL was much neglected in such customs enforcement cases.

A remarkable trend has occurred since 2023 that many regional customs like Ningbo Customs, Tianjin Customs, and Shenzhen Customs have enforced "the basic legal liabilities provision under ECL combined with the leniency provisions of the *Administrative Penalties Law*[36]". With this new approach, though the customs are

[35] Some scholars or lawyers have already noticed this issue. See, Chen, F., Chen, K.B., & Chen, H.J. (2022, October 19). Reviews of Customs Administrative Penalty Cases after the Implementation of the Export Control Law. Retrieved October 8, 2023, from https://mp.weixin.qq.com/s/7KC_pNWdlqRdnk9uwTo6pw; Wang, Y.L. (2023, July 3). The Export Control Law should be stringently enforced. Retrieved October 8, 2023, from https://mp.weixin.qq.com/s/rxAqWmUwx_jjy2vD2PcmyA.

[36] Article 32 of the *Administrative Penalties Law* prescribes that a lighter or mitigated administrative penalty shall be imposed if the party concerned: (1) has taken the initiative to eliminate or lessen the

vigorous in enforcing ECL, the fines are still far below the statutory penalty range of ECL. However, it can be reasonably foreseen that the customs will enforce ECL pursuant to ECL provisions, especially after the official issuance of Dual-use Draft Regulations, given the importance of national security and non-proliferation concepts underlying ECL enactment. One of such signs shows in some criminal cases where MOFCOM was also involved in investigations against ECL violations.

7.3.2 Criminal Cases

Several criminal cases related to the violations of export control laws and regulations are released on the website of China Judgment Online.

7.3.2.1 Case Summaries

Case 1: A person surnamed Hu, conspired with another defendant surnamed Fang, exported a total of three tickets of sodium carbonate (soda ash) with a total of 361.505 tons to Yangon of Myanmar by falsely declaring the export destination country with a knowledge that such export requires a Dual-use Export License during a period from January 2019 through May 2021. Both two accused were found guilty of smuggling goods and articles prohibited for import and export (Article 151(3) of the *Criminal Law*). Respectively, Hu was sentenced to fixed-term imprisonment of two years, subject to probation of two years, and a fine of CNY 100,000. Fang was sentenced to fixed-term imprisonment of one year and six months, subject to probation of one year and six months, and a fine of CNY 50,000. Besides, all the illegal proceeds were forfeited, and the seized smuggled goods and belongings used for the crime were confiscated.[37]

Case 2: Since February 2012, the accused surnamed Jin has continuously exported diluent containing more than 40% toluene to North Korea through an international freight forwarding company. Another accused surnamed Wang, the legal representative of this company, agreed to help Jin falsely declare the toluene content with the knowledge that the export of diluent with toluene content exceeding 40% was subject to the Dual-use Export License. It was calculated that Jin exported a total of 93.12 tons of diluent through this forwarding company from September 2012 to December

harmful consequences brought about by the unlawful act, (2) was coerced or induced by another to commit the unlawful act, (3) has taken the initiative to confess an unlawful act that the administrative organ was not yet aware of, (4) has performed meritorious deeds while working in coordination with the administrative organ to investigate unlawful acts, or (5) there are other circumstances that give rise to a lighter or mitigated administrative penalty in accordance with laws, regulations, and rules.

[37] (2021) Hu 03 Xing Chu 127, (2021) 沪03刑初127号, Shanghai Third Intermediate People's Court, 2 December 2021.

2017. All three accused were found guilty of smuggling goods and articles prohibited for import and export (Article 151(3) of the *Criminal Law*). Respectively, Jin was sentenced to fixed-term imprisonment of three years, subject to probation of five years, and a fine of CNY 250,000. Wang was sentenced to fixed-term imprisonment of three years, subject to probation of four years, and a fine of CNY 100,000. The company was imposed a fine of CNY 150,000.[38]

Case 3: From October 2019 through December 2020, a person surnamed Xie, conspired with others, exported ammonium chloride with a total of 743.7 tons to Myanmar by placing the items to the bottom of the truck and falsely declaring that the items were ammonium sulfate, with a knowledge that such export requires a Dual-use Export License. Xie was also found guilty of smuggling goods and articles prohibited for import and export (Article 151(3) of the *Criminal Law*) and was sentenced to fixed-term imprisonment of six years, and a fine of CNY 100,000. All the smuggled goods were confiscated accordingly.[39]

Case 4: From November 2015 through November 2016, an individual surnamed Zhang, who was in charge of a chemical fertilizer manufacturing company, willfully exported a total of 10,453.24 tons of ammonium chloride to Myanmar by falsely declaring the export destination port as Singapore and altering relevant customs declaration documents, with a knowledge that such export requires a Dual-use Export License. Both Zhang and the company were found guilty of smuggling goods and articles prohibited for import and export (Article 151(3) of the *Criminal Law*). Respectively, Zhang was sentenced to fixed-term imprisonment of two years, subject to probation of two years, and a fine of CNY 100,000. The company was sentenced to a fine of CNY 200,000. All the illegal proceeds were forfeited accordingly.[40]

7.3.2.2 Analysis and Comment

All the accused in the above cases were held in violation of Article 151(3) of the *Criminal Law of the PRC*, which is smuggling goods and articles prohibited for import and export. All the smuggled goods were precursor chemicals, including sodium carbonate (soda ash), toluene, and ammonium chloride. The following two points are worth noting from the above cases.

Firstly, the criminal violations constituting smuggling crimes involved a great amount of goods in quantity and value. For instance, the quantity of items in the above cases is 361.505 tons of sodium carbonate, 93.12 tons of diluent, 743.7 tons

[38] (2019) Liao 06 Xing Chu 8, (2019) 辽06刑初8号刑事判决, Liaoning Dandong Intermediate People's Court, 26 March 2019; (2019) Liao Xing Zhong 250, (2019) 辽刑终250号, Liaoning High People's Court, 29 May 2019.

[39] (2022) Yun 28 Xing Chu 2, (2022) 云28刑初2号, Intermediate People's Court of Xishuangbanna Dai Autonomous Prefecture, Yunnan Province, 16 March 2022.

[40] (2022) Liao 02 Xing Chu 37, (2022) 辽02刑初37号, Liaoning Dalian Intermediate People's Court, 30 May 2022.

of ammonium chloride, and 10,453.24 tons of ammonium chloride, which satisfies the triggering standard under the *Interpretative Opinion*.[41]

Secondly, it is important to ascertain the subjective knowledge level of the accused, which is also relevant to the criminal penalties. In all four cases, the accused were held to commit smuggling in a long preparation period with a manifest intent element, mainly by way of falsely declaring commodity descriptions or destinations of the exports. To establish such intent or knowledge, a series of evidence will be exhibited including witness testimony, the records of the transaction, and the communication scripts.

Please note that although the released reports of cases are rather limited, there may be more adjudicated criminal cases in practice. To our knowledge, a Chinese company was under investigation by MOFCOM and the customs in the initial stage and subsequently the ASB of the customs arrested one shareholder, put another shareholder on probation awaiting trial for their active involvement in the export of nuclear-related material without dual-use license to the U.S. The factory was in jeopardy as a result of the violations.

Again, for criminal risk alleviation and elimination purposes, the EBOs must set up an ICP of trade compliance, strictly implement the internal procedure to control the risks, and proactively resort to legal assistance for help in advance in ambiguous circumstances. Training on handling dawn raids is also desirable for the management and operational staff members to understand the boundaries of the legitimate operation of the business and how to protect the legal rights of the business and themselves.

[41] Article 11 of the *Interpretative Opinion*: Smuggling goods or articles prohibited from import or export by the State with any of the following circumstances shall, in accordance with Article 151(3) of the *Criminal Law*, be subjected to a fixed-term imprisonment of less than five years or criminal detention, and be concurrently or separately subject to a fine: ... (6) smuggling the used motor vehicles, cut-up cars, used electromechanical products or any other goods or articles of which the import or export is prohibited, with the quantity of not less than 20 tons but less than 100 tons or with the value of not less than CNY 200,000 but less than CNY 1 million... Any of the following circumstances shall be deemed to be "serious circumstances" under Article 151(3) of the *Criminal Law*: (1) the quantity or value of the smuggled goods or articles exceed the standards (1)–(6) in the above paragraph.

Chapter 8
Export Control Internal Compliance Programs

In this chapter, Sect. 8.1 outlines the advantages of setting up an export control internal compliance program ("China ICP") under MOFCOM guidelines; Sect. 8.2 specifies MOFCOM guidelines on China ICP; Sect. 8.3 analyzes the compliance logics of China ICP, providing some risk-based compliance advice from the perspective of controlled items, activities, and acting parties; Sect. 8.4 focuses on the practices of China ICP, summarizing a compliance sample and the regulatory trends. Section 8.5 concludes this chapter and emphasizes the necessity of installing China ICP.

8.1 Overview of China ICP

8.1.1 Why Is China ICP Necessary?

The International Organization for Standardization ("ISO") defines compliance as an ongoing process and the outcome of an organization meeting its obligations. According to ISO, compliance is made sustainable by embedding it in the culture of the organization and in the behavior and attitude of people working for it.[1] Therefore, compliance shall be better integrated into internal control processes tailored to the business operation.

According to the Basic Norms of Enterprises Internal Control issued by the Chinese government, internal control refers to the process implemented by the management and all employees of enterprises to achieve the control objectives.[2]

[1] ISO 37301:2021, Compliance management systems—Requirements with guidance for use. Retrieved October 10, 2023, from https://www.iso.org/obp/ui/#iso:std:iso:37301:ed-1:v1:en.

[2] Basic Norms of Enterprises Internal Control. Retrieved October 10, 2023, from http://www.gov.cn/zwgk/2008-07/02/content_1033585.htm.

D. Zhao, *Contemporary Export Control Law of China*, Modern China and International Economic Law, https://doi.org/10.1007/978-981-99-9825-8_8

China ICP is such an internal control compliance mechanism recommended by MOFCOM on export control compliance adopted by the members of the business community to proactively achieve the objective of regulatory compliance.

China ICP, which is basically an internal compliance control mechanism, focuses on the legality of export contents and procedures relevant to the cross-border transfer or export of controlled items, whether they are tangible goods or commodities, or intangible technologies or data. China ICP shall follow rules and regulations on export and desirably incorporate MOFCOM guidelines as appropriate and tailored such China ICP to the actuality of the business relevant to the exports from China.

For the business community, compliance in the context of the growing regulatory environment is not merely a matter of avoiding business abruption and corporate and personal liabilities, but also as a matter of fact of a competitive edge and image[3] in the given market.

Given the liabilities of EBOs under ECL are largely strict liabilities with severe consequences on the businesses, China ICP would help to detect past irregularities, avoid future non-compliances, ensure the smooth business operation and competitiveness without abnormal abruption, and enjoy trade and supervision facilitation benefits, e.g., multiple-use licenses and other facilitation measures[4] granted by the customs and other local authorities to the compliant businesses. There is also a trend in practice that MOFCOM may view EBOs without China ICP as high-risk entities, which may trigger inquiries from MOFCOM to examine their export records and practice and further trigger investigations by MOFCOM who may work in conjunction with the customs or ASB if any irregularities can be detected through such inquiries, formal or informal.

Regarding multiple-use licenses, according to Article 14 of ECL, for EBOs who have established China ICP, and whose systems operate well, MOFCOM may provide them with such licenses and other facilitation measures for their export of controlled items. A multiple-use license allows an EBO to export multiple dual-use items to multiple end-users multiple times within the scope and validity period (generally two years) of the license.[5] On 22 April 2022, MOFCOM announced the Draft Regulations on Export Controls of dual-use items, which prescribe four requirements to be satisfied for applying for the multiuse license, respectively, (i) have established a well-run China ICP, (ii) have been engaged in dual-use export activities for two or

---

[3] An effective and sound management of compliance-related risks should be regarded as an opportunity to pursue and take, due to the several benefits that it provides, including improving business opportunities and sustainability, protecting and enhancing an organization's reputation and credibility, increasing the confidence of third parties in the organization's capacity to achieve sustained success, and so forth. ISO 37301:2021, Compliance management systems—Requirements with guidance for use. Retrieved October 10, 2023, from https://www.iso.org/obp/ui/#iso:std:iso:37301:ed-1:v1:en.

[4] Article 14 of ECL.

[5] Article 3 of Order of the Ministry of Commerce [2009] No. 8—Administrative Measures for General License of Exports of Dual-use Items and Techniques. Currently, the validity of such a general license does not exceed three years as set forth in Article 6 of the Administrative Measures for General License of Export of Dual-use Items and Technologies.

more years and have obtained licenses many times, (iii) have relatively fixed sales channels and end-users, and (iv) meet other conditions as set forth by competent authorities.[6]

As a part of the China ICP, if the EBO takes the initiative to eliminate or mitigate the harmful consequences if brought by export control violations, the EBO may be given leniency in administrative penalties according to the Law of the People's Republic of China on Administrative Penalties.[7] The Draft Regulations further prescribe that service providers of dual-use item exports who have in place an ICP that runs well, so that the harmful consequences of a violation committed are prevented from further spreading, may be given a lighter punishment by the authority on a discretionary basis.[8] The China ICP may even serve as a possible factor in reaching a non-prosecution arrangement with the prosecutor where a company is charged with the criminal offense for violating ECL.[9]

8.1.2 Who Is to Consider Establishing China ICP?

EBOs in China, especially those constantly exporting controlled items, must have a comprehensive China ICP to identify and void export control exposures. In connection with such exporters, the service providers rendering agency, freight, delivery, customs clearance, third-party e-commerce trading platform, financial or other such services for exporters are expected to establish China ICP as well, since the cross-border services to such EBOs may also risk violations under ECL.[10]

As both tangible and intangible cross-border transfers of controlled items can constitute "controlled activities", the business entities must set up the China ICP over export or cross-border activities for pre-transfer risk control purposes. MOFCOM suggests that enterprises or scientific research institutes engaged in the research and development ("R&D") or production of dual-use items may, based on their operation activities, establish corresponding compliance mechanisms.[11] Practically, R&D activities may involve the export (outbound flow) of technologies or data. A webinar

---

[6] Article 23 of the Draft Regulations.

[7] Article 32(1) of the Law of the People's Republic of China on Administrative Penalties.

[8] Article 52 of the Draft Regulations.

[9] In practice, certain procuratorates in some pilot areas may reach a non-prosecution arrangement with the company which actively implements compliance rectifications. See Xu, H. (2021, November 23). *Exploration of the Prosecutorial Recommendation Model for Compliance with Non-prosecution in Case-Related Enterprises*. Procurator Daily. Retrieved October 10, 2023, from https://www.spp.gov.cn/spp/llyj/202111/t20211123_536133.shtml.

[10] According to Article 20 of the ECL, any organization or individual shall not provide agency, freight, delivery, customs clearance, third-party e-commerce trading platforms, finance, and other services for exporting business operators engaging in violations of export control.

[11] Guidance from the Ministry of Commerce on the Establishment of Internal Compliance Mechanisms for Export Control of Dual-Use Items by Export Operators, MOFCOM Announcement No. 10 of 2021, April 28, 2021.

or a visiting tour in a laboratory may cause the export or deemed export of dual-use technologies or data. Besides, the after-sale services provided by a production company may also involve the export of certain replacing components, technologies, and related services. Even an international business trip or non-business travel with a laptop may have export control risks, as the data in the laptop and samples in the luggage may be controlled items. In short, R&D institutes or R&D people of a business entity are likely to encounter export control risks, and China ICP corresponding to such R&D business is also desirable.

Furthermore, from the perspective of controlled items, China ICP is also desirable to the business entities engaging or likely to export controlled items specified on control lists, such as dual-use items, military items, and goods and technologies restricted or prohibited from export. Given that ECL adopts the catch-all control over exported items not so listed but posing national security risks,[12] the business entity must also take precautionary measures to avoid national security risks.

Apart from the business entities as EBOs in China, foreign importers and end-users of items controlled under ECL may consider China ICP as well. As analyzed in Chap. 6, foreign importers and end-users shall comply with the export and re-export controls and "in-country transfer" controls under ECL; otherwise, they may be designated onto the List of Controlled Parties in the case of violation and unable to further obtain items controlled under ECL and/or imposed with administrative penalties.[13]

8.2 How to Install China ICP?

8.2.1 Overview

On 28 April 2021, MOFCOM released the "Guidance of the Ministry of Commerce on the Establishment of Internal Compliance Mechanism of Dual-Use Item Exporting Business Operators" (MOFCOM Order No. 10, 2021) ("ICP Guidelines").[14] With the ICP Guidelines, the EBO will be able to implement China ICP to comply with ECL. Though not a binding obligation to set up China ICP, China ICP is crucial to the EBO in that it helps prevent or reduce non-compliance incidences and negative consequences as outlined above.

Three basic ingredients are essential in the contents of China ICP:

(a) Legality. The EBO must strictly adhere to ECL and related rules of law and place compliance above its commercial interests without eroding legality.

[12] Article 12 of the ECL.

[13] Article 18 and 37 of the ECL.

[14] Guidance from the Ministry of Commerce on the Establishment of Internal Compliance Mechanisms for Export Control of Dual-Use Items by Export Operators, MOFCOM Announcement No. 10 of 2021, April 28, 2021.

(b) Independence. China ICP must run independently and the export control compliance officer or manager must have independent power in controlling the export business for compliance purposes.
(c) Effectiveness. The compliance system must be placed into the internal control and audit procedures and implemented for the export business.

Out of the three ingredients, nine elements must exist in China ICP, which include (a) statement of policy and compliance commitment by the management (commitment policy); (b) designation of compliance responsibilities to an independent internal department/organ (independence); (c) comprehensive assessment of risks (self-examination); (d) internal control procedure (effectiveness); (e) emergency response measures (crisis solution); (f) training (awareness and competence); (g) compliance audits (retrospective health check); (h) document retention (evidence for defense); and (i) compilation of compliance manual (compliance formalization).

8.2.2 *China ICP Guidelines—Content Requirements*

8.2.2.1 Statement of Policy and Commitment

The main contents of the policy statement include but are not limited to:

(a) a statement of the basic purpose and importance of export control compliance;
(b) a commitment to abide by the export control laws and regulations;
(c) a commitment not to engage in business activities in violation of export control laws and regulations under any circumstances;
(d) a clear expression of support for export control compliance;
(e) a commitment to assess risks prior to commercial activities;
(f) an emphasis on the importance of familiarity of the employees with export control laws and regulations, and requirements for the employees to comply with relevant statutory provisions and not to conduct illegal exports under any circumstances;
(g) a list of risks and possible penalties for violating export control laws and regulations;
(h) the contact person responsible for export control compliance and the person's contact information.

Regarding the recipients of the compliance policy statement, firstly, the policy statement shall apply to all employees of the business entity (including employees directly and indirectly engaged in exporting, domestic employees, foreign employees, probationers, interns, and so forth). The business entity may require the employees to sign the undertaking letter of compliance. Secondly, the business entity may also distribute the policy statement to its transactional partners (e.g., suppliers, freight forwarders, distributors, sales agents, joint venture partners, technology exchange parties, other agents, and so forth). Wherever necessary, the business entity may require its transaction partners to sign the undertaking letter of compliance.

8.2.2.2 Designation of Compliance Responsibilities

The EBO is to establish a multilevel organizational structure, which is supported by the decision-making authority, led by the export control compliance department/organ, and implemented by each business unit. The exporting company shall determine the organizational structure at all levels, specify the recruiting criteria, job responsibilities, competence requirements, and contact information of the compliance personnel, and incorporate compliance performance into their overall performance assessment. The EBO may refer to the following organizational management framework or embed the export control compliance organizational structure into their existing compliance system.

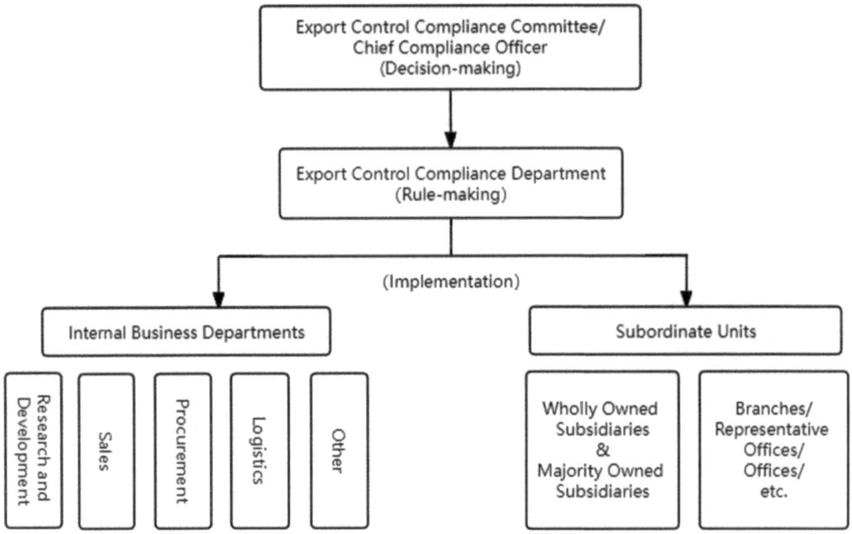

Note: (a) Subordinate units may implement their export control ICP under the guidance of the export control compliance department. Subordinate units may also establish their own separate ICP; (b) Internal Business Departments must implement the ICP as part of their duties in the business entity and accept compliance supervision and control by the Export Control Compliance Department.

8.2.2.3 Comprehensive Risk Assessment

A. Export control risks

A comprehensive risk assessment is the basis of China ICP, which must cover the export items, customers, technology research and development, internal operations, export control information updating, third-party transaction partners, risk prevention measures, and so on.

The business entity may refer to the Table 8.1 for potential compliance risks.

Apart from the potential risks above, there may be other different risks in business operations. EBOs are advised to develop prevention and control measures based on the specific risks and the actual conditions of their operations.

B. Risk assessment

The ICP Guidelines also provide detailed guidance on how to assess the risks.

(a) *Assessment of controlled items*

The assessment of controlled items is to be done in the following manners:

(i) Determine whether the items are included in the export control list (including the list of items subject to temporary export controls).
(ii) Sort out and classify the items to determine whether they fall under the jurisdiction of the import and export control laws and regulations of China, importing countries, or third countries (when involving transit, transshipment, re-export and so on).
(iii) Identify the main use of the items and figure out whether the following risks exist: the risk of endangering national security and interests, being used in

Table 8.1 Matrix of risks and responding measures

	Risks	Measures
1	Ambiguous nature of items	Classify controlled items onto a database
2	Difficulties in determining whether an export license is required	Promptly consult external professional agencies or the state export control administration department
3	Unknown end-users	Build automatic order screening system and seek information when known
4	Unknown end-uses	Check with the customer about the end-use and require the customer sign a statement on end-use
5	Risks of "deemed export" of controlled technologies	Develop control system for technologies
6	The product possibly containing the controlled items or technologies	Apply for a license as required by relevant laws and regulations; modify the design of products to avoid using sensible items
7	Lack of cooperation between the compliance department and the business departments	Enhance support from decision-making authority for the compliance department
8	Lack of compliance awareness among relevant transaction counterparties (suppliers, customers, third-party partners)	Appropriately communicate with counterparties about the export control ICP and clarify relevant compliance requirements

the design, development, production, or employ of WMD and their delivery vehicles, and being used for terrorist purposes.

(b) *Assessment of customers*

The assessment of customers' needs to consider the following ingredients:

(i) its main business scope, whether it involves military and other sensitive businesses;
(ii) whether the customer is a manufacturer, a distributor, or an end-user;
(iii) whether the customer is on the List of Controlled Parties under ECL, any other lists of parties prohibited or restricted from transactions of China, or the sanction list of the UN;
(iv) the risk level of the customer's country or region.

(c) *Assessment of technology and R&D*

The assessment of technology and R&D focuses on the following aspects:

(i) Determine whether their daily operations involve technologies subject to export control.
(ii) Examine whether the exchange and transmission of technologies may incur export control risks. Such export control risks may occur in technology information transfers by way of email, telephone, fax, domestic and international social networking software, and other electronic means. The access by a foreign party to an online data platform located in China for the storage or transmission of the software or technology may also incur export control risks.
(iii) Screen the employees engaged in work related to controlled technology and identify the hidden risk of providing controlled technology to foreign organizations and individuals even if in China without a license. In the case of engaging foreign employees to undertake the R&D work related to controlled technology or to acquire controlled technology information for business development or marketing purposes, e.g., at exhibitions, the EBO shall apply for an export control license before doing so.
(iv) Keep tracing records of the design and R&D data with alerts to the employees regarding the possible export control risks. If necessary, the EBO may consult the administration department of export control authorities.

(d) *Assessment of business partners other than customers*

The business partners other than the customers, which include cargo carriers, customs brokers, sales agents, R&D partners, financial service providers, third-party e-commerce trading platforms, and so forth, need to be assessed for possible compliance risks. The EBOs must exercise the due diligence work to identify the historical and current credit status of such business partners, domestic, or overseas. The due diligence may cover information of business licenses, board members, shareholders, actual controllers, and other items in order to avoid the non-compliance as may be caused by such business partners.

8.2.2.4 Internal Control Procedure

The EBO shall conduct internal control in advance of contract review, execution, performance, and application for export licenses.

Upon the review of any contract under negotiation, the EBO must conduct a comprehensive review of the transactional items, end-users, end-uses, transportation routes, and other related information. Besides that, the EBO may refer to Table 8.2 to identify whether there are any "red flags" in the proposed transactions.

Before signing the export contract, the EBO shall: (i) re-screen the relevant information of all parties involved in the transaction to prevent the risk of non-compliance arising due to changes in the list of parties prohibited or restricted from transactions and (ii) confirm whether all the previous reviews have been thorough, review the shipping information, and verify whether the license and the shipping documents match the cargo before shipping.

After signing the export contract, if the transaction involves controlled items or the EBO knows that the items may be subjected to the catch-all control, the EBO shall submit information to the export control administration department and apply for an export license in accordance with relevant laws and regulations. Additionally, the EBO shall also obtain the business qualifications as the operator for certain controlled items.[15] If it is difficult to determine whether relevant goods, technologies, and services are controlled items, the EBO may seek advice from external professional agencies or the state export control administration department. It is illegal for the EBO to export the controlled items before obtaining the export license.

8.2.2.5 Emergency Response Measures

The emergency response measures shall include the following contents:

(1) determine whether to initiate an internal investigation by the compliance department;
(2) determine the scope of the investigation;
(3) define the procedure of the investigation;
(4) prepare the investigation report;
(5) take remedial measures;
(6) feedback to the person who reports instances triggering internal investigations;
(7) report to the management;
(8) training on the lessons learned from such emergencies;

[15] For example, exporters engaging in the export of nuclear and nuclear dual-use items, biological dual-use items, certain chemicals and related equipment and technologies, missile and missile-related items and technologies, some other dual-use items, dredgers, high-pressure water cannons, and so forth shall register the operation qualification for sensitive items and technologies at the commerce departments. See Registration of the Operation Qualification for Sensitive Items and Technologies. Retrieved October 13, 2023, from http://egov.mofcom.gov.cn/xzxksx/18017/.

Table 8.2 Sample checklist of transactional red flags

Red flags	Yes	No
The customer		
The customer cannot be identified and is unwilling to answer questions related to its identity or transactions		
Information related to the customer cannot be found through normal channels (e.g., business registry, telephone directories, websites, and so on)		
The information of the customer (such as the Chinese or English name, address, and so on.) is the same as or close to the information of the individual or the entity on the List of Controlled Parties under ECL, other lists of parties prohibited or restricted from transactions of China, or the sanctions list of the UN		
The customer places its orders in a manner which is inconsistent with the general commercial practice		
The customer or the trade agent is unwilling to provide detailed information about the end-user or the end-use		
The customer evades answering or is ambiguous about whether the product or technology to be purchased will be used in the local country of the customer or will be re-exported		
The customer is unwilling to explain how to use the product to be purchased		
The customer is unwilling to answer the normal business or technical questions		
The customer is willing to buy at a price higher than prevailing market prices		
The customer is willing to buy an expensive product with cash		
The customer insists on buying the product without the knowledge of its functions or characteristics		
The customer refuses the normal procedures of installation, training, maintenance, guidance, and operation		
The Product		
The functions of the product ordered do not conform with the business scope of the customer		
The design or the normal use of the product ordered does not conform with the use as stated by the customer		
The product ordered does not conform with the technological level of the local country of the end-user		
The customer does not order the standard accessories of the product to be purchased		
The customer orders normally redundant accessories (e.g., buying components and parts more than necessary.)		
The transportation		
The address of the customer is too general		
The destination of delivery is unusual		
The destination of the products is different from the address of the end-user		
The customer has an unusual confidential requirement on the destination or detailed information of the products		
The customer has an unusual requirement on shipping or labeling of the products		

(9) voluntarily report to the state export control administration department in the case of serious violations.

Effective remedial measures require the coordination of departments and functions of the EBO at different levels. The management and the export control compliance department as well must attach importance to identifying and addressing risks. Business departments must take the initiative to promptly report risks to the compliance department and the management. Where necessary, the compliance department shall report risks to the State's export control administration department. In the meantime, corresponding corrections shall be made, including but not limited to suspending the contract, stopping shipments, retrieving goods in transportation, improving China ICP, and so forth.

8.2.2.6 Training

The EBO may implement training with contents responding to the employee's different job responsibilities.

(a) General staff members

The training to them must contain the concept and importance of export control compliance, the EBO's export control compliance policy and related management instruments, their compliance responsibilities, the contact person and contact information of the compliance department, risks of related violations, and so forth.

(b) Business departments

For the business departments involving management or operation of transactions subject to export control, such as manufacturing, research and development, procurement, and sales departments, in addition to the above training contents, the training must cover China ICP, the export control screening and review procedures, the focus of the end-user and end-use reviews, the operation of relevant information systems or screening tools, the procedure for reporting and handling detected violations, and so on.

8.2.2.7 Compliance Audits

The following process is desirable in the export control compliance retrospective audits:

(i) Determine the business department and personnel in the audit scope.
(ii) Prepare the audit process templates, such as interview questions, transaction audit checklists, and so forth.
(iii) Gather documentation from all business departments.
(iv) Conduct interviews with personnel at all levels of the business departments.

(v) Carefully review the above documentation, interview records and the actual business operation.

Apart from the comprehensive compliance audit at all levels, the EBO may conduct issue-specific audits focusing on certain departments (e.g., sales department, production department) or specific aspects of export transactions (e.g., shipment procedures, record keeping).

8.2.2.8 Document Retention

The EBO is advised to keep the documents and records relating to the abovementioned screening, identification of "red flags", and other compliance efforts.

In particular, the EBO must archive the following documents: (i) specifications of exported products; (ii) documents related to commercial transactions (such as records related to inquiries, order forms, contracts, invoices, bills of lading, freight bills, transfer records, and so forth); (iii) communications with relevant government departments; (iv) records of customer screening and correspondence; (v) documents proving the end-users and the end-uses; (vi) license application documents; (vii) license approval documents; (viii) records of carrying out export projects; (ix) export control-related internal rules, meeting minutes, resolutions, management documents; (x) violation found and measures taken; (xi) training records and materials; (xii) audit reports; (xiii) records of visits from foreign subcontractors, customers, and so on; (xiv) other documents to be filed.

The EBO may also adjust the document list above and prescribe specific document retention policies in line with its business operation. Such retained documentation would help the EBO in proving that the EBO did not or did not "knowingly" violate ECL, which may help to avoid or mitigate the EBO's legal liabilities in cases of governmental audit or investigation.

8.2.2.9 Compilation of Compliance Manual

The contents of such compliance manual may include, but are not limited to: (i) a policy statement signed by the management; (ii) summary of export control laws and regulations; (iii) the EBO's export control compliance policies and systems; (iv) export control compliance organizational structure and related responsibilities; (v) a list of the EBO's full-time (part-time) export control compliance personnel and their contact information; (vi) identification and screening system of controlled items operated or may be operated by the EBO, including relevant items that are not controlled items but may have risks listed in Article 12 of the Export Control Law, i.e., risks related to national security and interests, proliferation, and terrorism; (vii) the main content and result of the comprehensive risk assessment; (viii) export review process and priorities of the review; (ix) procedures for reporting and handling violations; (x) relevant training materials; (xi) contact information of state export

Table 8.3 Element similarities in ICP of China, the U.S., EU, and Japan

	China	U.S	EU	Japan
Policy statement/management commitment	√	√	√	
Establishment of organization/designation of personnel in charge	√		√	√
Risk assessment	√	√		
Screening process and procedures	√	√	√	√
Remedial actions	√	√	√	√
Training	√	√	√	√
Compliance audit	√	√	√	√
Recordkeeping and documentation	√	√	√	√
Compilation of manuals	√	√		
Physical and information security			√	

control administration departments and provincial authorities responsible for export control.

8.2.3 Global ICP Matrix

As revealed in practice, the subsidiaries in China of multinational groups are a bit confused about how to establish a China ICP when the group headquarters have already established an ICP that may aim to function globally.

According to MOFCOM, ICP Guidelines of China have drawn on some relevant contents of ISO 37301:2021, Compliance Management Systems—Requirements.[16] China ICP itself shares many similarities with some of the foreign countries' ICP, e.g., that of the United States. Such similarities are exhibited in Table 8.3 which is summarized based on our comparison of the China ICP and those of the U.S, EU, and Japan.

Similarly as it may seem from the table of comparison, the global ICP of a foreign company cannot function as a China ICP unless it contains every element as required by China ICP Guidelines. We recommend that the subsidiaries in China of foreign enterprises had better establish their own China ICP in Chinese by amending and updating its global ICP based on China ICP Guidelines, and installing the China export control elements into the existing internal control procedure. Overall, China ICP must be standardized according to China ICP Guidelines and made visible to the Chinese regulatory authorities to show compliance and responsibility.

[16] The Bureau of Industry Security and Import and Export Control of MOFCOM. (2022, June 13). *Q&As related to the Implementation of Internal Export Control Compliance Mechanisms by Export Business Operators (I)*. Retrieved October 13, 2023, from http://exportcontrol.mofcom.gov.cn/article/cjwt/202111/291.html.

8.3 China ICP: Compliance Logics

8.3.1 *Concept of EBO and Item-Based Compliance Obligations*

The identification of items subject to China export control is the crucial basis of China ICP. In practice, the failure to identify whether items to be exported fall within the scope of China export control may lead to illegal export without an export license, resulting in penalties imposed on the EBO.

It seems that under ECL, only the EBO has the obligation to comply with ECL, apart from some instances where the foreign importer of record and end-user is committed to its declared statement of end-user and end-use. However, the term EBO is not clearly defined under ECL. The author is of the opinion that (a) such EBO does not necessarily mean a company with a foreign trade business scope; (b) anyone who effects lawful or unlawful exports as an actual exporter, no matter as a business entity, an individual or otherwise, will likely count as such EBO subject to the export controls under ECL. The rationale for such an opinion is that export controls focus on the controlled items, and no matter who effects the exports, such an exporting party must be subject to the export controls and be liable for violations of export controls. This is also the general logic of export controls under EAR, and any party who effects exports of items subject to EAR must abide by EAR. By the same consideration, the party who conducts deemed export in China, or re-export or in-country transfer in a foreign country, may also constitute such EBO under ECL. In other words, EBOs are the exporters in China, re-exporters, and in-country transferors in a foreign country of controlled items under ECL.

Whether as a business entity in China or overseas, such EBO with the strict liability under ECL must screen the items to be exported or re-exported in accordance with risk assessment measures analyzed above. The EBO needs to be aware of the following compliance points.

(a) Tariff code for reference only

Though some EBOs routinely rely on the China 10-digit tariff code in determining export control items, such a practice is far from reliable and sufficient to avoid illegal export risks. The EBO must ensure export compliance by comparing the descriptions and specifications of the items on the control lists with their exported items.[17] For instance, according to the note of the Catalogue of Dual-use Items and Technologies Subject to Export License 2023, exporting any item included in the catalogue shall apply for the Dual-use Export License, regardless of whether the tariff code of the item is listed in the catalogue.[18]

---

[17] Ren, Q., & Zhao, D. (2020). Developments in Mainland China and Hong Kong. In Rachel Barnes et al. ed., *The Guide to Sanctions* (1st ed., p.241). London: Law Business Research Ltd.

[18] Announcement No. 42 of 2022 of the MOFCOM and the GAC, 30 December 2022.

That said, if an EBO correctly determines an export commodity not subject to export control, but its tariff code is enlisted in the Catalogue, the customs will likely not release the commodity for export unless the EBO can provide a certification from MOFCOM to prove that such commodity is not subjected to ECL. Therefore, the EBO must (a) make sure about the correctness of the tariff codes declared for the exports; (b) rightly classify the commodities to determine whether the commodities are subject to export control; and (c) prepare documentation to support the commodities not as export control items and apply for confirmation certification to MOFCOM if the tariff codes for such items appear on the Consolidated Catalogue of Dual-use Items.

(b) Overlap of controlled lists

In addition, different catalogues of controlled items may overlap with each other. Therefore, special attention shall be paid to licensing requirements for items overlapping different control lists. For instance, according to the annotations of the Catalogue of Goods Subject to Export License (2023),[19] for items listed in both this catalogue and the Catalogue of Dual-use Items and Technologies Subject to Export License, the EBO shall apply for the Dual-use Export License and be exempt from applying for the Export License for Goods (i.e., the license for goods listed in the Catalogue of Goods Subject to Export License).

(c) National security concerns

Goods, technologies, and services may be subjected to export control even if they are not listed in any catalogue relating to export control. The export control under ECL applies to the export of items related to safeguarding national security and interests.[20] Where the EBO knows or should have known that relevant goods, technologies, or services have such risks, they are obligated to apply for the export license for the export.[21] In this regard, EBOs shall invest compliance efforts in identifying export control risks of items not explicitly subject to export control but with national security concerns.

8.3.2 *Activity-Based Compliance Measures*

As far as the export control logic is concerned, apart from the focus of export control on the controlled items, MOFCOM and the customs devote their supervision and

[19] Ibid.

[20] Article 59 of the Draft Regulations.

[21] According to Article 12 of the ECL, … for the export of goods, technologies, and services not included in the control lists or not subject to temporary control, exporting business operators who know or should have known or are notified by the State's export control administrative departments that relevant goods, technologies, and services may have the following risks, shall apply for licenses to the State's export control administrative departments: (i) endangering national security and interests; (ii) being used to design, develop, produce or employ weapons of mass destruction and their delivery vehicles; or (iii) being used for terrorist purposes.

enforcement efforts to export activities of controlled items. Such export activities include export, re-export, and deemed export of controlled items, which also cover transferring intangible items from China to abroad or making such items accessible by overseas entities or persons. Therefore, the ICP must be implemented to effectively ensure compliance of the export activities to ECL.

8.3.2.1 Re-exports

According to ECL, transit, transshipment, thorough transport, and re-export of controlled items are also subject to export license,[22] posing risks to overseas importers and traders. The re-export of an item of China origin from overseas to a third country or region requires a license from Chinese authorities, on the condition that the export of that item from China to the same party in the third country or region requires a license.

If overseas individuals or entities re-export items controlled by ECL without a license, or re-export these items to parties in the List of Controlled Parties, they are in violation of ECL probably as foreign EBOs. Some foreign EBOs may wonder whether they can re-export the controlled items to other affiliates of the same group without a license. The answer is No, because the end-user of a controlled item shall not change without the approval of MOFCOM, for instance.

The buyers in the foreign re-export process may face a lower risk. If controlled items are re-exported without a license to a foreign buyer, as an end-user who does not know that it is the re-export of controlled items under ECL or the purchase transaction otherwise violates ECL, the foreign buyer would not be designated to the List of Controlled Parties. However, if such buyer is also a trader, it may also be treated as an EBO for re-exports and undertake the strict liabilities under ECL for not applying for the re-export license and may also be designated onto the List of Controlled Parties.

Unlike EAR, ECL does not contain a *de minimis* rule of control for foreign-made products, and such foreign-made products are presumably not controlled under ECL,[23] so that the further transfer or export of such foreign-made products does not need to apply for a license from MOFCOM. However, the test of determining a foreign-made product is not clear at this stage. The possible test can be the positive test of substantial manufacturing process which affords a foreign-made product status under ECL, or the negative test of simple processing, which does not afford the foreign-made status under ECL.

In conclusion, before re-exporting items of Chinese origin subject to export controls of China, foreign individuals and entities shall also take compliance measures pursuant to the ICP Guidelines, with an emphasis on screening the items, end-uses, and end-users and applying for the export license whenever necessary. It

[22] Article 45 of the ECL.

[23] Ren, Q., & Zhao, D. (2020). Developments in Mainland China and Hong Kong. In Rachel Barnes et al. ed., *The Guide to Sanctions* (1st ed., p. 242). London: Law Business Research Ltd.

is understandable that such a compliance effort may largely rely on the submission of documents and data from the upstream suppliers regarding the origin of the products, and a contractual indemnity clause may be desirable in the supply agreements with such supplier who is to indemnify the buyer for its incorrect or incomplete submission of information and data required by the buyer under this agreement.

8.3.2.2 Deemed Exports

According to ECL, controlled exports include deemed exports, which means that Chinese entities or individuals are prohibited or restricted from providing controlled commodities, technologies, or data for foreign entities or individuals, wherever the foreign entities are located.[24] Deemed exports may happen under various circumstances, such as visit to the EBO's plant or laboratory by a foreign visitor, the exchange of information in R&D activities, the employment of a foreign engineer, and showing the products or technology to foreign audience at an exhibition.

Currently, the EBO is advised to take prudent compliance measures to eliminate or alleviate risks related to deemed exports. Practically, the EBO must first identify technologies and products that are subjected to China export control; if providing them to employees, potential customers, visitors, or transaction parties of a foreign nationality, whether through face-to-face communications or electronic means, the EBO shall apply for the export license in advance of such deemed export.

8.3.2.3 Research and Development Activities

R&D activities usually involve exports of goods in smaller quantities or at a lower total value. Additionally, some exports involved in R&D activities are one time or temporary exports, which sometimes escape the internal compliance control system of the EBO. Nevertheless, such exports in R&D activities still constitute export activities regulated by export control laws and regulations of China, and the EBO is required to invest in compliance efforts in this arena.

Moreover, the export of intangible items frequently emerges in R&D activities. The EBO must pay particular attention to the fact that drawings, processing technologies, know-how, technical data or plans, and so forth may fall within the scope of controlled technologies.

Again, deemed exports are also of high risk with respect to intercompany R&D activities, where employees of different nationalities are working together and accessing technical information, drawings, and plans on a shared platform. The R&D activities of multinational companies in China and the overseas R&D activities of

[24] Article 2 of the ECL: "Export control of this Law refers to the prohibitive or restrictive measures taken by the State against...the act performed by a citizen, legal person or unincorporated organization of the People's Republic of China to provide any foreign organization or individual with controlled items."

Chinese companies may incur uncertain risks, and the EBO must take China ICP measures to tackle such risks. It remains to be seen whether a license exception may be made available to intercompany R&D activities which facilitates the necessary flow of technical information from China to related parties.

8.3.2.4 Employment of Expatriates

EBOs in China must maintain procedures designed to guard against the unauthorized release of controlled items, even to their employees. As analyzed above, sharing information with expatriates may constitute deemed export under ECL, posing risks of export control violations.

It is advised for EBOs in China to identify controlled products and technologies in their daily operation and establish a badge/classification system to indicate to employees whether they can share certain items with other employees,[25] especially expatriate employees.

For technologies and data subject to China export control, the EBO may take practical measures to safeguard them, including encrypting controlled technical data, restricting access to controlled technical data using network passwords, monitoring the flow of controlled technologies and so forth.[26]

8.3.2.5 Overseas Trips

In business travels, employees of an EBO might carry their laptops abroad, and thus, controlled technologies or data may be exported without a license. Therefore, the ICP of an EBO must include detailed rules addressing export control-related risks in overseas business travels, ensuring that the laptop, smart phone, and other belongings brought abroad do not contain any controlled technology or item without licenses.

8.3.2.6 Repair and After-Sale Service

When providing after-sales service, repair, or maintenance to equipment or commodities overseas, EBOs must review the following information: (i) whether the previous export of the equipment complied with export control laws and regulations; (ii) whether any party involved is on the list of parties prohibited or restricted from transactions; (iii) whether the service to be provided requires an export license; (iv) whether the export of the replacement part or accessory requires a license.[27]

---

[25] Dunn, T. L. (2005). Surviving United States Export Controls Post 9/11: A Model Compliance Program. *Denver Journal of International Law & Policy*, 33(3), 435–559.

[26] Weinberg, L. M., & Buren, L. V. (2006). The Impact of U.S. Export Controls and Sanctions on Employment. *Public Contract Law Journal*, 35(3), 537–561, at 557.

[27] The ICP Guidelines.

8.3.3 Third-Party Service Providers in China and Abroad

In addition to exporters and re-exporters as EBOs, third-party service providers are also obliged to comply with ECL and expected to establish the China ICP.[28] As required by ECL, any organization or individual shall not provide services such as agency, freight, delivery, customs clearance, third-party e-commerce trading platforms, finance, and other services for EBOs who engage in violations of export control.[29] This requirement applies extraterritorially, which means that services providers in both China and other countries or regions shall establish the ICP and alleviate risks of providing services for export control violations of ECL.

Although third-party service providers such as banks, insurance companies, and logistics service providers usually have limited information on transactions of their customers, they must screen key information of the transaction and identify "red flags".[30]

Furthermore, third-party service providers are also advised to incorporate export control compliance clauses in transaction contracts, bills of lading, and other relevant documents. Such clauses may include compliance commitments of customers and remedies if violations happen. Third-party service providers must procure commitments of their customers that the goods are not items subject to China's export control and will not be used for military usage unless the customers have provided the export licenses for such goods.

8.3.4 Overseas Importers and End-Users

Overseas importers and end-users must pay special attention to the following two aspects of compliance:

(a) Commitment to end-user covenant

The ECL requires the end-users of controlled items to make commitments that they shall not alter the end-uses of relevant controlled items or transfer them to any third party,[31] otherwise such end-users shall be listed in the List of Controlled Parties,

[28] Article 20 of ECL; Article 7 and 36 of the Draft Regulations.

[29] Article 20 of the ECL.

[30] Take typical "red flags" that transport service providers may encounter as an example. The ICP Guidelines have listed five "red flags" regarding transportation that require special attention in the due diligence, including: (i) the address of the customer is too general, (ii) the destination of delivery is unusual, (iii) the destination of the goods is different from the address of the end-user, (iv) the customer has an unusual confidential requirement on the destination or detailed information of the goods, and (v) the customer has an unusual requirement on shipping or labelling of the goods. See Appendix 1 "Red flags" Reference Table, the ICP Guidelines.

[31] Article 16 of the ECL.

in which case their transactions relating to controlled items may be prohibited or restricted.[32]

(b) Risks relating to national security of China

Overseas importers and end-users that may endanger national security and interests would be included in the List of Controlled Parties. The term "may endanger national security" can be interpreted broadly in practice, requiring foreign importers and end-users to take relevant compliance measures.

Given the ambiguity of "national security", overseas companies are advised to watch out for the touchy or sensitive political issues relevant to national sovereignty of China, territorial integrity, national unity, political party system, and so forth. A negative public comment, publication, or label on the product may trigger such sensitive issues and may be deemed as detrimental to the national security or interests of China, with a consequence of entry into the List of Controlled Parties, and/or even administrative or criminal penalties.[33]

8.3.5 Research Institutes and Universities

Export control regulatory requirements may restrict the flow of products, information, and people participating in international trade and investment as well as research and development activities in research institutes or universities.[34] Under Chinese law, there are no explicit rules stating that research activities at universities are exempt from export control norms. In practice, some universities have implemented their own export control ICP.[35]

Currently, China does not have an official guideline for export control compliance of research activities. In 2021, the European Commission promulgated recommendations on internal compliance programs for controls of research involving dual-use items under certain EU regulations.[36] Referring to the scenarios implicating dual-use

[32] Article 18 of the ECL.

[33] Article 43 of the ECL.

[34] Seyoum, B. (2017). National Security Export Control Regimes: Determinants and Effects on International Business. *Thunderbird International Business Review*, 59(6), 693–708, at 694.

[35] For example, Renmin University of China has implemented the "Measures for Compliance Management of Import and Export Control of Remin University of China (Trial)", which stipulates the designation of compliance responsibilities and liabilities of violating the measures. Retrieved October 13, 2023, from http://se-office.ruc.edu.cn/docs/2021-04/0281b2cb3b5147d6bc3fa286046ff141.pdf.

[36] Commission Recommendation (EU) 2021/1700 of 15 September 2021 on internal compliance programs for controls of research involving dual-use items under Regulation (EU) 2021/821 of the European Parliament and of the Council setting up a Union regime for the control of exports, brokering, technical assistance, transit, and transfer of dual-use items. Retrieved October 16, 2023, from https://eur-lex.europa.eu/legal-content/EN/TXT/PDF/?uri=CELEX:32021H1700&from=EN.

export controls as enumerated in the recommendations[37] and in light of ECL, the research institutes and universities in China must be aware of risks in the following scenarios:

- Teaching, consulting, collaborating, or working on research involving dual-use items in China with visiting foreign country researchers: providing controlled items for such researchers constitutes deemed export under the ECL and an export license may be required in advance.
- Organizing or participating in a conference, meeting, or seminar involving controlled items: an export license may be required if foreigners would have access to technologies shared in such academic events in China. In addition, Chinese citizens in foreign universities or research institutes shall be careful to avoid disclosures in violation of export control regulations.
- Publishing controlled technologies: the research institute or university could consider to amend or omit the specific parts that contain the controlled technology or restrict the access to these specific parts, otherwise an export license is required.
- Export of tangible controlled items: an export license is required, even for second-hand lab equipment.

As China ICP Guidelines and other compliance resources mainly focus on business entities, it is crucial for research institutes and universities to design their own export control ICP and arrange academic-specific export control training for faculty and staff, who might need help in figuring out whether an export license is required in specific scenarios or whether they may not be aware of any license requirement.

8.4 Compliance Practices

8.4.1 Flow of Business

Practically, EBOs shall compilate the compliance manual based on their actual business operation and following the instruction of the China ICP Guidelines. Apart from such compliance guidelines, EBOs are advised to embed export control compliance in all the flow of business operation, including ordering, procurement, contract signing, shipment, after-sale services, and so forth.

[37] Id, Appendix 2, Research scenarios of where export controls may come into place.

8.4.2 Regulatory Trends

On 12 February 2023, the Bureau of Industry Security and Import and Export Control of MOFCOM promulgated the Circular of the General Office of the Ministry of Commerce on Further Effectively Carrying out the Export Control of Dual-Use Items (Shang-Ban-An-Guan-Han [2023] No. 35, the "Circular"). The circular emphasizes seven key points of export control administration by governmental authorities, which are summarized as follows:

(a) "*Adhering to the holistic approach to national security and incorporating national security in every aspect of export control*". MOFCOM supervises the export control administration with an emphasis on national security, indicating that MOFCOM shoulders the political responsibility of safeguarding national security. MOFOCM is duty-bound to enforce export control laws and regulations strictly.
(b) "*Earnestly implementing export control laws and regulations and accurately understanding the scope of export control*". In relation to the identification of goods, technologies, and services (including data) and the related customs classification, MOFCOM may intensify enforcement-related training and utilize more technical measures to identify controlled items and export control risks through law enforcement or coordination with the Customs in practice.
(c) "*Strictly implementing licensing procedures and end-use and end-user regulations*". The requirements for the export licensing procedure and application materials, including details of the items and the end-use and end-user commitments, will be implemented without compromise.
(d) "*Establishing and improving the ICP to effectively prevent and mitigate trade-related risks*". MOFOCM takes China ICP established by business entities as an important method to resolve export control risks. MOFCOM may deem such business entities that fail to promptly establish export China ICP as high-risk enterprises. Accordingly, MOFCOM may exercise supervisory measures toward such enterprises and may request corrections or impose penalties on them when violations are found.
(e) "*Implementing multiple-use licensing and other facilitating measures to promote lawful trade*". MOFCOM may consider the impact of export control on cross-border supply chains, draw on relevant mechanisms of other countries, and grant multiple-use licenses and license exceptions for the compliant EBO with China ICP, with an aim to facilitate the development of cross-border trade.
(f) "*Strengthening the monitoring and enforcement of export control, and seriously punishing illegal acts*". Since ECL took effect in December 2020, the business community has had three years to prescribe and implement China ICP. Considering the national security concerns in export control policies, MOFCOM will take the initiative to enforce related regulations, impose administrative penalties, and conduct law enforcement in concert with the customs, which has the power to initiate criminal investigations. In the near future, there may be more cases of administrative and criminal penalties related to export control.

(g) "*Strengthening organization and implementation to promptly address concerns raised by enterprises*". It is expected that MOFCOM may provide more channels for interaction with the business community so that enterprises can receive prompt administrative guidance on practical issues they encounter in the process of complying with ECL.

8.5 Commentary

Export control is a piece of national policy of China in terms of ensuring national security and non-proliferation. In the absence of abusive export control practices of a foreign country, the Chinese government shows self-restraints in enforcing the extraterritorial provisions of ECL against abusive foreign export control measures.

Nevertheless, non-compliance with ECL may result in severe monetary and even criminal penalties or designation onto the List of Controlled Parties, so both EBOs in China and overseas and importers/end-users in a foreign company are advised to have a China ICP in place if they deal with exported, re-exported, or deemed exported items controlled under ECL. Admittedly China ICP incurs both financial and time costs[38] and may interrupt the free flow of information in the workplace.[39] However, considering the potential penalties and adverse impacts on businesses, such compliance investments are imperative.

[38] Seyoum, B. (2017). National Security Export Control Regimes: Determinants and Effects on International Business. *Thunderbird International Business Review*, 59(6), 693–708, at 704.

[39] Weinberg, L. M., & Buren, L. V. (2006). The Impact of U.S. Export Controls and Sanctions on Employment. *Public Contract Law Journal*, 35(3), 537–561, at 557.

Chapter 9
Countermeasures as Economic Sanctions

This chapter is an essential introduction to economic sanctions system of China, and such sanctions are generally taken in the form of countermeasures under international law.

Countermeasures are a conjecture covering both export controls and economic sanctions, which will also enable the reader to understand the economic sanctions framework under Chinese law.[1] This chapter introduces the countermeasures in the form of export controls or sanctions under Chinese laws against foreign country's abuse of export controls or economic sanctions, as well as the dilemma in compliance practices as between countermeasures of China and the foreign abuses.

Specifically, Sect. 9.1 analyzes the rationale of the countermeasures based on national security and interest concerns in the context of international law and specifies the categories of such countermeasures under Chinese legal frameworks. Section 9.2 introduces the Blocking Rules relevant to foreign export controls or sanctions that may affect dealings of Chinese parties with a party in a third country. Section 9.3 centers around the List of Unreliable Entities and the reasons and consequences of designations of a foreign party by MOFCOM. Section 9.4 identifies the foreign discriminative restrictive measures ("DRMs") that interfere with the internal affairs of China as well as the countermeasures against those DRMs under *Anti-Foreign Sanctions Law of China* ("AFSL"). The compliance advice is suggested accordingly in each of Sects. 9.2 through 9.4.

[1] According to the definition of this term under the *Max Planck Encyclopedia of Public International Law*, countermeasures are unilateral measures adopted by a State in response to the breach of its rights by the wrongful act of another State that affect the rights of the target State and are aimed at inducing it to provide cessation or reparations to the injured State.

D. Zhao, *Contemporary Export Control Law of China*, Modern China and International Economic Law, https://doi.org/10.1007/978-981-99-9825-8_9

9.1 Rationale and Manifestations of Countermeasures

As explored in Chap. 5, apart from the multilateral non-proliferation controls, unilateral export controls are not legitimate under international law unless necessary for safeguarding national security. Accordingly, ECL empowers those unilateral export controls based on national security and interest considerations. That said, ECL also authorizes counter measures to tackle or counter the foreign abuse of export controls that endangers national security or interest of China.[2] Such unilateral export controls are the manifestation of the sanction mechanism under Chinese law that sanctions are introduced only when justified under international law as countermeasures. Such countermeasures, whether taken against abuse of export controls or unilateral sanctions on the part of a foreign State, can also be viewed as economic sanctions.

Pursuant to Article 33 of the *Law on Foreign Relations of the People's Republic of China* which became effective on 1 July 2023, China has the right to take respective countermeasures or restrictive measures against acts that endanger its sovereignty, national security, and development interests in violation of international law or fundamental norms governing international relations. This article further authorizes the State Council and its departments to adopt administrative regulations and departmental rules as may be necessary to further adopt and enforce such measures. Such countermeasure decisions if made pursuant to this article are final. It can be concluded that China only takes countermeasures in terms of sanctions against a foreign party only if there is a violation of international law or norm where its sovereignty, national security, and development interests are endangered.

Such respective countermeasures or restrictive measures, in nature, are unilateral sanctions[3] adopted by the Chinese government. As a concept outside the scope of the traditional international law theory, unilateral sanctions have been a product of decades of state practice, and its legality was somewhat termed as in a "grey area".[4] Nevertheless, it seems that a rule of customary international law has come into existence according to which unilateral sanctions are unlawful if not consistent with the UN Charter and other principles of international law.[5] As an authoritative

---

[2] Article 48 of the ECL prescribes that the People's Republic of China may, depending on the actual situation, take reciprocal measures against any country or region whose abuse of export control measures endangers the national security and interests of the People's Republic of China.

[3] Unilateral sanctions are defined as "the use of economic, trade or other measures to compel a change of policy of another State or to pressure individuals, groups, or entities in targeted States to influence a course of action". See The Office of the High Commissioner for Human Rights. (2017). Technical Mission to the State of Qatar, Report on the Impact of the Gulf Crisis on Human Rights, para. 61. Retrieved October 30, 2023, from https://www.nhrc-qa.org/storage/news/2018/01/OHCHR-TM-REPORT-ENGLISH-1.pdf.

[4] Hofer, A. (2017). The Developed/Developing Divide on Unilateral Coercive Measures: Legitimate Enforcement or Illegitimate Intervention? *Chinese Journal of International Law*, Vol. 16, 177.

[5] Subedi, S.P. (2021). Conclusions: The Current Law on Unilateral Sanction, Remedies against Unlawful Use of such Sanctions and Recommendations. In S.P. Subedi (ed.), *Unilateral Sanctions in International Law* (p. 329), Hart Publishing.

interpretation of the UN Charter, the 1970 Declaration on Principles of International Law concerning Friendly Relations and Cooperation among States in accordance with the UN Charter (Resolution 2625 (XXV)) affirms that no State or group of States has the right to intervene, directly or indirectly, for any reason whatever, in the internal or external affairs of any other State. "No State may use or encourage the use of economic political or any other type of measures to coerce another State in order to obtain from it the subordination of the exercise of its sovereign rights and to secure from its advantages of any kind."[6] Judging from the declaration, unilateral sanctions that intervene in the internal affairs of States and violate the principle of sovereign equality are contrary to international law. Moreover, bilateral or multilateral treaties establish a State's international obligations, and unilateral sanctions contrary to the relevant treaties are also contrary to international law.

To justify the legality of such unilateral sanctions, the concept of "countermeasures" under customary international law may be invoked. Theoretically, countermeasures are one of the circumstances precluding wrongfulness of an act of a State established in Article 22 of the *Draft Articles on the Responsibility of States for Internationally Wrongful Acts* ("Draft Articles on State Responsibility"), which have been widely recognized in practice by institutions and States, including the International Court of Justice.[7] According to the Draft Articles on State Responsibility, four requirements shall be satisfied, respectively, and firstly, countermeasures must be reversible. Second, countermeasures must be commensurate with the injury suffered. Third, countermeasures may only be against a State which is responsible for an internationally wrongful act, not a third State. Last, the injured State shall notify the responsible State of any decision to take countermeasures and offer to negotiate with that State.[8]

In practice, China has adopted sanctions or countermeasure schemes against such foreign unilateral sanctions that violate international law or norms. Apart of mentioning countermeasures against foreign abuse of export controls in general under ECL, other China sanctions focus on three aspects as illustrated in the following sections, respectively: (**i**) blocking foreign export controls and sanctions relevant to third-country transactions under the Blocking Rules; (ii) sanctions against foreign stoppage of supplies under the Provisions on the Unreliable Entities List ("PUEL"); and (**iii**) sanctions under AFSL against the DRM which interferes with the internal affairs of China.

[6] United Nations. (1971). Declaration on Principles of International Law concerning Friendly Relations and Cooperation among States in accordance with the Charter of the United Nations. Retrieved October 30, 2023, from https://digitallibrary.un.org/record/202170.

[7] Crawford, J. (n. d.). *Responsibility of States for Internationally Wrongful Acts*. Retrieved October 30, 2023, from https://legal.un.org/avl//pdf/ha/rsiwa/rsiwa_c.pdf.

[8] Articles 49, 51 and 52 of the Draft Articles on State Responsibility.

9.2 The Blocking Rules

The full name of China Blocking Rules is *the Rules on Blocking Unjustified Extra-Territorial Application of Foreign Legislation and Measures* (the "Blocking Rules").[9] The Blocking Rules are departmental rules leaving much room for interpretation. Though MOFCOM can interpret its departmental rules, it is reluctant to do so thus far.[10] It seems that MOFCOM intends to retain some flexibility. Obviously, the Blocking Rules need time to develop itself against the changing landscape of export control and sanctions' environment.

9.2.1 Why Are the Blocking Rules Issued in a Prompt Manner?

Given the constantly mounting economic sanctions' pressure from the US against Chinese companies, China at that time was under severe political pressure to plant every possible defensive and countermeasures. As China did not have any rules of law that can protect the interests of Chinese companies who transact or intend to transact with their counterparts in countries subject to US economic sanctions, e.g., Iran, China at a minimum and as a political gesture must have something in place similar to the Blocking Statute of EU,[11] as prompt as possible.

9.2.2 What Are the Hardships that the Blocking Rules Intend to Resolve?

The Blocking Rules possibly consider resolving the following difficulties afflicted on the part of Chinese companies: Chinese companies are prohibited under the law of the US from engaging in transactions over certain commodities subject to US export controls or other transactions with a third-country party subject to the US sanctions ("Blocked Third Country Transactions"). Under the Blocking Rules, Chinese companies normally mean companies established under the laws of the PRC, no matter who may be the shareholders of such companies.

---

[9] Order No. 1 of 2021 of MOFCOM, 1 September 2021.

[10] The MOFCOM has released an official interview related to the Blocking Rules after its enactment. See MOFCOM (2021, January 12). Head of MOFCOM's Department of Treaty and Law Answered Questions from the Press on the Rules on Blocking Unjustified Extra-Territorial Application of Foreign Legislation and Measures. Retrieved October 30, 2023, from http://english.mofcom.gov.cn/article/newsrelease/policyreleasing/202101/20210103031441.shtml.

[11] Council Regulation (EC) No 2271/96 of 22 November 1996 on protecting against the effects of the extraterritorial application of legislation adopted by a third country, and actions based thereon or resulting therefrom.

Such Blocked Third-Country Transactions block re-export to the third country of an item subject to EAR or block Chinese companies' transactions with a party of a third country under the US primary sanctions which though only bind the US person but also forbid any person from engaging in any activity that causes a US person to violate a US primary sanctions[12] or under US secondary sanctions regimes where non-US person must follow such US sanctions against the third country.[13]

If foreign export controls or sanctions apply to transactions of Chinese companies with a third-country party, it may be viewed under the Blocking Rules as having an extraterritorial effect, and the Blocking Rules intend to block such foreign statutory laws and mandatory decisions from being applied, observed, and enforced in China.[14]

9.2.3 What Are the Countermeasures Planted Under the Blocking Rules?

The Blocking Rules adopt the following countermeasures to protect Chinese companies from being affected by the foreign statutory laws and mandatory decisions:

A. **Reporting mechanism**

As under Article 5 of the Blocking Rules, it is generally understood that Chinese companies are not supposed to report the existence of every foreign law not in their favor, but must report the instances they encountered of normal business or trade activities with a counterparty in a third country (the "Foreign Party"), which are prohibited or restricted by foreign law or foreign mandatory measures.[15] It seems that the obligation of Chinese companies to report the instances of prohibition or restriction under foreign law can be triggered mostly upon satisfaction of the following conditions on the part of the Chinese company: (**i**) there is a business case where a meaningful business model exits, and (**ii**) a reasonably detailed transaction is contemplated with a given foreign party.

[12] For example, § 1705 of the *International Emergency Economic Powers Act* prescribes that it shall be unlawful for a person to violate, attempt to violate, conspire to violate, or cause a violation of any license, order, regulation, or prohibition issued under this chapter.

[13] Some scholars hold that the Blocking Rules are specifically targeting those secondary sanctions. See MOFCOM. (2021, January 11). Safeguarding legitimate interests and international trade order: experts taking questions on the Rules on Counteracting Unjustified Extra-Territorial Application of Foreign Legislation and Other Measures. Retrieved October 30, 2023, from http://english.mofcom.gov.cn/article/newsrelease/significantnews/202101/20210103031442.shtml.

[14] Shang, S. (2021). Challenges and Priorities in Constructing China's Extraterritorial Regulatory System: Concurrently on the Rules on Blocking Unjustified Extra-Territorial Application of Foreign Legislation and Measures. *Study on International Law*, 2021(02), 63–80.

[15] Under Article 5 of Blocking Rules of China, the affected citizen, legal person, or other organization of the PRC **shall** report such matters to the competent department of commerce of the State Council within 30 days.

Though any Chinese company can report the negative impact of a foreign law, it is another matter whether the company is held liable for not discharging the reporting obligation. If a business case or a reasonably detailed contemplated transaction cannot be proved, it is difficult for MOFCOM to ascertain that the company has a serious business case to report. Accordingly, it seems administratively unreasonable to impose administrative sanctions against such company for not so reporting.

In the event that a business case and specific contemplated transaction is indeed impacted by a foreign law or a foreign mandatory decision, the Chinese company is to report such impact. However, the Blocking Rules fail to identify the specific penalties, which will be prescribed by MOFCOM. Pending such a prescription, it seems that the Chinese company failing to report will not be sanctioned by serious penalties, but only subject to a warning, and rectification of the failure within a given timeframe only.[16]

The reporting mechanism is significant to MOFCOM. It may rely on the data of reports to assess the impact of a given foreign law or measures and determine which foreign law to block.

B. **The scheme of blocking foreign laws**

An inter-departmental working mechanism led by MOFCOM will determine which foreign law to be blocked with following elements: (**i**) violation of international law and the basic principles of international relations, (**ii**) potential impact on national sovereignty, security and development interests of China, (**iii**) potential impact on the legitimate rights and interests of the citizens, legal persons or other organizations of China, and (**iv**) other factors that shall be taken into account.[17]

Regarding the first element, the working mechanism will examine the international law basis and/or the sufficiency of factual evidence for the jurisdiction of or measures taken under a given foreign law. For instance, the working mechanism will determine whether the inclusion of a third-country company into the Entity List of BIS is based on due process and sufficient factual evidence for the alleged inclusion reasons. The second element involves the overall national security assessment based on the reported and other data. As for the third element, this is a consideration of the negative impact on the specific transactions, actual or contemplated. Regarding the fourth element, i.e., other factors that shall be considered, this may include consideration of response to the same foreign law or measures from other countries (e.g., the EU) or the difficulty of implementing the blocking measures.

If the working mechanism determines that a foreign law or decision is not justified over its extraterritorial jurisdiction, MOFCOM will publicize an order of injunction not to recognize, enforce or comply with the blocked foreign law or

[16] Article 13 of Blocking Rules of China prescribes that where a citizen, legal person, or other organization of China fails to truthfully report as required or fails to comply with the prohibition order, the competent department of commerce of the State Council may give a warning, order he/it to rectify within a specified period, and may concurrently impose a fine according to the severity of the circumstances.

[17] Article 6 of the Blocking Rules.

measures ("Blocked Foreign Law"). The legal risks for Chinese companies lie in their compliance, if any, with such Blocked Foreign Law.

C. **Prohibition from compliance with the Blocked Foreign Law**

Chinese company is not supposed to comply with the Blocked Foreign Law, unless it has been granted an exemption not to follow the order of injunction. The grant of exemption is a discretionary power by MOFCOM, which can be positive or negative but must be made within 30 days or promptly if it is an urgent case.[18]

It is always difficult and problematic to determine what behavior of the Chinese company can constitute compliance with the Blocked Foreign Law. Given the objective of protecting the lawful rights and interests of Chinese companies,[19] all Chinese companies still retain the freedom to sign or not sign a transaction agreement with a counterparty. Accordingly, no transaction per se with a foreign party or another Chinese party on the Entity List of BIS does not mean compliance with the Blocked Foreign Law. The Blocking Rules do not force a Chinese company to transact with a certain country or a certain party.

However, if a Chinese company terminates a negotiation or agreement with a foreign party pursuant to a Blocked Foreign Law, or with a Chinese party who has violated a Blocked Foreign Law and thus has been listed on the US export control or sanctions blacklists, the Chinese company may be held in violation of the order of injunction not to follow the Blocked Foreign Law and thus may incur the administrative consequences of a warning and an order to rectify its failure to follow the order of injunction and/or certain amount fines if the fines are specified in the future.[20]

"An order to rectify" means that the Chinese company must proceed with the negotiation or transaction with the other party. If the Chinese company refuses to rectify, the company will face administrative fines as well as claims of damages by the counterparty, foreign or domestic, in courts in China.

D. **Judicial remedies through Chinese courts**

(a) Legal action for damages against a Chinese party

Under Article 9.1 of the Blocking Rules, a Chinese company may according to law seek legal action at a Chinese court for the damages it suffers from the compliance with Blocked Foreign Law by a counter party.[21]

Given the qualification "according to law", it seems that Article 9.1 does by itself confer on the Chinese plaintiff an independent cause of action. However, the Blocking Rules only nullify in effect the Blocked Foreign Law so that the Chinese party cannot rely as a legal defense on compliance with the Blocked Foreign Law. Rather, it is a violation of the Blocking Rules. However, whether the plaintiff can

---

[18] Ibid., Article 8.

[19] Id., Article 1.

[20] Id., Article 13.

[21] Please note that such party is unofficially construed as a Chinese party only.

establish a valid claim for damages depends upon its ability to prove such damages as well as causation between the illegal compliance and such damages according to the law of tort under the *Civil Code of the PRC*.

(b) Legal action for compensation against a foreign company

Assuming there is a judgment (most likely a foreign court judgment in practice) against a Chinese party based on the Blocked Foreign Law and a Chinese party suffers loss occasioned by the judgment, this Chinese party may lodge a lawsuit against the counterparty benefiting from the foreign court judgment to cover the loss.[22]

According to the unofficial oral construction by MOFCOM, such benefiting counterparty potentially liable under the compensation proceedings in China can be Chinese or foreign companies.[23]

9.2.4 *What Do the Blocking Rules Mean to Chinese and Foreign Companies?*

A. **Subsidiaries in China**

The Chinese subsidiaries of foreign companies will face twofold legal risks under the Blocking Rules as follows.

(a) The obligation to report the impact of a foreign law or measures

Such obligation would likely arise when a meaningful business case or a reasonably detailed transaction is contemplated with a given foreign party. In practice, the Chinese subsidiary has to monitor whether there is a meaningful business case and specific actual or contemplated transactions with a Foreign Party in a country unilaterally sanctioned by a foreign country.

(b) Risks of compliance with a Blocked Foreign Law

It is not clear what constitutes such compliance. In practice, the issue depends upon whether the Chinese subsidiary can adduce sufficient commercial justification for discontinuing or terminating any business with a foreign party or a Chinese party on the BIS Entity List, for instance, so that such discontinuing or terminating decision is not coerced by the Blocked Foreign Law. In this connection and with such sufficient

[22] Article 9.2 of the Blocking Rules.

[23] The MOFCOM has released an official interview related to the Blocking Rules after its enactment. See: MOFCOM. (2021, January 12). Head of MOFCOM's Department of Treaty and Law Answered Questions from the Press on the Rules on Blocking Unjustified Extra-Territorial Application of Foreign Legislation and Measures. Retrieved October 30, 2023, from http://english.mofcom.gov.cn/article/newsrelease/policyreleasing/202101/20210103031441.shtml.

commercial justification, a unilateral termination right under a given agreement can be a useful tool.

If compliance with a Blocked Foreign Law is deemed existing by MOFCOM, the Chinese subsidiary will be ordered to take rectification measures to continue the discontinued business. Such an order may be difficult to follow, and the Chinese subsidiary will be exposed to a certain amount as fines.

The same subsidiary may also be sued in a Chinese court for its compliance with Blocked Foreign Law. If the subsidiary discontinues the business with some Chinese companies on the BIS Entity List or other foreign unilateral blacklists and the inclusion of these companies into such list is based on the Blocked Foreign Law, the Chinese subsidiary will be liable to the Chinese plaintiff.

B. **Foreign companies**

Foreign companies generally are not subject to the Blocking Rules. However, if a foreign company wins or benefits from a foreign lawsuit against a Chinese party based on a Blocked Foreign Law, the foreign company will face a lawsuit in China by the Chinese party for compensation of losses. The Chinese court may enforce its judgment against the equity interest held by such foreign party in its subsidiary in China or the assets in China owned by such foreign party, unless the same party is insulated from such enforcement by holding no shares in any Chinese companies and owning no assets in China.

Please note that foreign companies may be included in the Unreliable Entity List of China as illustrated in Sect. 9.3 for their stoppage of supplies to Chinese companies on BIS Entity List or other foreign unilateral blacklists, in which case its business and trade with China will be substantially affected.

9.2.5 Preliminary Conclusions

It remains to be seen whether the Blocking Rules will indeed substantially resolve the difficulties that Chinese companies are facing with the US Blocked Transactions or the US Re-export Restrictions, or the Stoppage of Supplies.

If MOFCOM intensifies enforcement of the Blocking Rules, the consequence may be to force the foreign subsidiaries in China and ultimately their parent companies to take sides between the U.S. and China, and the global market and technology will be segregated into two blocks, one is U.S. block, another is non-U.S. block. The question is how many foreign companies and their subsidiaries will choose the side of China.

Given that there is no sign of compromising the economic sanctions and export control measures on the part of the U.S. even after the EU adopts its Blocking Statute, the U.S. may likely follow the same pattern even with the advent of Blocking Rules of China. Strategically the only way a foreign company and its subsidiaries in China can avoid the risks of confronting U.S. or China regulations would be to find a supply chain without any commodity, technology, software, and labor of the US origin. If that supply chain immune from the bite of any US origin elements can be developed, the foreign company and its subsidiaries will be able to emancipate themselves from the constraints of US economic sanctions and the Blocking Rules of China.

The potential market and technology segregation as mentioned above will be the most sensitive issue that MOFCOM must consider carefully and seriously in enforcing the Blocking Rules and the Rules of Unreliable Entity List. Please note that China has not yet determined which foreign law is to be blocked. This can be viewed as an element of the prudence of MOFCOM in enacting the Blocking Rules.

9.3 The Provisions on the Unreliable Entities List

On 16 February 2023, MOFCOM announced to designate two US corporations onto the Unreliable Entities List ("UEL") for their involvement in arms sales to the Taiwan region of China, i.e., Lockheed Martin Corporation and Raytheon Missiles & Defense.[24] This is the first instance of designation under the provisions on the PUEL ever since the official release of China of PUEL in September of 2020.[25]

9.3.1 Factors Triggering Sanctions Under PUEL

According to Article 2 of PUEL, the unreliable entity list mechanism aims at adopting measures against the foreign party for its following behaviors in international economic, trade, and other relevant activities: (**i**) endangering national sovereignty, security or development interests of China ("Endangerment of National Security"), and (**ii**) suspending normal transactions with a Chinese party or applying discriminatory measures against such Chinese party, which in either case violates the normal market transaction principle and afflicts damage to the legitimate rights and interests of the Chinese party ("Stoppage of Supplies or Business Discrimination"). Such foreign or Chinese party includes enterprises, other organizations, or individuals.

Reading literally from the above provisions, a foreign party may be designated as a UEL party only when it both satisfied the pre-conditions of Endangerment of National Security and Stoppage of Supplies or Business Discrimination as well. However, in designating the above two US corporations, MOFCOM makes it clear that such UEL designation is based on the consideration of safeguarding national sovereignty, security, or development interests of China. It can be inferred that MOFCOM views

---

[24] Order No. 1 of Announcement of the Working Mechanism on the Unreliable Entities List, 16 February 2023.

[25] Order No. 4 of 2020 of the MOFCOM, 19 September 2020.

the two pre-conditions of UEL designation as alternative triggering events, rather than as co-existing ones.

9.3.2 Consequences of UEL Designation

Pursuant to Article 10 of PUEL, one or several of the following measures may be taken by MOFCOM against the designated foreign party: (**i**) trade restriction or prohibition relevant to China, (**ii**) investment restriction or prohibition in China; (**iii**) restriction or prohibition from entry into China of personnel or transportation means relevant to such party, (**iv**) restriction or revocation of work permission, stay or residence in China for such relevant personnel, (**v**) discretionary amount of administrative fine according to severity of the circumstance, and (**vi**) other necessary compulsory measures. In essence, the consequences of being a UEL party under Chinese law are almost equivalent to the consequence of SDN designation by OFAC under US law.[26]

Notably, MOFCOM has imposed all prohibitive measures against the two US corporations, with the entry and work prohibitions confined to their senior management. MOFCOM also imposed a fine to each of the two US enterprises up to twice the amount of its arms sales to the Taiwan region of China since the implementation of PUEL.

9.3.3 Compliance Considerations Under PUEL

As a foreign party, it is prudent not to "endanger" the national security or interests of China which is a vague concept with a wide coverage and difficult to follow in practice. To avoid such a risk, it is desirable for a foreign company to comply with the export control and countermeasure laws and regulations and avoid triggering politically sensitive events against China.

For a company in China, UEL screening is a must to avoid direct and indirect trade, investment, and cooperation projects with the UEL party, unless the company in China notifies in advance MOFCOM and obtains its consent or approval of the proposed dealing with a UEL party.

---

[26] According to Liao Fan, the legal consequences of being designated as a PUEL party can be summarized as import and export restrictions, investment restrictions, entry and stay restrictions, loss of goodwill and reputation, and civil litigation risks. See, Liao, F. (2021). A Comparative Analysis of the Unreliable Entity List. *Study of Comparative Law*, 2021(01).

9.4 The Anti-foreign Sanctions Law

Issued and implemented on 10 June 2021, AFSL may impact Chinese and/or foreign parties in the following two ways: (**i**) not to deal with parties on "the List of Parties Subject to Counter Measures" ("LCM"), which includes those foreign persons and entities advancing the DRMs against a person or entity in China, and (**ii**) the exposure of legal actions in China for following the DRMs of a foreign country.

9.4.1 Identification of DRMs Under AFSL

The term "DRMs" under Article 3 of AFSL is an uncertain legal concept which is highly abstract, and vague in substantive connotation and extension. Legally construed, four elements must be satisfied to constitute such DRMs, which include: (**i**) violating international law and the basic norms of international relations, (**ii**) using various pretexts or according to its own laws to contain or suppress China, (**iii**) being discriminatory in nature as against Chinese citizens and organizations, and (**iv**) interfering in internal affairs of China. Among others, the upmost important and decisive element is interfering in internal affairs of China, considering that the legislative aim and value of AFSL are to safeguard the national sovereignty, security, and development interests of China, as prescribed in Article 1. The other three elements are easy to be proved by the Chinese government in practice, as the foreign unilateral sanctions or export controls most often satisfy the first three elements.

Since AFSL came into effect on 10 June 2021, China has imposed several sanctions against targeted individuals or companies by designating them onto LCM for their direct or indirect involvement in the formulation, decision, and implementation of the DRMs as mentioned above.

On 23 July 2021, China announced sanctions on seven US individuals and entities in accordance with AFSL and in response to the reaction of the US to the Hong Kong issue.[27]

On 21 December 2021, China announced countermeasures against Nadine Maenza, Nury Turkel, Anurima Bhargava, and James W Carr of the US Commission on International Religious Freedom for their reactions to the alleged human rights issue in Xinjiang.[28]

On 21 February 2022, the Chinese government announced countermeasures in accordance with AFSL on the infringing acts of Raytheon Technologies Corporation

[27] Ministry of Foreign Affairs of the PRC. (2021, July 23). Foreign Ministry Spokesperson's Remarks on China's Decision to Impose Sanctions on Relevant US Individuals and Entity. Retrieved October 31, 2023, from: https://www.fmprc.gov.cn/eng/xwfw_665399/s2510_665401/2535_665405/202107/t20210723_9170832.html.

[28] Ministry of Foreign Affairs of the PRC. (2021, December 21). Foreign Ministry Spokesperson Zhao Lijian's Regular Press Conference. Retrieved October 31, 2023, from: https://www.fmprc.gov.cn/eng/xwfw_665399/s2510_665401/2511_665403/202112/t20211221_10473754.html.

and Lockheed Martin Corporation, both of which are military industrial enterprises that have long participated in the US arms sales to the Taiwan region.[29]

On 5 August 2022, China announced sanctions on Nancy Pelosi and her immediate family members in accordance with relevant Chinese laws in response to her visit to the Taiwan region.[30]

On 12 August 2022, China announced sanctions on Agnė Vaiciukevičiūtė, Deputy Minister of Transport and Communications of Lithuania, in response to her visit to the Taiwan region.[31]

On 16 August 2022, China announced sanctions on several Taiwan independence advocates.[32]

On 16 September 2022, the Chinese government announced sanctions on Gregory J Hayes, chairman and chief executive officer of Raytheon Technologies Corporation, and Theodore Colbert III, president and chief executive officer of Boeing Defense, Space & Security, who were involved in the latest arms sales to the Taiwan region.[33]

On 23 December 2022, China announced sanctions on Miles Maochun Yu and Todd Stein in accordance with AFSL for their responses to the alleged human rights issue in Tibet.[34]

On 15 February 2023, China announced sanctions on US entities (not specified) for their responses to the entry of a Chinese civilian unmanned airship into the US airspace.[35]

---

[29] Ministry of Foreign Affairs of the PRC. (2022, February 21). Ministry Spokesperson Wang Wenbin's Regular Press Conference. Retrieved October 31, 2023, from: https://www.fmprc.gov.cn/eng/xwfw_665399/s2510_665401/2511_665403/202202/t20220221_10644075.html.

[30] Ministry of Foreign Affairs of the PRC. (2022, August 5). Foreign Ministry Spokesperson Announces China's Sanctions on U.S. House Speaker Nancy Pelosi. Retrieved October 31, 2023, from: https://www.fmprc.gov.cn/eng/xwfw_665399/s2510_665401/2535_665405/202208/t20220805_10735509.html.

[31] Ministry of Foreign Affairs of the PRC. (2022, August 12). Foreign Ministry Spokesperson Announces China's Sanctions on Lithuanian Deputy Minister of Transport and Communications Agnė Vaiciukevičiūtė. Retrieved October 31, 2023, from: https://www.fmprc.gov.cn/eng/xwfw_665399/s2510_665401/2535_665405/202208/t20220812_10742448.html.

[32] Xinhua. (2022, August 16). Diehard "Taiwan independence" separatists to be sanctioned: spokesperson, 16 August 2022, available at: https://english.news.cn/20220816/662a03d49b79488db590f68ff2323b30/c.html.

[33] Ministry of Foreign Affairs of the PRC. (2022, September 16). Foreign Ministry Spokesperson Mao Ning's Regular Press Conference. Retrieved October 31, 2023, from:
https://www.fmprc.gov.cn/eng/xwfw_665399/s2510_665401/2511_665403/202209/t20220916_10767123.html.

[34] Ministry of Foreign Affairs of the PRC. (2022, December 23). Foreign Ministry Spokesperson Mao Ning's Regular Press Conference. Retrieved October 31, 2023, from: https://www.fmprc.gov.cn/mfa_eng/xwfw_665399/s2510_665401/2511_665403/202212/t20221223_10994393.html.

[35] Ministry of Foreign Affairs of the PRC. (2023, February 15). Foreign Ministry Spokesperson Wang Wenbin's Regular Press Conference. Retrieved October 31, 2023, from: https://www.fmprc.gov.cn/eng/xwfw_665399/s2510_665401/2511_665403/202302/t20230215_11025476.html.

On 7 April 2023, China announced sanctions on Hudson Institute, the Ronald Reagan Presidential Library & Museum and four related individuals for allowing Tsai Ing-wen to enter the US and engage in political activities there.[36]

As shown above, the DRMs identified by the Chinese government in practice are generally related to Taiwan region, Hong Kong, Xinjiang or Tibet, and so forth, especially when it comes to such issues as territory integrity issues, or human rights including forced labor allegations, independence, and arms sales, which interferes with internal affairs of China.

9.4.2 Overview of AFSL's Impact

AFSL may impact Chinese and/or foreign companies in the following two scenarios:

A. **Not to deal with LCM Parties**

As mentioned above, LCM includes those foreign persons and entities advancing the DRMs against a person or entity in China. Chinese persons and entities must not transact with the LCM parties.

Please note that "advancing" as aforementioned means under AFSL the "directly or indirectly" involvement in the DRM formulation, decision, or implementation. The term "implementation" normally refers to an act by a public authority and usually does not cover corporate compliance with the DRM. Therefore, corporate compliance with the DRM will normally be treated as carrying out or execution of the DRMs but may trigger risks of being sued in Chinese court, rather than being enlisted on the LCM as sanctioned parties.

B. **Exposure of legal action in China for following the DRMs**

A Chinese or a foreign person or entity is supposed not to follow the DRMs taken by a foreign country. Otherwise, the party following such DRMs will be exposed to the potential legal action in Chinese courts by the aggrieved person or an entity in China. Such aggrieved party is entitled under AFSL to seeking the legal remedy of cessation of the infringing act and damages.

[36] Ministry of Foreign Affairs of the PRC. (2023, April 7). Decision on Taking Countermeasures Against Hudson Institute, the Ronald Reagan Presidential Library and Museum and Their Leaders. Retrieved October 31, 2023, from: https://www.mfa.gov.cn/eng/zxxx_662805/202304/t20230407_11056272.html.

9.4.3 AFSL Compliance Obligations

A. **Companies in China**

(a) To comply with LCM sanctions

A subsidiary in China of a foreign company under Article 11 of AFSL must comply with the LCM sanctions and shall not conduct transactions and cooperation with LCM parties. This means that such a subsidiary may lose foreign business partners who are the LCM parties.

If the subsidiary conducts transactions or cooperation with such LCM parties, the subsidiary's business in China will be restricted or prohibited by the Chinese government.

(b) Not to follow DRMs

If such DRMs are followed, the subsidiary would face the risk of being sued by the Chinese party who suffered from the obedience by the subsidiary to the DRMs.

B. **Foreign Companies**

A foreign company will have the same obligations and risks as illustrated above with the subsidiary in China. The only difference is that such foreign company will not be subject to the business restriction or prohibition if dealing with the LCM parties.

If a foreign company is sued for following the DRMs, its assets including equity shares of its subsidiaries in China may be subject to the judicial attachment and may be later enforced to honor the Chinese court judgment if in favor of the aggrieved plaintiff in China.

9.4.4 AFSL Compliance Measures

A. **LCM screening**

With a view to avoiding transaction or cooperation with the LCM Parties, both the foreign company as well as its subsidiarics in China must proccss thc LCM scrccning of their business partners and employees.

Please note that the LCM screening must cover those parties subject to the catch-all countermeasures ("Catch-all Parties") as set forth in Article 5 of AFSL. Such catch-all parties, though not enlisted as LCM parties, will be subject to the same sanctions applied to the LCM parties if the Chinese government expressly so determines. Such catch-all parties include the following parties: the spouse and direct lineal family members of the LCM party, the senior executives or actual controller of the LCM party, the entity in which the LCM party serves as a senior executive, and the entity which the LCM party *de facto* controls, or sets up or operates as a participating party.

B. **Identification of the DRMs**

Given the risk of being sued by the aggrieved Chinese parties, all companies must identify themselves which foreign export control and economic sanctions and the blacklists thereunder are the DRMs under AFSL. For instance, the addition of five Chinese entities to the Entity List by BIS with the so-called reason of involvement in alleged human rights violations and abuses[37] may be treated as a DRM under AFSL.

C. **Exposure assessment of being sued by the Chinese customer**

Both foreign and Chinese companies must assess such risks in a manner as follows:

(a) to list all Chinese customers affected by the DRMs;
(b) to assess the potential damages if any that the affected Chinese customers may claim against a company in China or overseas;
(c) to analyze the evidence, document, and supply chain model to determine whether a prima facie case can be made by the Chinese customers;
(d) to make internal protocol as to the internal management of interacting and dealing with the Chinese customers.

Only after the valuation of all facts and evidence can a company formulate a sensible strategy as to whether to comply with the DRMs and if so, what are the consequences.

D. **Export control and sanctions provisions of agreements**

In practice, the export control and sanctions provisions of the agreement are normally founded on the compliance requirements of the US and EU export control and sanctions. In such a case, the provisions need to be adjusted so as not to be repugnant to the mandatory laws and regulations in China, including but not limited to AFSL.

---

[37] Bureau of Industry and Security. (2021, June 24). Addition of Certain Entities to the Entity List. Retrieved October 31, 2023, from: https://www.federalregister.gov/documents/2021/06/24/2021-13395/addition-of-certain-entities-to-the-entity-list.

Appendix A
Export Control Law of the People's Republic of China (Translation for Reference Only)

Chapter I General Provisions

Article 1 This law is formulated for purposes of safeguarding national security and interests, fulfilling non-proliferation and other international obligations, and strengthening and normalizing export control.

Article 2 This law shall apply to the State's export control of dual-use items, military items, nuclear items, and other items such as goods, technologies, services that relate to maintenance of national security and interests, or fulfillment of non-proliferation or other international obligations (hereinafter collectively referred to as the "controlled items").

The term "controlled items" referred to in the preceding paragraph includes the data such as technical information and so forth related to such items.

Export control of this law refers to the prohibitive or restrictive measures taken by the State against the transfer of controlled items from within to outside the territory of the People's Republic of China, and the act performed by a citizen, legal person or unincorporated organization of the People's Republic of China to provide any foreign organization or individual with controlled items.

Dual-use items of this law refer to goods, technologies, and services that can be used for both civil and military purposes or contribute to elevating military power potentials, especially those can be used to design, develop, produce, or employ weapons of mass destruction and their delivery vehicles.

Military items of this law refer to equipage, specialized production equipment and other relevant goods, technologies, and services used for military purposes.

Nuclear items of this law refer to nuclear materials, nuclear equipment, non-nuclear materials used for reactors, and relevant technologies and services.

Article 3 Export control shall adhere to the holistic view of national security, safeguard international peace, coordinate security and development, and improve administration and services of export control.

D. Zhao, *Contemporary Export Control Law of China*, Modern China and International Economic Law, https://doi.org/10.1007/978-981-99-9825-8

Article 4 The State implements a unified export control regime administrated through formulating control lists, directories, and catalogues (hereinafter collectively referred to as the "control lists") and carrying out export licensing.

Article 5 The departments of the State Council and the Central Military Commission that perform the function of export control (hereinafter referred to as the "State's export control administrative departments") shall undertake export control-related functions according to their assigned responsibilities. Other relevant departments of the State Council and the Central Military Commission shall discharge functions related to export control in accordance with their assigned responsibilities.

The State shall establish a coordination mechanism for export control to overall plan and coordinate major issues of export control. The State's export control administrative departments and relevant departments of the State Council shall closely cooperate and strengthen share of information.

The State's export control administrative departments shall, in conjunction with relevant departments, establish an expert consultation mechanism to provide advice on export control work.

The State's export control administrative departments issue guidelines on export control for the related industries in due course and guide export operators in establishing sound export control internal compliance systems and normalizing their operations.

The relevant departments of the people's governments of provinces, autonomous regions, and municipalities directly under the central government shall carry out relevant export control responsibilities in accordance with laws and administrative regulations.

Article 6 The State shall strengthen international cooperation on export control and take part in the formulation of international rules relating to export control.

Article 7 Exporting business operators may lawfully establish and join relevant chambers of commerce, associations or other self-regulatory industrial organizations.

Relevant chambers of commerce, associations, or other self-regulatory industrial organizations shall abide by laws and administrative regulations, provide services related to export control for their members according to their bylaws, and exert their functions of coordination and self-regulation.

Chapter II Control Policies, Lists, and Measures

Section 1 General Provisions

Article 8 The State's export control administrative departments shall, in conjunction with relevant departments, formulate export control policies, the major ones of which shall be submitted to the State Council or both the State Council and the Central Military Commission for approval.

The State's export control administrative departments may assess the countries and regions as destinations of the export of the controlled items to determine their risk levels and take corresponding control measures.

Article 9 In accordance with this law and related laws and administrative regulations as well as export control policies, the State's export control administrative departments shall, in conjunction with relevant departments, formulate and adjust export control lists for controlled items pursuant to prescribed procedures, and shall publicize such lists in a timely manner.

Pursuant to the need to safeguard national security and interests, and fulfill non-proliferation and other international obligations, upon approval of the State Council or both the State Council and the Central Military Commission, the State's export control administrative departments may exercise temporary control over any goods, technologies and services not included in the export control lists and make public announcement of such control. The duration of the temporary control shall be no longer than two years. An assessment shall be conducted in a timely manner before the expiration of the temporary control period, and a decision to cancel the temporary control, extend the temporary control, or include the temporary control items into the export control lists shall be made depending on the assessment results.

Article 10 Pursuant to the need to safeguard national security and interests, and fulfill non-proliferation and other international obligations, upon approval of the State Council or both the State Council and the Central Military Commission, the State's export control administrative departments, in conjunction with relevant departments, may prohibit the export of relevant controlled items, or prohibit the export of relevant controlled items to particular destination countries or regions, or particular organizations or individuals.

Article 11 Exporting business operators who export controlled items shall comply with the provisions of this law and related laws and administrative regulations; shall obtain such qualifications as may be statutorily required for export operations of related controlled items.

Article 12 The State shall implement a licensing system for the export of controlled items.

For the export of controlled items included in the control lists or items subject to temporary control, exporting business operators shall apply for licenses to the State's export control administrative departments.

For the export of goods, technologies, and services not included in the control lists or not subject to temporary control, exporting business operators who know or should have known or are notified by the State's export control administrative departments that relevant goods, technologies, or services may have the following risks, shall apply for licenses to the State's export control administrative departments:

1. endangering national security and interests;
2. being used to design, develop, produce, or employ weapons of mass destruction and their delivery vehicles; or
3. being used for terrorist purposes.

Where exporting business operators are uncertain about whether the goods, technologies, or services to be exported fall under the scope of the controlled items prescribed under this law, and thus consult the State's export control administrative departments, the State's export control administrative departments shall reply in a timely manner.

Article 13 The State's export control administrative departments shall consider as a whole the following factors to review applications of exporting business operators for the export of controlled items and make the decision to or not to grant the license:

1. national security and interests;
2. international obligations and external commitments;
3. types of export;
4. degree of sensitivity of the items;
5. countries or regions as export destinations;
6. end-users and end-uses;
7. related credit records of exporting business operators; and
8. other factors stipulated by laws and administrative regulations.

Article 14 For exporting business operators who have established internal compliance program on export control which operates well, the State's export control administrative departments may provide them with multiple-use licenses and other facilitation measures for their export of relevant controlled items. Specific provisions are to be formulated by the State's export control administrative departments.

Article 15 Exporting business operators shall submit the end-user and end-use certification of the controlled items to the State's export control administrative departments, which shall be issued by end-users or by a national or local government agency in the place where such end-users are located.

Article 16 End-users of controlled items shall covenant that, without the approval of the State's export control administrative departments, they shall not alter the end-uses of relevant controlled items or transfer them to any third party.

Exporting business operators or importers who discover that end-users or end-uses are likely to be altered shall, pursuant to prescribed provisions, immediately report it to the State's export control administrative departments.

Article 17 The State's export control administrative departments shall establish a risk administration system for end-users and end-uses of controlled items, assess and verify end-users and end-uses of controlled items, and strengthen the administration of end-users and end-uses.

Article 18 The State's export control administrative departments shall establish a list of controlled parties which comprises those importers and end-users who:

1. violate administrative requirements of end-users or end-uses;
2. may endanger national security and interests; or
3. use the controlled items for terrorist purposes.

For importers and end-users designated onto the list of controlled parties, the State's export control administrative departments may take necessary measures such as prohibiting or restricting transaction relating to controlled items and ordering the suspension of the export of relevant controlled items.

Exporting business operators shall not transact in violation of prescribed provisions with any importer or end-user that is designated onto the list of controlled parties. Exporting business operators, who, under special circumstances, do need to transact with importers and end-users on the list of controlled parties may apply to the State's export control administrative departments.

Importers and end-users on the list of controlled parties who eliminate the circumstances referred to in paragraph (1) upon implementation of relevant measures may apply to the State's export control administrative departments for removing them from the list of controlled parties; the State's export control administrative departments may, in accordance with the actual situation, determine to remove such importers and end-users from the list of controlled parties.

Article 19 When exporting controlled goods, consignors or customs brokers of the goods for export shall submit the license granted by the State's export control administrative departments to the customs for verification, and go through customs clearance in accordance with relevant provisions of the State.

Where consignors of the goods for export fail to submit the license by the State's export control administrative departments to the customs for verification, and the customs have evidence that the goods for export may fall within the scope of export control, the customs shall raise queries to the consignors of the goods for export; the customs may request classification by the State's export control administrative departments, and shall deal with it lawfully in accordance with the classification conclusion made by the State's export control administrative departments. The customs shall not release the goods for export during the classification or query.

Article 20 Any organization or individual shall not provide agency, freight, delivery, customs clearance, third-party e-commerce trading platforms, finance, and so on for exporting business operators engaging in violation of export control.

Section 2 Export Administration on Dual-Use Items

Article 21 Exporting business operators shall truthfully submit related documents in accordance with laws and administrative regulations to apply for export of dual-use items to the State's export control administrative departments of dual-use items.

Article 22 The State's export control administrative departments of dual-use items shall accept applications for export of dual-use items, review the applications independently or in conjunction with relevant departments in accordance with this law, related laws and administrative regulations, and make a decision to or not to grant the license within a statutory period. Where the licensing decision is made, it is the duty of the license issuing authority to issue the export license.

Section 3 Export Administration on Military Items

Article 23 The State implements a monopoly system for the export of military items. Operators engaged in export of military items shall obtain the monopoly privilege for exporting military items and conduct exporting business of military items within the permitted business scope.

The monopoly privilege of exporting military items shall be reviewed and granted by the State's export control administrative departments of military items.

Article 24 Exporting business operators of military items shall, in accordance with control policies and product attributes, apply for review and approval of the export project proposal, program as well as contract for military items to the State's export control administrative departments of military items.

The major export project proposal, program as well as contract for military items shall be reviewed by the State's export control administrative departments of military items in conjunction with relevant departments and be submitted to the State Council and the Central Military Commission for approval.

Article 25 Before the export of military items, exporting business operators of military items shall apply to the State's export control administrative departments of military items for the export license of military items.

When exporting the military items, exporting business operators of military items shall submit the license issued by the State's export control administrative departments of military items to the customs for verification and go through customs clearance in accordance with the relevant provisions of the State.

Article 26 Exporting business operators of military items shall entrust approved military items export transportation companies to handle the export, transportation, and relevant operations of military items. Specific regulations shall be formulated by the State's export control administrative departments of military items in conjunction with relevant departments.

Article 27 Exporting business operators or research institutes and manufacturers of military items who intend to participate in international military items exhibitions shall go through the review and approval formalities of the State's export control administrative departments of military items pursuant to procedures.

Chapter III Supervision Administration

Article 28 The State's export control administrative departments shall, in accordance with law, supervise and inspect the activities of export of controlled items.

The State's export control administrative departments may take the following measures to investigate the suspected violations of this law:

1. entering the business premises of parties under investigation or other relevant places to carry out investigations;

2. interviewing parties under investigations, interested parties or other relevant organizations or individuals, and requesting them to provide explanations related to the investigated matters;
3. examining and duplicating relevant vouchers, agreements, accounting books, business correspondence, and other documents and data of the parties under investigation, interested parties, or other relevant organizations or individuals;
4. checking the vehicles used for the export, stopping the loading of suspicious items to be exported, and ordering transport back of illegally exported items;
5. sealing up and detaining relevant items involved in the investigation; and
6. examining the bank accounts of parties under investigation.

It shall be approved in writing by principals of the State's export control administrative departments to take the measures specified in Item (5) and Item (6) of the preceding paragraph.

Article 29 The State's export control administrative departments shall perform their duties in accordance with law, and relevant departments of the State Council, local people's governments as well as their relevant departments, shall provide assistance.

The State's export control administrative departments carry out supervision and investigation independently or in conjunction with relevant departments, with which departments the relevant organizations and individuals shall cooperate with no refusal or obstruction.

Relevant State authorities and their functionaries shall be legally obligated to maintain the confidentiality of any State secret, commercial secret, personal privacy, and personal information as learned during the investigation.

Article 30 To strengthen the administration of export of controlled items, and prevent the risks of illegal export of controlled items, the State's export control administrative departments may conduct a supervision interview, issue a warning letter, or take other measures.

Article 31 Any organization or individual has the right to report the suspected violation of this law to the State's export control administrative departments. The State's export control administrative departments shall deal with the report upon receipt thereof in a lawful and timely manner, and shall keep the information of the reporting party confidential.

Article 32 The State's export control administrative departments shall, pursuant to the international treaties concluded or acceded to by the State, or according to the principle of equality and reciprocity, develop cooperation and exchanges with other countries, regions, and international organizations and so forth.

Any provision of information related to export control by an organization or individual within the territory of the People's Republic of China to those outside the territory of China shall be conducted in accordance with law; any such provision that may endanger national security and interests shall be prohibited.

Chapter IV Legal Liabilities

Article 33 Exporting business operators who export relevant controlled items without obtaining the qualification for export operations of related controlled items shall be given a warning, be ordered to stop the illegal act, and their illegal gains shall be confiscated, and where the illegal business amount is not less than RMB500,000, a penalty of not less than five times but not more than ten times the illegal business amount shall concurrently be imposed; where no illegal business amount is involved or the illegal business amount is less than RMB500,000, a penalty of not less than RMB500,000 but not more than RMB5 million shall concurrently be imposed.

Article 34 Exporting business operators who commit any of the following acts shall be ordered to stop the illegal act, and their illegal gains shall be confiscated, and where the illegal business amount is not less than RMB500,000, a penalty of not less than five times but not more than ten times the illegal business amount shall concurrently be imposed; where no illegal business amount is involved or the illegal business amount is less than RMB500,000, a penalty of not less than RMB500,000 but not more than RMB5 million shall concurrently be imposed; where the circumstances are serious, an order to suspend business for rectification or even revoke the qualification for export business of related controlled items may be imposed:

1. exporting controlled items without licenses;
2. exporting controlled items beyond the scope specified in the export licenses; or
3. exporting controlled items that are prohibited from export.

Article 35 Where any party obtains the export license for controlled items by fraud, bribery or other illegal ways, or illegally transfers the export license for controlled items, the license shall be revoked, the issued export license shall be forfeited, the illegal gains shall be confiscated, and where the illegal business amount is not less than RMB200,000, a penalty of not less than five times but not more than ten times the illegal business amount shall concurrently be imposed; where no illegal business amount is involved or the illegal business amount is less than RMB200,000, a penalty of not less than RMB200,000 but not more than RMB2 million shall concurrently be imposed.

Where any party forges, alters, or trades the export license for controlled items, the illegal gains shall be confiscated, and where the illegal business amount is not less than RMB50,000, a penalty of not less than five times but not more than ten times the illegal business amount shall concurrently be imposed; where no illegal business amount is involved or the illegal business amount is less than RMB50,000, a penalty of not less than RMB50,000 but not more than RMB500,000 shall concurrently be imposed.

Article 36 Any party that knowingly provides agency, freight, delivery, customs clearance, third-party e-commerce trading platforms, finance, and other services for exporting business operators engaged in violations of export control shall be given a warning, be ordered to stop the illegal act, and its illegal gains shall be confiscated, and where the illegal business amount is not less than RMB100,000, a penalty of not less than three times but not more than five times the illegal business amount shall concurrently be imposed; where no illegal business amount is involved or the illegal business amount is less than RMB100,000, a penalty of not less than RMB100,000 but not more than RMB500,000 shall concurrently be imposed.

Article 37 Exporting business operators who violate this law to transact with importers or end-users designated in the list of controlled parties shall be given a warning, be ordered to stop the illegal act, and their illegal gains shall be confiscated, and where the illegal business amount is not less than RMB500,000, a penalty of not less than ten times but not more than twenty times the illegal business amount shall concurrently be imposed; where no illegal business amount is involved or the illegal business amount is less than RMB500,000, a penalty of not less than RMB500,000 but not more than RMB 5 million shall concurrently be imposed; where the circumstances are serious, an order to suspend business for rectification or even revoke the qualification for export operations of related controlled items shall be imposed.

Article 38 Exporting business operators who refuse or obstruct the supervision and inspection shall be given a warning, and a penalty of not less than RMB100,000 but not more than RMB300,000 shall be imposed; where the circumstances are serious, an order to suspend business for rectification or even revoke the qualification for export operations of related controlled items shall be imposed.

Article 39 For exporting business operators who are penalized due to violations of this law, from the effective date of the penalty, the State's export control administrative departments can refuse to accept their applications for export licenses in the subsequent five years; persons in charge directly responsible for the violations as well as other persons who are directly responsible for the violations may be prohibited from engaging in the relevant export business operations in the subsequent five years, and those who are convicted of criminal penalties due to violations of export control shall not engage in relevant export business for lifetime.

The State's export control administrative departments shall include such exporting business operators' violations of this law into their credit records in accordance with law.

Article 40 The State's export control administrative departments shall be responsible for imposing penalties as to the violations of export control prescribed in this law; to the extent that the customs are authorized by laws and administrative regulations to impose penalties, the customs shall impose penalties in accordance with this law.

Article 41 Any organization or individual that does not accept the State's export control administrative departments' decision not to grant the license may apply for administrative reconsideration in accordance with the law. The administrative reconsideration decision shall be the final verdict.

Article 42 State functionaries of export control administration who neglect their duties, play favoritism and commit irregularities, or abuse their powers, shall be subject to disciplinary measures in accordance with law.

Article 43 Any party that violates the administrative provisions on export control in this law and endangers national security and interests shall, in addition to the penalties prescribed in this law, be dealt with and punished in accordance with relevant laws and administrative regulations.

Any party that, in violation of this law, exports controlled items prohibited from export by the State or exports controlled items without a license shall be subject to criminal liabilities in accordance with law.

Article 44 Any organization or individual outside the territory of the People's Republic of China that violates the administrative provisions on export control in this law, endangers the national security and interests of the People's Republic of China, or obstructs the fulfillment of non-proliferation and other international obligations, shall be dealt with and held liable in accordance with law.

Chapter V Supplementary Provisions

Article 45 Relevant provisions of this law shall apply to the transit, transshipment, through transport and re-export of controlled items, or the export to overseas of such controlled items from customs special supervision areas such as bonded areas and export processing zones, and bonded supervision places such as export supervision warehouses and bonded logistics centers.

Article 46 For the export of nuclear items and other controlled items, if no provisions are prescribed in this law, provisions of relevant laws and administration regulations shall apply.

Article 47 The export of military items for overseas use of armed forces, foreign military exchanges, and military assistance shall follow the provisions of relevant laws and regulations.

Article 48 The People's Republic of China may, depending on the actual situation, take reciprocal measures against any country or region that abuses export control measures and endangers the national security and interests of the People's Republic of China.

Article 49 This law shall be implemented as of 1 December 2020.

Appendix B
Draft Regulations on the Export Control of Dual-Use Items [Translation for Reference Only]

Released by MOFCOM on April 22, 2022, for the purpose of soliciting public opinion.

Chapter I General Provisions

Article 1 With a view to safeguarding national security and interests, fulfilling non-proliferation and other international obligations, and strengthening and normalizing export control of dual-use items (the "dual-use export control"), the Regulations are enacted in accordance with the Export Control Law (the "ECL") of the People's Republic of China.

Article 2 The Regulations shall apply to the dual-use export control by the State.

Export control under the Regulations refers to the prohibitive or restrictive measures taken by the State against the transfer of controlled items from within to outside the territory of the People's Republic of China, and the act performed by a citizen, legal person or unincorporated organization of the People's Republic of China to provide any foreign organization or individual with controlled items.

Dual-use items of the Regulation refer to goods, technologies, and services that can be used for both civil and military purposes or contribute to elevating military power potentials, especially those can be used to design, develop, produce, or employ weapons of mass destruction and their delivery vehicles.

Article 3 Dual-use export control shall adhere to the holistic view of national security, safeguard international peace, overall plan and coordinate security and developments, and improve administration and services of export control.

Article 4 The State implements a unified export control regime administrated through formulating control lists, carrying out export licensing, and conducting lawful supervision and inspection.

Article 5 The commerce authority under the State Council (the "State Council commerce authority") shall be in charge of dual-use export control. Other relevant

D. Zhao, *Contemporary Export Control Law of China*, Modern China and International Economic Law, https://doi.org/10.1007/978-981-99-9825-8

authorities under the State Council shall discharge functions related to export control in accordance with their assigned responsibilities.

The National Coordination Mechanism for Export Control is to coordinate major issues of export control. The State Council commerce authority and other relevant authorities under the State Council shall closely cooperate and strengthen share of information.

The commercial authority under the people's governments of provinces, autonomous regions and municipalities directly under the central government shall assist in the receipt of license application, supervision and inspection, investigation and other efforts related to dual-use export control.

Article 6 The State Council commerce authority shall, in conjunction with relevant authorities, to establish an expert consultation mechanism for dual-use export controls to provide advice on the development and adjustment of the legislation, rules, and policies for dual-use export controls, the development and adjustment of control lists, the identification of dual-use items, and the review of export applications and so forth.

The expert consultation mechanism for dual-use export controls shall consist of experts in relevant fields. The experts shall follow the principle of being objective, impartial, and meticulous when giving advisory opinions.

Article 7 The State Council commerce authority will develop, adjust and issue, as appropriate, guidelines on export control of dual-use items in due course, and guide export business operators in establishing sound dual-use export control internal compliance programs and normalizing operations. For export business operators with an established internal dual-use export control compliance program that runs well, the State Council commerce authority may grant facilitations such as a multiple-use license for the export of related dual-use items.

Business operators provide agency, freight, delivery, customs clearance, third-party e-commerce trading platforms, finance, and other services for the export of dual-use items and may establish export control compliance programs accordingly.

The State Council commerce authority may organize evaluations for the operation of their internal dual-use export control compliance programs.

Article 8 Export business operators of dual-use items and relevant organizations and individuals may lawfully establish and join relevant chambers of commerce, associations, or other self-regulatory industrial organizations.

Relevant chambers of commerce, associations, or other self-regulatory industrial organizations shall abide by laws and administrative regulations, provide services related to export control for their members according to their bylaws, guide their members to strengthen internal compliance construction, and play their roles in coordination and self-regulation.

Article 9 The State Council commerce authority and foreign affairs authority shall, in conjunction with other relevant authorities, strengthen international cooperation on dual-use export controls, and participate in the development of international rules related to export controls.

The State Council commerce authority shall conduct cooperation and exchanges on export controls with other countries or regions, international organizations, and so forth in accordance with the international treaties signed or acceded to by China, or in accordance with the principles of equality and reciprocity. Other relevant authorities under the State Council shall conduct cooperation and exchanges on export controls based on the division of responsibility among them.

Article 10 The State Council commerce authority shall, in accordance with the principle of equality and reciprocity, issue and administer Statements of End-User and End-Use upon application to the governments of other countries and regions. Applicants shall strictly abide by the undertakings provided by them when applying for the issuance of the Statement of End-User and End-Use.

The administrative measures for the Statement of End-User and End-Use shall be separately provided for by the State Council commerce authority.

Chapter II Control Policies, Control Lists, and Control Measures

Section 1 Control Policies

Article 11 The State Council commerce authority shall, in conjunction with relevant departments, formulate export control policies, the major ones of which shall be submitted to the State Council or to both the State Council and the Central Military Commission for approval.

Article 12 The State Council commerce authority shall, in conjunction with relevant authorities including the foreign affairs authority under the State Council, assess the countries and regions of destination for the export of dual-use items, identify their risk levels, and adopt control measures accordingly.

Factors to consider in the assessment include:

(1) impact on national security and interests;
(2) the need to fulfill any international obligation identified in the international convention to which China is a contracting party or in the resolution of the United Nations Security Council;
(3) the needs of foreign policy;
(4) the cooperation in export control areas between a country or region of destination and China, and
(5) other factors to be considered.

Section 2 Control Lists

Article 13 The State Council commerce authority shall, based on ECL, the Regulations and the dual-use export control policy in conjunction with relevant authorities, develop and adjust the dual-use export control list as per the prescribed procedure, and issue them in a timely manner. Items in this list shall be assigned control codes.

When formulating and adjusting the dual-use export control list, consultation shall be sought by appropriate methods, and necessary industrial surveys and assessments shall be conducted. The following factors shall be considered:

(1) impact on national security and interests; and
(2) impact on the fulfillment of non-proliferation and other international obligations.

Article 14 The State Council commerce authority will, in conjunction with relevant authorities, implement temporary controls, and shall make a public announcement of the items subject to temporary controls and the temporary control period. Such temporary control period shall not exceed two years.

Before the expiration of the temporary control period, the State Council commerce authority shall conduct an assessment in a timely manner, and take measures as follows depending on the assessment results:

(1) issuing a public announcement to cancel the temporary control measure if the conditions for implementing temporary controls no longer exist;
(2) issuing a public announcement to extend the period of the temporary control by not more than two years if the conditions for implementing temporary controls still exist and it is still not appropriate to include the temporarily controlled items in the dual-use export control list; or
(3) include the temporarily controlled items in the dual-use export control list if it is appropriate to do so.

Article 15 As needed for the safeguard of national security and interests or fulfillment of non-proliferation or other international obligations, subject to the approval of the State Council or both the State Council and the Central Military Commission, the State Council commerce authority may, in conjunction with relevant authorities, forbid the export of any relevant dual-use items, or forbid the export of any relevant dual-use items to a specified country or region of destination or to a specified organization or individual, and make a public announcement.

Section 3 Licensing Scheme

Article 16 The State implements a licensing scheme for the export of dual-use items included in the dual-use export control list and temporarily controlled dual-use items.

An individual license allows an export business operator to export one dual-use item to an end-user once within the validity period of the license. A multiple-use license allows an export business operator to export multiple dual-use items to multiple end-users for multiple times within the scope and validity period stated in the license.

Article 17 The State Council commerce authority shall, alone or in conjunction with relevant authorities, review the application for the export of a dual-use item and decide whether or not to grant a license based on ECL. If permitted, the license shall be uniformly issued by the State Council commerce authority. If refused, the applicant shall be notified in a timely manner of the decision and the reasons thereof.

Article 18 The State Council commerce authority shall decide whether or not to grant a license within 45 business days of the date of accepting a license application. If the decision cannot be made within 45 business days, subject to the approval of the head of the State Council commerce authority, the period may be extended by 10 business days, and the applicant shall be notified of the extension and its reasons.

For the export of dual-use items with a material impact on national security and interests or foreign policy, the State Council commerce authority may report the case to the State Council or to both the State Council and the Central Military Commission for approval before a decision; and the time required for approval shall not count against the period in the first paragraph.

If the State Council commerce authority needs to organize an expert review for an export application, the time required for the review shall not count against the period in the first paragraph.

Article 19 The validity period of an individual Dual-use Export License shall generally not exceed one year, and the validity period of a multiple-use Dual-use Export License shall not exceed two years.

Article 20 An applicant for the Dual-use Export License shall file an application with the State Council commerce authority, with a truthfully filled out dual-use export application form and the following documentation:

(1) a copy of the dual-use export contract or agreement;
(2) the technical specifications or test report of the dual-use item to be exported;
(3) an end-user and end-use certificate;
(4) statement of importer and end-user information;
(5) identity credentials of the applicant's legal representative and main business manager, and the person submitting the application; and
(6) other documentation as required by the State Council commerce authority.

Article 21 If any change is needed for the Dual-use Export License already issued to an exporter, the export business operator may file an application with the State Council commerce authority. The authority shall in turn decide after review whether or not to approve the change.

Article 22 Where the following risks are found with the export of any dual-use item, the State Council commerce authority shall revoke the related license during its validity period and promptly notify the export business operator of the revocation:

(1) endangering national security and interests;
(2) being used to design, develop, produce, or employ weapons of mass destruction and their delivery vehicles; or
(3) being used for terrorist purposes.

Article 23 An export business operator who satisfies the following conditions may apply for a multiple-use Dual-use Export License:

(1) having in place an internal dual-use export control compliance program that runs well;
(2) having been engaged in dual-use export activities for two or more years, and been granted a Dual-use Export Licenses many times;
(3) having relatively stable sales channels and end-users;
(4) meeting any other condition as set forth by the State Council commerce authority.

The export business operator is required to submit proof of meeting the above conditions to the State Council commerce authority when applying for a multiple-use license.

Article 24 The export business operator granted a multiple-use license shall regularly report uses of the license to the State Council commerce authority and accept its inspections.

Article 25 The export of any dual-use item which falls under the following circumstances may be exempted from applying for a license:

(1) return of the item to its original exporting place within a reasonable period after its entry into China for repair, testing or inspection purposes;
(2) return of the item to its original place of export immediately after the end of any exhibitions held in China which it has participated in;
(3) export of civil aircraft components to be repaired overseas; or
(4) any other circumstances as regulated by the State Council commerce authority.

If an export business operator believes that an export falls under the above circumstances, the exporter shall register the export with the State Council commerce authority before the export. When the export business operator knows or should have known that the export no longer falls under the above circumstances, the exporter shall suspend the export. The exporter shall apply to the State Council commerce authority for a license if continues the export. The State Council commerce authority may require the export business operator in the preceding paragraph immediately stop an export and notify the export business operator.

The specific measures for exemption from applying for licenses shall be separately regulated by the State Council commerce authority.

Article 26 A multiple-use license or license exemption does not apply in the following circumstances:

(1) where the export business operator has been subject to criminal or administrative punishment within recent five years due to an export control violation;
(2) where the export business operator has been subject to a regulatory interview or written warning by the competent commerce authority within recent one year due to any related activity or conduct with risk of violations of dual-use export controls; or
(3) any other circumstance as provided for by the State Council commerce authority.

Article 27 For the export of any goods, technology, or service other than the dual-use items on the dual-use export control list or subject to temporary controls, if the exporter knows or should have known, or has been notified by the State Council commerce authority of the following risks that may be involved in the export, the export business operator shall take active measures to suspend the export, and shall apply to the State Council commerce authority for a license if the exporter still needs export:

(1) endangering national security and interests;
(2) being used to design, develop, produce, or employ weapons of mass destruction and their delivery vehicles; or
(3) being used for terrorist purposes.

If an export business operator, within three years of completion of an export, finds any risks identified in the preceding paragraph with any goods, technology, or service exported in that export, the exporter shall promptly report to the State Council commerce authority.

Section 4 End-User and End-Use Management

Article 28 An export business operator shall submit an end-user and end-use certificate issued by the end-user when applying for an export license. The State Council commerce authority may, as needed, require an export business operator to also submit an end-user and end-use certificate issued by the government authority of the host country or region of the end-user.

Where an export business operator finds that the end-user and end-use certificate is forged, has expired, or was obtained by fraud, bribery, or other illegal ways, the export business operator shall promptly report to the State Council commerce authority, and assist the State Council commerce authority to investigate and verify related matters.

Article 29 The end-user of a dual-use item shall, as required by the State Council commerce authority, make a covenant in the end-user and end-use certificate. Without the approval of the State Council commerce authority, the end-use of the controlled item concerned shall not be altered, nor shall the controlled item concerned be transferred to any third party.

Article 30 If there is a need for the change of end-user or end-use of a dual-use item already exported, the change shall be subject to the approval of the State Council commerce authority before it can be made to the extent permitted. The end-user or importer may have the application made to the State Council commerce authority through the original Chinese domestic export business operator.

Where the export business operator or importer of a dual-use item finds that the end-user or end-use of a dual-use item has changed or may change the exporter or importer shall immediately report to the State Council commerce authority.

If the item or part of it has not been exported, the export shall be immediately suspended.

Article 31 Where, as found in an investigation by the State Council commerce authority, an importer or end-user falls under any of the circumstances set forth in the first paragraph of Article 18 of ECL, the State Council commerce authority shall include the importer or end-user in the list of controlled parties.

The State Council commerce authority may take the following measures against the export of any dual-use item to an importer or end-user on the list of controlled parties:

(1) prohibiting all or part of the export;
(2) not granting the related license application;
(3) revoking the related license that has been issued;
(4) ordering the suspension of the related export that has not been completed; and
(5) taking any other necessary measure.

Article 32 Export business operator shall not violate provisions by trading with any importer or end-user on the list of controlled parties. If, under special circumstances, an export business operator does need to trade in any dual-use item with an importer or end-users on the list of controlled parties, an application may be made to the State Council commerce authority.

Multiple-use licenses, license exemption, and other licensing facilitation measures are not applicable to any export involving an importer or end-user on the list of controlled parties.

Article 33 Where an importer or end-user on the list of controlled parties has given a relevant undertaking to the State Council commerce authority and fulfilled that undertaking in full, or has acted otherwise which removes all circumstances under which the importer or end-user should be included in the list of controlled parties, the State Council commerce authority may decide upon application or ex officio, to remove the importer or end-user from the control list depending on the actual situation.

Article 34 The State Council commerce authority may, in conjunction with relevant authorities, establish a management scheme for end-users and end-uses of dual-use items to assess, investigate and verify the end-users and end-uses of dual-use items and enhance end-user and end-use administration.

Section 5 Other Control Measures

Article 35 When exporting dual-use items, consignors or customs brokers of the goods for export shall submit the license granted by the State's export control administrative departments to the customs for verification and go through customs clearance in accordance with relevant regulations of the State.

The customs authority shall not release the goods for export if the export license stated in the preceding paragraph is not provided.

Article 36 Any organization or individual shall not provide agency, freight, delivery, customs clearance, third-party e-commerce trading platforms, finance, and other services for exporting business operators engaging in violation of dual-use export control.

Organizations and individuals engaged in agency, freight, consignment and delivery, customs clearance, third-party e-commerce trading platform, financial, or other services shall immediately stop services to an export business operator found to be engaged in activities in violation of dual-use export controls and report to the State Council commerce authority.

Article 37 Export business operator shall, in accordance with ECL, the Regulations and the dual-use export control list, identify whether any goods, technologies or services to be exported fall within the scope of controls before declaring them for export, and may consult with the State Council commerce authority if it is indeed unable to make such an identification. The State Council commerce authority shall reply timely and if necessary, may organize an expert evaluation.

Article 38 Where a consignor of goods for export fails to submit a license issued by the State Council commerce authority to the customs authority for inspection when declaring the goods for export, the customs authority may question the export if they have evidence proving that the goods to be exported may fall within the scope of dual-use export control.

If the consignor of goods for the export or the customs declaring agent for the export provides the customs authority with a reply obtained under Article 37 of the Regulations, or other materials proving that the goods to be exported are not within the scope of dual-use export controls, the customs authority may after verification process the export formalities in accordance with the regulations.

During the period of customs queries, the customs authority may request identification to be organized by the State Council commerce authority. Depending on the conclusion of the identification, the goods to be exported may be legally released by the customs authority if they do not fall within the scope of dual-use export controls or may be lawfully dealt with by the customs authority if they fall within the scope of dual-use export controls. During the period of customs questioning or identification, the customs authority shall not release the goods to be exported.

Where a consignor of goods for export or the customs declaring agent for the export registers for the export with a license exemption certificate, the customs authority shall not release the goods for export and shall legally deal with the goods if they are notified by the State Council commerce authority, or if there is evidence proving that the actual circumstances of the export may be inconsistent with the registered information.

Article 39 Export business operator shall properly retain duplicates of license application documents, duplicates of licenses, forms and vouchers, agreements, accounting books, business correspondence and other documents and materials related to the export of dual-use items for a period of not less than five years. The State Council commerce authority shall have the right to access and copy relevant materials.

Chapter III Supervision and Administration

Article 40 The State Council commerce authority shall, in accordance with law, supervise and inspect the export of dual-use items. For suspected violations of ECL and the Regulations, the State Council commerce authority may conduct investigations under the second paragraph of Article 28 of ECL.

Article 41 The State Council commerce authority shall, in conjunction with foreign affairs, national security, customs and other authorities, establish an interdepartmental dual-use export control law enforcement coordination mechanism to organize, guide, and coordinate in a centralized manner, the departmental or regional law enforcement efforts for dual-use export controls, including the monitoring and alerting, risk assessment, and investigation and handling of suspected violations of dual-use export control laws and regulations, enhanced collection, analysis, use and exchange of law enforcement-related information, and lawful transfer of cases.

Article 42 The State Council commerce authority shall lawfully perform administrative responsibilities for dual-use export controls, while the authorities with public security, national security, customs, transport, financial regulation, market regulation, postal administration, and other regulatory responsibilities as well as local people's governments and their relevant departments shall aid within the scope of their respective responsibilities.

The State Council commerce authority shall, alone or in conjunction with relevant authorities, conduct lawful dual-use export control supervision, inspection, and investigation, which any organizations or individuals concerned shall collaborate with, and must not refuse to accept or obstruct.

Article 43 To supervise and inspect dual-use export activities, or to investigate suspected violations of dual-use export control laws and regulations, the State Council commerce authority shall, in conjunction with relevant authorities, designate the professional institutions to conduct the identification of dual-use items. The State Council commerce authority may authorize as necessary other professional institutions or experts to conduct such identification.

The institution or individual authorized to conduct the identification of dual-use items shall employ scientific technology or expertise to carry out the identification through inspection, testing, and other methods based on relevant technical rules and standards, and issue an identification opinion within the prescribed timeframe, and shall keep confidential any State secrets or trade secrets learned during the identification activity.

Article 44 To strengthen the administration of export of dual-use items, and prevent the risks of illegal export of controlled items, the State Council commerce authority may take measures including conducting a supervision interview, issuing a warning letter, or taking other measures toward the relevant organizations and individuals pursuant to Article 30 of ECL.

Article 45 Any provision of information related to dual-use export control by an organization or individual within the territory of the People's Republic of China to those outside the territory of China shall be conducted in accordance with law; any such provision that may endanger national security and interests shall be prohibited.

Without the approval of the State Council commerce authority, no Chinese citizen, legal person, or other organization may undertake to accept, or accept, any export control-related on-site visit or inspection from a foreign government.

Chapter IV Legal Liability

Article 46 In the case of an export business operator exporting any dual-use item without a license, exporting dual-use item beyond the scope of the export license, or exporting any dual-use item prohibited from export, the exporter shall be subject to a penalty by the State Council commerce authority in accordance with Article 34 of ECL.

Where the circumstance of an actual export is inconsistent with the information registered by the export business operator for license exemption, this shall be deemed as exporting without a license, for which a penalty shall be imposed in accordance with Article 34 of ECL.

Where an export business operator, after obtaining a license for export and before completing the export, knows or should have known that the export falls under the circumstances set forth in the second paragraph of Article 30 of the Regulations but still uses the license to export, such a activity shall be deemed as exporting beyond the licensed scope stated in an export license, for which a penalty shall be imposed in accordance with Article 34 of ECL.

Article 47 Where any party obtains the export license for dual-use items by fraud, bribery, or other illegal ways, or illegally transfers the export license for dual-use items, or forges, alters, or trades the export license for dual use items, a penalty shall be imposed by the State Council commerce authority in accordance with Article 35 of ECL.

Article 48 Any party that knowingly provides agency, freight, delivery, customs clearance, third-party e-commerce trading platforms, finance, and other services for export business operators engaged in violation of export control shall be subject to a penalty imposed by the State Council commerce authority in accordance with Article 36 of ECL.

Article 49 Any export business operator who violates the Regulations by trading with an importer or end-user on the list of controlled parties shall be subject to a penalty by the State Council commerce authority in accordance with Article 37 of ECL.

Article 50 Any export business operator who fails to perform the reporting obligation set forth in Article 27, 28, or 30 of the Regulations shall be ordered to make corrections and given a warning by the State Council commerce authority; and in serious cases, a penalty between CNY100,000 and CNY300,000 shall concurrently be imposed.

Whoever fails to perform the reporting obligation set forth in Article 36 of the Regulations while providing agency, freight, consignment and delivery, customs declaration, third-party e-commerce trading platform, financial or other services to any export business operator of dual-use items shall be ordered to make corrections and given a warning by the State Council commerce authority; and in serious cases, a penalty between CNY100,000 and CNY300,000 shall concurrently be imposed.

Article 51 An applicant for a Statement of End-User and End-Use who violates the covenant to the State Council commerce authority or otherwise violates the administrative provisions for the Statement of End-User and End-Use, may be given a warning, be confiscated of illegal proceeds, and be fined between five times and ten times the illegal business income if the illegal business income exceeds CNY200,000, or fined between CNY200,000 and CNY2 million if the illegal business income is below CNY200,000, by the State Council commerce authority.

Article 52 An export business operator, or an organization or individual concerned engaged in agency, freight, consignment and delivery, customs declaration, third-party e-commerce trading platforms, financial or other services for the export of dual-use items, shall be given a lighter or reduced penalty under any of the following circumstances:

(1) where the person has taken proactive actions to eliminate or mitigate the harmful consequences of a violation as committed;
(2) where the person was coerced or induced by another into committing a violation;
(3) where the person has voluntarily confessed to a violation committed which has not yet been known to the State Council commerce authority; or
(4) where the person has cooperated with an investigation by the State Council commerce authority into a violation of dual-use export control, with meritorious conduct.

An export business operator or an organization or individual concerned engaged in agency, freight, consignment and delivery, customs declaration, third-party e-commerce trading platforms, financial or other services for the export of dual-use items who has in place an internal export control compliance program that runs well, so that the harmful consequences of a violation committed is prevented from further spreading, may be given a lighter punishment by the State Council commerce authority on a discretionary basis.

Article 53 For export business operator penalized for a violation of the Regulations, the State Council commerce authority may refuse their export license applications within five years of the date when the penalty decision takes effect; and any directly liable executive or other directly liable employee of the exporter may be banned from engaging in related export business activities for five years, and those who have been subject to criminal penalties for an export control violation shall be banned forever from engaging in related export business activities.

Article 54 Violations of ECL or the Regulations by export business operators shall be entered into relevant credit records by the State Council commerce authority in accordance with law.

Article 55 When the State Council commerce authority imposes penalties for a violation of dual-use export controls under ECL and the Regulations, the illegal proceeds determined shall be all actual income derived from the violation of dual-use export control; and the illegal business income means the monetary amount of any dual-use items exported in the illegal export, or the monetary amount paid for any relevant service provided for the illegal export.

Article 56 Any violation of dual-use export control specified in the Regulations shall be subject to penalties by the State Council commerce authority; except where it shall be subject to penalties by the customs authority according to any laws or administrative regulations, in which case, it shall be subject to penalties under tECL and the Regulations imposed by the customs authority.

Article 57 In the case of a violation of the administrative provisions relating to dual-use export controls in ECL and the Regulations, which endangers national security and interests, it shall be handled and penalized in accordance with any relevant laws and administrative regulations, in addition to the penalties imposed under ECL and the Regulations.

For a violation of ECL and the Regulations by exporting any dual-use item prohibited by the State from export, or exporting any dual-use item without a license that constitutes a criminal offense, criminal liability shall be pursued in accordance with law.

Chapter V Supplementary Provisions

Article 58 The transit, transshipment, transit, or re-export of dual-use items, or export of dual-use items from special customs supervision zones or bonded supervision premises to overseas shall be governed by the relevant provisions of ECL and the Regulations.

Article 59 The export of the controlled chemicals among dual-use items shall be governed by the Regulations on the Administration of the Controlled Chemicals; and any matter not covered thereby shall be governed by reference to the Regulations.

The Regulations shall apply to the export control of the other goods, technologies, services and other items related to the protection of national security and interests or fulfillment of non-proliferation and other international obligations specified in Article 2 of ECL, which shall be administered by reference to the management of dual-use items and included in the dual-use export control list; except where there are other provisions in any laws or administrative regulations, in which case such other provisions shall prevail.

Article 60 The Regulations shall come into force on [DD/MM/YYYY], the Regulations on the Export Control of Nuclear-Related Dual-use Items and Technologies, the Regulations on Export Control of Missiles and Missile-related Items and Technologies, the Regulations on the Export Control of Dual-use Biological Items and Related Equipment and Technologies, and the Measures on Export Control of Certain Chemicals and Related Equipment and Technologies shall be abolished simultaneously.

MIX
Papier aus verantwortungsvollen Quellen
Paper from responsible sources
FSC® C105338
FSC
www.fsc.org

If you have any concerns about our products,
you can contact us on
ProductSafety@springernature.com

In case Publisher is established outside the EU,
the EU authorized representative is:
Springer Nature Customer Service Center GmbH
Europaplatz 3, 69115 Heidelberg, Germany

Printed by Libri Plureos GmbH
in Hamburg, Germany